JOSSEY-BASS

CASH FLOW STRATEGIES

Innovation in Nonprofit Financial Management

Richard and Anna Linzer

John Wiley & Sons, Inc.

Published by Jossey-Bass
A Wiley Imprint
989 Market Street, San Francisco, CA 94103-1741   www.josseybass.com

Jossey-Bass books and products are available through most bookstores. To contact Jossey-Bass directly call our Customer Care Department within the U.S. at 800-956-7739, outside the U.S. at 317-572-3986, or fax 317-572-4002.

Jossey-Bass also publishes its books in a variety of electronic formats. Some content that appears in print may not be available in electronic books.

Library of Congress Cataloging-in-Publication Data

Linzer, Richard.
    Cash flow strategies: innovation in nonprofit financial management/Richard and Anna Linzer.
        p. cm.
    Includes bibliographical references and index.
        ISBN-13: 978-0-7879-8147-1 (cloth)
    1. Nonprofit organizations—Finance.   2. Cash flow.   I. Linzer, Anna.   II. Title.
    HG4027.65.L548   2008
    658.15′244—dc22

                                                                                    2007026867

Printed in the United States of America
FIRST EDITION
HB Printing   10 9 8 7 6 5 4 3 2 1

CONTENTS

FIGURES AND EXHIBITS

FIGURES

EXHIBITS

ACKNOWLEDGMENTS

It takes courage to try new ideas. Over the years our clients have shown great courage. They shared their concerns and problems; we offered our counter-intuitive advice. As one client noted, "It's heresy, but it works." That our ideas have flourished and been helpful is very gratifying.

Our thanks to Michael Herschensohn, Irene Namkung, and John Ullman at Northwest Folklife, and to Edward Frodel, James Kolb, Terry Webster, and Nellie Baker at West Sound Academy for allowing their experiences to be used as case studies. Special thanks to James Kolb, who took a keen interest in this ap-proach and worked closely with us to make it succeed for his school.

The senior staff of the Pennsylvania Council on the Arts: Philip Horn, Brian Rogers, Heather Doughty, Karl Blischke, Charon Battles, Amy Gabrielle, and Michael Faison have provided thoughtful comments and a keen willingness to put these new ideas to the test.

Our editor Jesse Wiley was keen-eyed and crystal clear. His insights and per-sistence made this a much better book. The production staff at Jossey-Bass were indulgent and kind even when we got tangled up in cross-platform computer shuf-fles. Our agent, Carol Franco, provided worldly wisdom and graceful wit that helped ensure smooth sailing as the passage of this publication progressed.

Special thanks go to Carl Morgan, who translated our hypotheses into the first format for the Cash Flow Forecaster. Alan Bicker brought his financial expertise and computer literacy to the development of the Real Estate Calculator. Both Carl and Alan's efforts will benefit nonprofit decision makers for years to come.

Warren Cook researched a difficult accounting problem and found the right answer, for which we are grateful. An extra helping of ice cream to Martha Perry, who offered our ideas to her colleagues in the foundation community. Thanks to Professor Henry Hansmann for a footnote that sparked one of the most crucial ideas in this book.

And, speaking of ideas, intuitive or counterintuitive, we courageously take full responsibility for them as well as for any errors and omissions.

THE AUTHORS

Richard Linzer provides consultation for businesses, nonprofit organizations, and government agencies. He works with organizations in the areas of financial management, board development, group facilitation, institutional analysis, and strategic planning. Since 1965, Richard Linzer has consulted with more than five hundred businesses, government agencies, and nonprofit institutions in the arts, humanities, education, health care, social services, and environmental fields.

Anna Linzer is a poet and writer and long-distance cold-water swimmer. Her novel, *Ghost Dancing*, was published by Picador of St. Martin's Press and received an American Book Award in 1999. In addition, her poetry and stories have appeared in literary magazines and anthologies, including *Kenyon Review, Carolina Quarterly*, and *Blue Dawn, Red Earth*.

Richard and Anna are coauthors of *The Cash Flow Solution: The Nonprofit Board Member's Guide To Financial Success, It's Simple! Money Matters for the Nonprofit Board Member, Money Matters! A Kit for Nonprofit Board and Staff Members*, and *It's Easy! Money Matters for Nonprofit Managers. It's Simple!* received the 2000 Terry McAdam Award, Honorable Mention, for outstanding contribution to the advancement of the nonprofit sector from the Alliance for Nonprofit Management.

Richard and Anna Linzer work together as cofacilitators. They have developed a method of facilitation for retreats that uses sequences of exercises in the form of kits and workbooks. The five publications that Richard and Anna have designed to be used as organizing structures for retreats and meetings are: *The Board Retreat Kit, The Board Development Kit, The Corporate Retreat Kit, The Collaboration Workbook,* and *The Strategic Planning Kit for Public Agencies.*

Richard and Anna Linzer live on Dabob Bay in Washington State. (Visit their Web site at www.linzerconsulting.com.)

INTRODUCTION

Money makes the world go round. And money matters occupy a lot of our thoughts, particularly in the nonprofit sector. Raising money, earning money, saving money, spending money, the financial drumbeat seems to go on forever. Financial management is a primary consideration for all nonprofit institutions. Some managers have said that after mission, money is the most time- and energy-consuming aspect of organizational life.

You are about to take a fresh look at financial management in the nonprofit sector. New themes and unconventional ideas await you. Since we are practitioners who work with nonprofit clients every day, the prose is tailored to your interests, the information is focused on the operational and strategic aspects of financial management, and the tools and templates provided are designed to make new concepts immediately applicable to your institution.

Since we know that you are busy—leaders in the nonprofit world are rarely idle—our response to the press of time is to offer you methods and tools that simplify and clarify your money matters. To that end, we keep technical terminology on a short leash and provide you with plenty of illustrative examples to match up with your experience.

In *The Cash Flow Solution*, we focused specifically on the questions that nonprofit board members frequently ask us. In *Cash Flow Strategies*, we have expanded the scope to include case studies, forms, and agreements, as well as software for implementing our approach to financial management. This book is meant for board members and staff of organizations and institutions that receive donations, earn revenue, and engage in the host of activities that are defined by a public service mission. However, it is important to understand that our cash flow principles are also applicable to a wide variety of institutions, including NGOs (nongovernmental organizations) and religious institutions, as well as other noncommercial entities that seek to provide benefits to society.

This book presents our approach to fiscal matters, the tools and techniques we use with our clients, three case studies drawn from our practice, and some thoughts about the future. The attached CD includes two programs that will make your life easier:

- Cash Flow Forecaster: Automates cash flow budgeting, forecasting, and fiscal monitoring
- Real Estate Calculator: Allows you to compare and contrast different strategies for dealing with real estate questions

The steps outlined here are tried and true. Our clients have tested them for you. The challenge of using our approach to cash flow financial management is that it requires a shift in perception. You will need to think about money in a different way. Our job is to show you how thinking about money differently can assist you in achieving a successful financial future.

What's In Store

Our approach to money matters in the nonprofit sector is very simple: understand and manage your cash flow, learn how to bridge gaps or deal with surpluses effectively, and work to make all the resources in the nonprofit world flow more efficiently. That's a one-line prescription for administrators, board members, donors, consultants, and others with an interest in the financial health and welfare of organizations in the nonprofit world. There it is in a nutshell. But, as some say, the devil is in the details, so together we need to take a longer look at all those devilish little particulars.

Our intent with this book is to offer you a simple and easy approach to using cash flow for budgeting, forecasting, and monitoring. As you will see, this approach will make the financial side of your operation understandable to all decision makers. We will show you how cash flow analysis can resolve complex problems and allow you to formulate strategies that will enable your institution to achieve more mission for less money.

We describe a whole new category of volunteers in the nonprofit sector: the *creditholders,* people whose effortless assistance will open the door to the use of fully secured credit. Credit provides the key to dealing with gaps in income, and curiously enough, it also can help you deal with surpluses. It seems counterintuitive, but it works, and this book shows you how.

Finally, we discuss a means to make all the resources in the nonprofit world flow more efficiently.

Like ancient Gaul, this book is divided into three parts. Each part explores two overarching issues about money matters that have emerged over the years as a focus for our work as consultants.

Part One is all about understanding and managing your cash flow. These are the two overarching issues in Part One:

- Too many board and staff members of nonprofit organizations find budgets and financial reports difficult to read and understand.
- Financial projections and reports requiring a great deal of time and energy to produce often fail to assist decision makers in making strategic choices.

Part Two looks at new ways to bridge gaps and deal effectively with surpluses, so that you establish true financial security. These are the two overarching issues addressed in this section:

- Ensuring financial security for nonprofit institutions in an uncertain environment poses a difficult challenge to administrators.
- Cash reserves, endowments, and other forms of capital accumulation often fail to enhance a nonprofit's ability to fulfill its mission.

Part Three examines how administrators and board members can work to make all the resources in the nonprofit sector flow more efficiently. And these are the two overarching issues in this section:

- Nonprofit institutions need to obtain higher levels of working capital to fulfill their mission.
- Nonprofit institutions must reach beyond the world of philanthropy to a much broader basis of societal support.

Addressing these issues over the past four decades has convinced us that revamping the relationship of nonprofit institutions to money matters starts with establishing a cash flow–based system for budgeting, forecasting, and monitoring as a supplement to conventional approaches.

In Chapter One we discuss the benefits that cash flow concepts and tools bring to administrators and their boards. Cash flow thinking is a strategic approach to financial management. We examine the incentives for using cash flow strategies to deal with the ebb and flow of income and expense each year. We make a few critical distinctions regarding access to capital to demonstrate why nonprofit institutions are different from businesses.

Chapter Two graphically presents financial statements based on conventional budget formats and contrasts them with cash flow budget formats. We use the experience of one of our clients to illustrate why cash flow budgets provide more strategic information than conventional budgets.

What would the world be like without words? Chapter Three introduces the use of financial footnotes as a way to enhance cash flow budgets. Footnotes bring fiscal insights for those on the board and staff who are more comfortable with language than with numbers.

Imagining the future can provide a direction toward which a nonprofit organization can move and align itself. The key question is how much time and energy should be allocated to trying to predict an unknowable future. In Chapter Four we show you a quick and easy method for forecasting that uses the Cash Flow Forecaster on the attached CD.

In Chapter Five we show how cash flow budgets lend themselves to greater participation in monitoring by all decision makers. Analysis of fiscal information yields unexpected outcomes, as demonstrated in Chapter Six, where we discuss the importance of cash flow analysis in the context of the challenge conventional financial materials pose for conducting research and comparative analysis. In Chapter Seven, we explore ways donors and granting agencies can use the information that cash flow thinking generates to improve their understanding of nonprofit institutions.

Alas, this book can't be all wine and roses. Money matters have their own dark side. Chapter Eight looks at the troubling circumstances in which nonprofit organizations operate today. Strategy is a balancing act in which an institution's strengths and weaknesses are weighed by decision makers and then matched up with the opportunities and obstacles the environment presents. In this chapter, issues of income and asset allocation in the nonprofit sector provide a context for strategic action by nonprofit institutions dedicated to being more self-sufficient.

Help is on the way in Chapter Nine. Cash flow budgets and multiple-year cash flow forecasts can create access to a new resource for working capital: the prudent use of fully secured borrowing. We will show you how credit can be a powerful tool for short-term and long-term financial stability. To get credit from banks you need collateral. To get extra credit you need terrific collateral—and collateral has always been something of a problem for most nonprofits. In Chapter Ten, we demonstrate how cash flow presentations can be used to enlist the services of creditholders (individuals who support an institution's mission by placing assets, either their own cash or stocks and bonds in the bank, to trigger low-interest financing). Solving the puzzle of collateral in the nonprofit world opens the door to the use of conventional credit. We provide the instructions necessary for any nonprofit organization, from the smallest to the largest, to gain access to the working capital that it needs from commercial sources. Banks and bankers will never look the same to you after you read this section.

Chapter Eleven shows you how to apply what you now know about cash flow and credit to safely set up a fully secured line of credit. To make it clear that this really is possible, we present a case study featuring an organization that used our approach to obtain a line of credit. We also include letters and documents from the case study that you can use as the basis for your own efforts in securing a line of credit.

Chapter Twelve advocates the use of credit for coping with deficits, which may seem like a highly controversial approach for nonprofit organizations, but it works very well, and we show you how. Having a game plan ready and in place before shortfalls occur is wonderful, but if you don't, this chapter will tell you how to respond when deficits happen. And, trust us, they do! The Northwest Folklife case study will show you how one organization, at a moment when it looked like every loan officer's worst nightmare, was able to borrow safely and resolve its deficit.

In Chapter Thirteen we look at gifts and surpluses from a cash flow perspective. The results may surprise you almost as much as an unanticipated bequest from an unknown donor. We show you how to get much more mission for less money, even as you feel that you are rolling in dough.

Chapter Fourteen, which discusses the use of credit for venture, may not be for the faint of heart. We share with you a case study about a small private school that reveals how you can create a new institution with the help of your friends and your banker.

Owning versus leasing space is a question that is a never-ending issue in the nonprofit world. Truthfully, it is complicated and can be confusing. But consistent with our goal of making concepts simple and easy, we present some ideas that may help to clarify matters in Chapter Fifteen. With help from the Real Estate Calculator, the other new cash flow tool on the attached CD, we show you how to compare and contrast the advantages to nonprofit organizations of different real estate strategies.

Chapter Sixteen presents an example of how all the elements of our approach fit together to assist an organization in the midst of a serious financial crisis. This chapter includes a description of how a major cultural institution proposed to deal with its financial situation and the advice we would offer instead.

In Chapter Seventeen we take a look at some of the challenges to earned revenue that nonprofit organizations confront. Discounts are something everyone loves. But in the nonprofit sector discounts may have some less-than-positive consequences.

Chapter Eighteen inspects the track record of philanthropy and the way in which current investment practices by foundations and donor-advised funds may be undercutting the ability of nonprofit institutions to fulfill their mission. We also examine the money management policies of large institutions, particularly those with sizable endowments, from a cash flow point of view.

Is it possible for nonprofit institutions to exert more control over their financial destiny? Chapter Nineteen looks at philanthropy in the future. This chapter will lead you into the exploration of a philanthropic realm unlike any other in the field. The notion of a cash flow based future, with plenty of access to working capital enhanced by the securing of insurance and investment by the sector's giants, creates a practical vision of a brand-new nonprofit world.

All nonprofits operate within the general framework of contemporary philanthropy. We believe it is time to change the rules of the game: the rules that dictate how funds are handled and disbursed by foundations, by donor-directed financial service businesses, or by endowments. The promise of these changes is an enormous increase in the amount of working capital available to nonprofit organizations to pursue their mission. Since none of the rules of the current system are mandated or carved in stone, the change is largely one of perception, with help from the simple piece of proposed legislation sketched in this chapter.

The actions outlined in this book will have an immediate and positive effect on nonprofit organizations that adopt them. Creating cash flow budgets, using cash flow forecasting tools, and carefully monitoring cash flow will make the financial affairs of a nonprofit institution clear to everyone. Organizing creditholders to provide collateral will enable nonprofit institutions to qualify to use credit from their bank. By familiarizing themselves with good practices in obtaining and managing credit, institutions not only obtain working capital for their own needs, they help to make the case for a national market to provide working capital for all nonprofit organizations.

With legislative help, using the accumulated capital in the nonprofit sector from private and community foundations, financial service donor-directed programs, endowments, and other public service capital pools, access to working capital for all nonprofit organizations can be achieved.

Cash flow strategies provide the basis for some powerful innovations in nonprofit financial management. We welcome you to join us as we explore these ideas.

Quilcene, Washington   Richard and Anna Linzer
September 2007

PART ONE

COMPREHENDING AND USING FINANCIAL INFORMATION

Budgets and financial reports are as basic as it gets for any nonprofit organization that has moved beyond keeping its accounts in a shoe box. Yet, time after time, we have observed administrators and their board members struggle with even the most rudimentary aspects of nonprofit financial management. And they are not alone. Foundation officials, donors, administrators of government agencies, and even consultants to the field often express frustration with financial materials that are opaque. Since this is a bedrock issue, one that affects all aspects of a nonprofit organization's operations, we devote time in the first chapters to addressing this lack of clarity on financial matters.

- *Too many board and staff members of nonprofit organizations find budgets and financial reports difficult to read and understand.*

To address this issue, we examine both conventional budget formats and the system of accounting used in the field. Our solution is to propose the use of new tools to create cash flow budgets, forecasts, and reports and to use these documents and the information in them as a supplement to conventional financial statements.

As the size and complexity of nonprofit institutions increases, the amount of time devoted to planning and budgeting increases as fast or faster. Much of this effort is directed toward making financial forecasts. Since none of us can know the future with certainty, this raises the fundamental issue of whether too much effort is being spent in trying to interpret the future, time that might be better spent on other activities.

• *Financial projections and reports requiring a great deal of time and energy to produce often do not assist decision makers in making strategic choices.*

Our response to this issue is to propose new tools and methods for cash flow forecasting and monitoring that require much smaller and more reasonable inputs of information. The methods we suggest rapidly produce alternative scenarios that can enable administrators and their board members to move strategically into the future.

CHAPTER ONE

THE CASE FOR CASH FLOW THINKING

Cash flow thinking involves focusing on the arrival of revenues and the departure of expenditures that occur during an institution's fiscal year. It's simple to understand cash flow thinking, and it is easy to use it to address some of the toughest fiscal problems confronting decision makers in the nonprofit world.

First and foremost, cash flow thinking is a supplement—not a substitute—for the accrual basis accounting systems most nonprofit institutions employ. Cash flow thinking allows everyone at the board and staff levels to comprehend the financial position of their institution. By making the fiscal picture simple to grasp, the organization encourages greater participation. With cash flow thinking, more than just the members of the Finance Committee can be actively involved in decision making. This means that all board members are able to exercise their responsibility for due diligence, and it allows the staff an opportunity to understand and share the fiscal information that is vital to the well-being of the institution.

Nonprofit organizations are set up and run differently from commercial enterprises. As we show later in this chapter, the two types of organizations are just different enough to make cash flow thinking especially pertinent to nonprofit institutions. Which is not to say that cash flow is not a powerful driving force in business and in markets, but the special role that cash flow has in the nonprofit arena is what needs to be clearly understood.

Key Questions

Should we create a cash reserve or manage our risk with a fully secured line of credit with the bank? This is just one of a host of questions that cash flow thinking can answer definitively. We explore some of the other questions in this chapter and the answers later in the book.

Cash flow thinking creates a platform for the creation of budgets, forecasts, and reports that are easily generated and understood. It has also stimulated the development of tools such as the Cash Flow Forecaster and the Real Estate Calculator, and techniques such as the creditholder concept, which provides collateral for fully securing an institution's borrowing. Finally, cash flow thinking opens the door to the analysis of a variety of topics that have a direct bearing on the fiscal health of your organization:

- Should we establish an endowment?
- Are we better off owning or leasing our facilities?
- What impact will earned income have on our budget?

Why does the simplicity and ease of cash flow thinking matter to leaders in the nonprofit world?

Cash flow is the term used to describe the revenues that flow into an institution's coffers and the expenses that are paid out when bills are due. Cash flow implies a very literal approach to both money and time. This means that income has to be in hand before it is counted; promises that the check is in the mail don't count. And bills are considered paid only when the checks really are in the mail.

We are advocates of concentrating on cash flow as one of the financial tools available to nonprofit decision makers. Over the years, we have encountered many decision makers and nonprofit professionals who did not fully understand their own institution's financial statements. Adding to the problem, the same individuals who failed to grasp the meaning of their institution's fiscal affairs often counted on someone else to be responsible for understanding the budget and the financial reports. *Just talk to our accountant,* or *let the chief financial officer answer that question* have often been the responses to our financial interrogations. And the situation in the boardroom is rarely much better.

Members of the Finance Committee—an eager stockbroker, an overworked CPA, an amiable local banker—are typically drafted to take care of business and to be responsible, while the rest of the board members focus on other issues. The problem is that all members of the board are equally responsible for the financial well-being of their institution, and they endure considerable liability in their capacity as board members. It is vital for everyone on the board to understand the numbers.

Trustee ownership and understanding of financial matters has been a running debate in the field. This issue has evoked a variety of responses ranging from suggestions to mandate financial training for executives and nonprofit board members to notions of designating specialists to work alongside board and staff to supervise and coach them in money matters.

While we appreciate the benefits of training and the obvious profit potential for consultants working as capacity builders to nonprofit institutions, we instead advocate starting out by making things so simple and so easy that anyone who sits on the board or in a managerial capacity can quickly grasp the essential financial issues confronting the institution.

The clarity of cash flow thinking starts to deliver positive benefits the moment you adopt it. Everyone will be able to read and understand your budgets, forecasts, and reports. For the numerically challenged, cash flow is straightforward in much the same way that a checkbook is immediately accessible. For those who like pictures, cash flow lends itself to helpful graphic images. English majors, who may hate numbers, will appreciate the almost poetic footnotes that accompany your materials.

Why is cash flow thinking particularly relevant to nonprofit organizations?

How many times have you heard a colleague or a board member lament that your nonprofit organization should be more like a business? It's a refrain that we have heard from many people who are or have been successful in their nine-to-five business lives. For these people the importance of a cash flow approach to nonprofit institutions needs to be especially emphasized. These folks frequently see the nonprofit sector as just an underdeveloped version of the commercial world. And many translate their notion of good business practices directly into recommendations for financial policies for their nonprofit institution. While nonprofits can learn a lot from businesses, the differences between the financial practices of the two sectors need to be understood in the context of the very real differences between them.

For example, the cash flow concepts that we advocate place very little emphasis on the accumulation of assets by nonprofit institutions. This is often baffling to businesspeople. Yet it makes perfect sense once you grasp the importance of mission to the nonprofit sector, and the way restricted funds turn into smoke and mirrors for many institutions.

In both the commercial world and the nonprofit sector, cash flow is important, particularly as a tool for understanding operations. Yet, as anyone in business will tell you, the bottom line in the commercial sector is all about the assets and liabilities left at the end of the fiscal year. On the other hand, for nonprofit institutions, cash flow is uniquely important, because assets don't always have the same impact on the bottom line as they do in commercial settings. Here are three reasons why things are different:

First, businesses are creatures of the marketplace; nonprofits are creatures of the IRS. After all, without a charter from the feds, tax-exempt organizations could not offer deductions for contributions and avoid most of the taxes businesses pay. Another way of looking at this issue is to say that while businesses are created by markets, nonprofits are often the creatures of market failure. Market failure occurs when customers are unable or unwilling to pay the full price of the services or goods they receive. In the nonprofit field this means that a third party, such as a donor, foundation, or government agency, is needed to supplement the cost of the activity.

Second, the ways in which the two types of organizations are allowed to raise money are not the same. The rules that apply to this money create some profound differences. Businesses sell equity (ownership) to investors in the form of stocks, bonds, partnerships, and venture arrangements. Once the equity has been sold, businesses have a great deal of flexibility in how and for what they spend their money. The notion that in business *cash is king* is just another way of paraphrasing Yogi Berra when he says: "Cash, why it's just as good as money."[1]

Yet in the remarkably regulated financial environment in which nonprofits operate, even cash is not always a liquid asset. *Liquid assets* consist of unrestricted cash, and of money in a mutual fund or savings account that can easily be converted into unrestricted cash. Restricted cash may be in the bank account but not available for any purpose other than the specific one dictated by the funding source. This alone can create a fiscal crisis for seemingly solvent nonprofit institutions.

Nonprofits are prohibited from selling equity to anyone. Instead, they are allowed to receive tax-deductible gifts and grants, which often come with strings attached. Businesses can use profits to pay for their activities. Nonprofit institutions are often contractually bound to observe government or foundation requirements that any funds left over from grants be returned to the source rather than switched into different budgetary areas.

Both businesses and nonprofit institutions can borrow money. So the major difference is this: businesses sell equity and distribute profits to investors and to the government in the form of taxes; nonprofits receive tax-deductible grants and gifts that are meant to be spent for the social purpose for which the organization was formed.

Third, businesses have a very different annual fiscal cycle from that of their nonprofit counterparts. Businesses mobilize money through the sale of equity, or they use profits or borrowing to provide the funds they need to operate. At the end of the fiscal year they distribute earnings in the form of dividends and taxes.

Nonprofit organizations are continually soliciting gifts and grants, attempting to earn revenue, and occasionally borrowing. But because they have no equity to sell, nonprofit organizations do not engage in distribution to investors and in many cases pay little, if anything, in federal, state, or local taxes. Therefore, the fiscal cycle for a nonprofit organization is only about cash flow: income in and expenses out. It is this characteristic of nonprofit institutions that makes cash flow thinking so relevant to understanding how they work.

Arthur Levitt, the former chairman of the Securities and Exchange Commission, states in *Take on the Street* that to understand the quality of the financial situation of an enterprise, you need to look at the cash flow report.[2] We agree, which is why we focus on cash flow budgeting, cash flow forecasting, and cash flow monitoring. The assets and liabilities are important too, but in nonprofit organizations cash flow thinking needs to be accorded a special place at the table when fiscal decisions are made.

Why add a cash flow–based approach to supplement our existing system?

Before you read on, you may want to buy your bookkeeper a bottle or two of over-the-counter heartburn medication. Then it will be ready when you announce that you are considering adding another level of financial record keeping to that already busy schedule. You can imagine the warm embrace we receive from our clients when we strongly urge them to do just that. What we often hear in response to our request is that they already have a perfectly fine system of accounting that has been mandated by the Federal Accounting Standards Board (FASB).

Our answer to this objection is that cash flow budgeting, forecasting, and monitoring make it possible for everyone, not just the accountants and members on the Finance Committee, to understand what is going on. Using cash flow budgets, forecasts, and reports to complement an existing system of financial management may at first seem like an added chore. After all, having an accrual basis accounting system in place generates lots of information in the form of balance sheets, income and expense statements, statements of changes in net assets, and statements of cash flows. The difficulty is that not everyone is comfortable with the information provided.

Accrual basis accounting is a system that recognizes income when it is earned and expenses when they are incurred, rather then when cash actually changes hands. To someone versed in finance and accounting the accrual basis system is finely detailed and comprehensible. To those without a financial management background, accrual basis accounting can be something of a challenge.

Accountants and lots of other people understand accrual accounting and consider it the appropriate standard for all financial environments. Accrual basis accounting uses a system that identifies payables and receivables in a virtual time frame. So, if you have been notified that a grant has been awarded, your bookkeeper "books" the amount at the moment of the award. But if, as sometimes happens, the grant is slow in arriving, and your fiscal year ends, you still have the receivable on your books. You account for it within the fiscal year time frame, but you still do not have the money that was meant to be spent on the program for which the funds were designated. For folks who understand this approach, it makes sense; they have a mental model that allows for everything to balance in the institution's accounts over time.

As that popular source "The Motley Fool" noted in November 2006: "Be Careful When It Comes to Accruals."[3] Unless you understand that the money in the last report may not be money in the bank, you can find yourself in financial trouble. The problem, as we see it, is that the way for-profit businesses almost universally use this system of accounting gives it a lot of authority, but people in business generally know that there can be a disconnect between receivables and sales. In the nonprofit setting the impact of booking third-party-payer revenues well in advance of receipt of funds can be much more problematical. The typical line we hear is, "Well, we got the grant, so what's the problem?" Well, the problem is that if the grant or contact check has not arrived, or the funds are restricted—something that does not happen in business—then other funds on hand may not be available for either operations or programs. The same thing happens with endowments or restricted cash reserves. The money is there on the balance sheet, but that does not mean that it can be spent to deal with today's expenses.

On the other hand, income and expense are empirical phenomena—that is, you can see them as they happen—in cash flow thinking. Everyone may be aware that money is coming, but until it lands in the bank, it is not booked. The same is true with expenses paid. This is familiar from daily life: the float attached to your credit card purchases means that you don't feel the actual impact on your wallet until you write the check to pay off your bill.

Cash flow thinking requires reporting only those events that involve the exchange of cash. It acknowledges but sets aside any transactions that do not involve cash, such as depreciation or amortization. Cash flow budgets, reports, and forecasts merge actual time with real money. They are dynamic—unlike conventional budgets and balance sheets. A balance sheet is a snapshot of a fiscal moment in time. A cash flow budget, report, or forecast is like watching a movie in which income and expense costar with time to express the ebbs and flows of your organization's financial position.

With accrual basis accounting, income and expenses are posted before they are received or paid. This creates a virtual world that can sometimes be confusing. For example, when multiple-year pledges that have been posted do not arrive on schedule, your organization can be much poorer than it looks on paper. Our cash flow approach focuses exclusively on the income that arrives at your door and the expenses that are recorded as checks as they sail off in the mail. A sense of practical reality accompanies cash flow thinking.

Because these two systems (accrual and cash basis accounting) treat money in relation to time differently, a cash flow approach must be kept separate from your accrual basis accounting system. To make the separation easy, simply use the Cash Flow Forecaster tool that comes with this book. That will be much better for the bookkeeper than all that heartburn medication.

Can thinking about cash flow answer our perennial fiscal questions?

In our approach to thinking about cash flow, this inherently simple system is also the key to an in-depth understanding of many of the most complex issues in nonprofit financial management. If this seems like a paradox, read on.

Here are some related questions many leaders ask:

- Should we stockpile cash in unrestricted reserves or a restricted endowment, or both?
- Should we own our facilities or should we lease them?
- Why should we establish a line of credit and pay the bank interest, when we could build a healthy cash reserve and collect interest ourselves?
- Should we be cautious before starting a money-making enterprise to supplement our other sources of revenue?

The list goes on and on, and in each case, thinking about cash flow can help to provide clear answers.

Most leaders in the nonprofit sector pay careful attention to the assets and the liabilities of their institutions. But in some cases that focus on the pluses and minuses can make it difficult to answer complex fiscal questions. For example, one of the difficulties some larger institutions face is that their balance sheets can look strong, particularly if they have endowments, while their access to spendable dollars is quite limited. Decision makers may be unclear about the financial position of their institution because the restricted assets provide a false sense of fiscal security. Decision makers ask us whether it is cheaper to have a cash reserve or a fully secured line of credit. We tell them that without doing a cash flow analysis and a direct comparison, you cannot establish the precise difference in benefits of one approach or the other.

The same concerns influence decisions about which dollar to use to cover which purpose in the budget. If all dollars cost the same, then it makes no difference. But dollars can have very different costs, and cash flow lets you focus on the differential cost of money. So if the bank account is low this month, it makes sense to use the cheapest dollar—namely the borrowed one—to fill up the tank, rather than those expensive dollars that have been earned at high cost to your institution.

The benefits of applying cash flow principles to financial problems are most clearly demonstrated in the area of real estate. Leaders in the nonprofit world spend countless hours each year trying to figure out whether it is better to own or lease space, or whether a capital campaign is the right approach to adopt, versus a host of alternative strategies for dealing with facility issues. The Real Estate Calculator that comes with this book will reduce these difficult questions into understandable alternatives that can be compared and contrasted quickly. The software does this by providing standardized terms to follow and by establishing a common cash flow basis so that comparison of different approaches is possible. Typically, real estate discussions swing between hard issues, such as costs and financial consequences, and soft issues, such as the desire to own rather than rent because the notion of ownership just feels better. Without a clear differentiation among the factors that drive the choice, real estate decisions are often more art than science.

Are there other incentives and benefits to thinking about cash flow?

Cash flow budgeting, forecasting, and monitoring set the stage for strategic thinking for leaders, particularly in the area of financial risk management. Understanding how a nonprofit organization works today, and how it is likely to perform in the coming years, is fundamentally rooted in an understanding of its cash flow. Ongoing awareness of when funds enter and leave the institution's coffers is necessary to ensure the health and stability of the organization. Thinking about cash flow can set the stage for the use of credit to address both financial shortfalls and windfalls. It also makes it possible to communicate clearly with the individuals and institutions that will make the credit you require available to you. And in the process our recommended procedures for budgeting will dynamically illuminate your financial game plan.

Using cash flow tools such as the Cash Flow Forecaster makes generating useful forecasts or quickly preparing financial reports, and many other financial tasks, turn out to be much easier and far less time-consuming to perform. Our cash flow–based electronic tools enable you to generate useful forecasts in much less time—forecasts that can be easily advanced as you move through the fiscal year. The same tools make financial monitoring a breeze. These savings in time and energy may bring you back into the good graces of your bookkeeper.

Cash flow thinking can also help leaders analyze their financial policies in new and different ways. By using cash as a common basis, fiscal data from different institutions can be used for comparing and contrasting patterns and trends that would otherwise be inaccessible. These benefits of cash flow presentations can be shared with donors, foundations, and government agencies. Cash flow budgets can provide them with real insight into your circumstance—bolstering your requests—and bring a much-needed financial reality to discussions about their policies for restricting grants and gifts.

For example, some foundations have a policy that prohibits them from funding organizations that have incurred a deficit, even if it is only on paper and actually a matter of timing, not money. Other funders refuse to pay for the operational expenses necessary to administer their funded programs. Using a cash flow–based approach, you can control your own destiny by understanding the impact of these issues on your bottom line. You may not be able to convince the funders that you need more operational dollars to sustain their grants, but you will be prepared to take constructive action to mend this situation on your own through the use of credit.

Cash flow financial management alerts you to potential shortfalls and windfalls. Knowing in advance how the budget will be affected by these changes can be a lifesaver for administrators focused on fulfilling their mission. Cash flow thinking also opens the door to a new resource for nonprofit organizations, the use of fully secured credit to fill in income gaps or to hedge against future risks.

Why should board members support the use of cash flow thinking?

People sign up to be board members and staff of nonprofit organizations for a variety of reasons, but struggling with fiscal systems is rarely one of them. Just saying the words *financial management* to many people in the nonprofit sector evokes a wince. Yet, like it or not, all nonprofit board members are responsible for the financial well-being of their organization. They are legally liable for the finances, just as administrators, acting as agents for the board, are obliged to ensure that budgets and reports are accurate. Because fulfilling the mission is inherently dependent on good fiscal practices, it is important that financial reporting and analysis be comprehensible to all.

The case for using a cash flow approach begins with the clarity that cash flow concepts bring to budgets, forecasts, and reports. Everyone associated with a nonprofit institution is more likely to grasp financial management issues when cash flow tools are used and shared.

The simplicity and clarity of cash flow has special applicability for the board members of nonprofit institutions. Cash flow budgeting and reporting means that board members are encouraged to participate more fully in problem solving and decision making.

Having clear, readable financial information means that board members, even those who are allergic to budgets and numbers, can assume their rightful responsibilities as trustees. These responsibilities include providing financial oversight and the problem solving and decision making necessary to sustain or attain financial health for their organization. Having the Finance Committee examine fiscal issues in great detail may be wonderful, but *due diligence* demands that all board members understand the implications and consequences of their votes on critical issues.

Here's a simple formulation for this concept: *Cash flow approach = better understanding of fiscal matters = greater comprehension by board and staff = wider participation in decision making = better decisions and due diligence.*

A solid grasp of the relationship between income and expense and the assets and liabilities of the institution is an important ingredient in nonprofit financial management. But for many board members, it is a challenge to understand the terminology and the relationships associated with nonprofit financial thinking. This is where cash flow tools and techniques, in the form we present them here, are so helpful. It is possible to use cash flow as a guide for performing the key fiscal functions asked of board and staff members.

And this is why cash flow budgeting, forecasting, and monitoring are so important in the nonprofit sector. Traditional accounting, with all the bells and whistles that pertain to nonprofit institutions, has an important role to play in generating periodic financial reports and the audits so often requested by funding agencies. But you still need to set up a cash flow budgeting, forecasting, and monitoring system to provide the supplemental information that leaders need to run things.

Why should nonprofit managers and administrators adopt the cash flow approach?

The case for cash flow is slightly different for administrators and staff than it is for board members. Cash flow concepts are inherently rooted in operational considerations. All nonprofit institutions, whether large or small, must integrate their money with time. This is most dramatically clear in situations that trigger shortfalls or windfalls. Interestingly, having too much money on hand is just as significant in terms of fiscal decision making as having too little. Of course, most of us would opt for the surpluses, the surprise gifts, or the mystery bequests, but the principle is the same. Having more or less money than your operation requires right now means that the issue of what to do with this money must be addressed. It is here that cash flow analysis really pays off. The decision of what to do with all that extra money—or the flip side, what to do when the cookie jar is empty— can be greatly enhanced if decisions are made using cash flow analysis.

Cash flow budgets, forecasts, and reports allow for nimble financial management. As we lay out in forthcoming chapters, strategy is an integral part of forecasting, balancing preparation with adaptability. Strategy involves making choices in a temporal context. So any decision—to advance, or to hold, or to retreat—has an awareness of time built into it. Since cash flow merges money with time, it sets the stage for strategic financial thinking. We have witnessed too many nonprofit planning sessions that simply did not take time into consideration, which is why we sometimes have heard the nonprofit sector called *the land that time forgot.* Cash flow thinking forces everyone to see things in relation to time because it is about actual cash that is only counted when it is in hand or out the door.

As time becomes increasingly precious, both in the office and in the boardroom, the essential requirements of accurate financial reporting by staff, along with comprehension and oversight by board members, remain the same. These functions will always demand attention, regardless of the size or complexity of the institution. Yet without an ongoing awareness of how funds enter and leave the institution's coffers, annual budgets or records of past years, no matter how laboriously composed, offer little help in understanding how a nonprofit organization works today and how it is likely to perform in the coming years. An annual cash flow budget, starting with the cash in the bank and then divided into monthly segments, is arguably one of the most valuable tools that the administrator of any nonprofit needs to maintain the health and stability of the organization. Our approach to cash flow and the tools that accompany it dramatically reduce the time needed to prepare and use financial forecasts and reports.

Income is on everyone's mind in the nonprofit world. One of the most compelling reasons that nonprofit institutions try to increase their earned revenue is that the surpluses thus obtained are *unrestricted:* they have no strings attached. There is a real need for unrestricted funds that can be plugged into operational categories, avoiding the restrictions that so often come with gifts and grants. Cash flow analysis and concepts can help you understand the impact of earned income. Knowing when to be entrepreneurial and when to stick to your knitting can be very valuable. Access to working capital is the single greatest challenge to nonprofit institutions. Moreover, the key to confronting this daunting issue is to be found by thinking about cash flow. More about this in Chapter Nineteen, where we present some ideas for legislation that will increase nonprofit institutions' access to working capital—those operational dollars that are now so scarce.

Looking Ahead

We are making some serious claims for thinking about cash flow as simple and easy. In the coming chapters we show you why cash flow thinking really is simple for everyone—and we substantiate these claims by making it easy for you to use these ideas. We provide case studies, sample forms, contractual agreements, and actual letters so that you don't have to reinvent the wheel to get on board with cash flow.

Speaking of hopping on board, in Chapter Two we share with you the terrible plight of one of our clients' chief financial officers. And we show you how a little cash flow thinking solved the problem for this gifted CFO by making it simple for her board to see their actual fiscal position.

CHAPTER TWO

BEGINNING WITH BUDGETS— CONVENTIONAL AND CASH FLOW

Budgets are the bedrock on which most nonprofit organizations build their financial strategy. The allocation of income and expenses for a given period, usually one year, represents a quantitative plan for the coming year. So why do so many participants in the nonprofit sector find budgets and financial reports difficult to read and understand? A glance at the various forms that budgets can assume is enough to answer that.

In this chapter we show two different versions of the same budget. One is an annual summary budget of the type used by most nonprofit institutions, and the other is a cash flow budget we use with our clients. In addition to providing the basis for comparison, the two budgets show a fundamental aspect of our approach to money matters. We also demonstrate a streamlined version of the cash flow budget for those of you who prefer your financial materials stylishly svelte.

Financial management typically starts with the preparation of a budget, but the different audiences that budgets must satisfy tend to have competing requirements. Budgets need to be clear and comprehensible enough for board members to approve them. Staff members require budgets that provide guidelines for the operations they are charged with implementing. Donors bring their own ideas and priorities—sometimes at odds with those of the people preparing the budgets. Government agencies must match budgets up with the mandates that they observe. Administrators face disparate audiences, with different requirements for formats and degrees of specificity.

So it is small wonder that new clients will sometimes share with us a handful of budgets, each designed to fulfill a different need. Our response is always to ask them to prepare cash flow budgets and reports as a supplement to the conventional financial statements they are currently using. This apparently extra work actually saves effort, because cash flow budgets and reports can answer a number of crucial questions in nonprofit financial management.

Practical Financial Matters

Why not assign all fiscal matters to the Finance Committee? The problem with this, as you know, is that all members of the board share responsibility—and liability–for the financial well-being of their institution, and inability to understand the numbers doesn't relieve a jot of their obligation. What's needed is to make things so simple and so easy that everyone who sits on the board or in a managerial capacity can quickly grasp the essential financial issues confronting the institution.

The best way to start is by showing you a conventional annual summary budget and then comparing it with a cash flow budget. The comparison helps point out the benefits of the cash flow budget to leaders at all levels in nonprofit institutions.

How does the budget we see at every board meeting compare with a cash flow budget?

If a picture is worth a thousand words, then the graphic presentation of a budget has to be worth at least a couple of hundred numbers. The budget that most organizations use is what we call an Annualized Summary Budget (ASB). We use that name because the ASB budget format presents the total income and expenses for one year in a single column. Exhibit 2.1 presents the old budget format you know and love.

In looking at Exhibit 2.1 your eye typically runs rapidly down the column to the bottom line, which in this case is an intentional—though rare—zero. You might be tempted to glance at the income figures to see where the money is coming from, perhaps noting the $225,000 for earned income, or even wondering why grants, donations, and gifts are presented in separate categories. You might think that the salaries in the expense column are not so hot, but those consulting fees are just outrageous. And what about printing? Isn't printing excessive at 13 percent of the total budget?

Typically, these questions, and many others, will have to remain unanswered until explained by the one who constructed the budget in the first place. If you're among the administrators or staff who worked with the details associated with the budget, these questions have been covered. You understand the detail. But what

EXHIBIT 2.1. ANNUALIZED SUMMARY BUDGET.

Income	
1. Grants	120,000
2. Donations	50,000
3. Gifts	35,000
4. Earned Revenue	225,000
Total Income	430,000
Expense	
5. Salaries	244,992
6. Fringe Benefits	53,892
7. Part-Time Wages	15,000
8. Consulting Fees	7,500
9. Rent	22,000
10. Utilities	5,500
11. Legal and Accounting Fees	13,500
12. Supplies	12,616
13. Printing	55,000
Total Expense	430,000
Balance	0

about board members, or staff in large institutions unfamiliar with the entire scope of the institution's operations? What about funding agencies or donors who may be reviewing your financial information for the first time? Important questions left unanswered may have considerable consequence. For example, a program officer might interpret your costs as out of line and deny a grant. Or a board member might apply different criteria to your line items—criteria that do not reflect the operational reality of your institution.

Because it is a convention, you may not notice, at least not consciously, that all the numbers are a summary for the entire year. That can leave the uninformed reader clueless about what is happening on a daily, weekly, monthly, or even quarterly basis.

On the other hand, the cash flow budget, with its accompanying footnotes, reveals a great deal more information. An annual cash flow budget, one that starts with the cash in the bank and is divided into monthly segments, integrates money with the time that will be passing as the year progresses. It thus clarifies and simplifies financial matters. The cash flow budget in Exhibit 2.2 uses the same raw data as the Annualized Summary Budget, but it looks much more interesting.

EXHIBIT 2.2. SAMPLE CASH FLOW BUDGET.

	Jan.	Feb.	Mar.	Apr.	May	June	July	Aug.	Sept.	Oct.	Nov.	Dec.	Total
INCOME													
1. Grants	0	5,000	15,000	20,000	30,000	0	0	5,000	15,000	1,000	10,000	10,000	120,000
2. Donations	5,000	10,000	5,000	2,000	5,000	2,000	1,000	3,000	2,000	5,000	4,000	6,000	50,000
3. Gifts	4,000	4,000	0	7,000	2,000	3,000	4,000	2,000	1,000	3,000	2,000	3,000	35,000
4. Earned Revenue	21,000	13,000	18,000	16,000	13,000	35,000	25,000	15,000	2,000	17,000	24,000	26,000	225,000
Total Income	30,000	32,000	38,000	45,000	50,000	40,000	30,000	25,000	20,000	35,000	40,000	45,000	430,000
EXPENSE													
5. Salaries	20,416	20,416	20,416	20,416	20,416	20,416	20,416	20,416	20,416	20,416	20,416	20,416	244,992
6. Fringe Benefits	4,491	4,491	4,491	4,491	4,492	4,492	4,492	4,492	4,492	4,492	4,492	4,492	53,900
7. Part-time Wages	5,000	8,000	2,000	0	0	0	0	0	0	0	0	0	15,000
8. Consulting Fees	0	0	0	0	0	0	0	3,000	4,500	0	0	0	7,500
9. Rent	2,000	2,000	2,000	2,000	2,000	2,000	2,000	2,000	2,000	2,000	2,000	2,000	22,000
10. Utilities	500	500	500	500	500	500	500	500	500	500	500	500	5,500
11. Legal and Accounting Fees	3,500	2,000	2,500	500	500	500	500	500	1,000	1,000	1,000	0	13,500
12. Supplies	2,093	1,593	1,093	1,093	592	1,092	1,092	1,092	1,092	1,092	592	92	12,608
13. Printing	3,000	1,000	2,000	3,000	1,500	6,000	11,000	13,000	8,000	5,500	1,000	0	55,000
Total Expense	41,000	40,000	35,000	32,000	30,000	35,000	40,000	45,000	42,000	35,000	30,000	25,000	430,000
Running Total	−11,000	−19,000	−16,000	−3,000	17,000	22,000	12,000	−8,000	−30,000	−30,000	−20,000	0	0

In this case, notice that all items of income and expense are viewed on a monthly basis. Some items are the same month after month; these are called *fixed income* or *fixed expenses*. Other items increase or decrease on a monthly basis, and these are called *variable* income or expenses. It is likely that your organization's budget will contain a mixture of fixed and variable income and expenses. Yet the conventional budget may not give you a clear understanding of which is which, since the summary totals do not distinguish between them.

What are the benefits of the cash flow budget that we don't obtain from the annualized summary budget?

Purely for illustrative purposes we started both budgets with zero dollars in the bank and end the same way. The annualized summary budget provides a sense of the projected solvency of the institution at the end of the year. It does not directly provide much information about operations and their relationship to time. In contrast, the cash flow budget allows your eye to quickly chart out the ebb and flow of funds during the year. As you move along the running or cumulative total line, you may notice that the first four months of the year and four of the five last months of the year all end with negative numbers. Sweat could be pouring from the brow of board members as they glance at all these negative figures. Perhaps they are rethinking their tenure on your board. Then, suddenly, they are reassured by seeing that this organization earns its money in May, June, and July, and usually has a strong finish in December.

Imagine a new board member, sitting in monthly board meetings during those first four months and wondering if this is a sinking ship. The annual summary budget is not going to be much help when the institution hits those months of negative numbers. Did anyone warn new board members that the financial picture in this organization could make them feel seasick?

Time is increasingly precious, and perhaps nowhere more than in the boardroom. Your board members are called upon to plan, decide, and direct the financial aspects of an organization—all this without micromanaging you or your staff. Your responsibility is to provide information that establishes the groundwork and the framework for each of these board functions. Remember: all board members are legally liable for the finances of the organization. You and your staff members, acting as agents of the board, are obliged to ensure that budgets and reports are accurate.

One of the virtues of cash flow thinking is that information can be compressed to ever more basic levels, allowing for a quick review by board members and other staff. Exhibit 2.3 presents a minimalist summary cash flow budget—a format that the busiest board member can grasp at a glance. The information has been pared down so that only months, income and expense totals, and the running total are presented. People who want more detail can easily refer to an annual cash flow

EXHIBIT 2.3. SUMMARY CASH FLOW BUDGET.
(All Sums in Thousands)

	Jan.	Feb.	Mar.	Apr.	May	June	July	Aug.	Sep.	Oct.	Nov.	Dec.	Total
Income	30	32	38	45	50	40	30	25	20	35	40	45	430
Expense	41	40	35	32	30	35	40	45	42	35	30	25	430
Running total	–11	–19	–16	–3	17	22	12	–8	–30	–30	–20	0	0
Cumulative Total	–11	–19	–16	–3	17	22	12	–8	–30	–30	–20	0	0

Note: In this example, we started the preceding year at zero, so the cumulative total is identical to the running total for each month.

budget or the monthly cash flow projections that have been used to create this summary.

This ultra-slim budget can be used to quickly convey information to the reader. In a summary budget, you might add a note that states the beginning balance of cash on hand, which leads to the cash pluses or minuses at the end of the year. The summary cash flow budget also provides the basic information necessary to generate charts or graphs to help readers understand the dynamic quality of your annual cash flow.

Our contention is that a four-line summary cash flow budget and some light reading of the footnotes is enough to enable the majority of members of the board and staff to grasp the fiscal reality of the organization's circumstances.

Now, obviously, to get to this point, someone has to back up these notes and numbers, so there is all sorts of detail to explore for the financial whizzes. But for the average board member, you will be providing the basic financial picture that they need to understand in order to govern or run any nonprofit institution.

By way of analogy, when driving a car, you pay attention to the dashboard, scanning it for the status of the engine, the speed, and the amount of fuel. Although you know that hundreds of vital individual components need to work in tandem to propel the machine, you can't pay attention to each of them while driving. Board members and staff of nonprofit organizations need something like a dashboard to keep track of the essential financial affairs of their institutions, and the summary cash flow budget serves that purpose very well.

Why does a graph of cash flow information tell us more than the detailed numbers about the financial position of the organization?

Sometimes portraying numbers graphically aids understanding. A high percentage of people are visual learners. Pictures and graphs give these folks a way to see the numbers you are offering. Translating a conventional summary budget into graphic form helps them a little, but presenting a monthly cash flow budget in graphic form is a definite winner. When you capture the curve of income and expense in a graph, everyone can see at a glance the overarching ebb and flow of money. Instead of focusing on each individual item within the budget, they can rapidly gain an understanding of the global fiscal position of the institution. Again, the simplicity of cash flow thinking, as portrayed graphically, allows everyone in a leadership capacity to understand and to participate in the financial decision-making process. The rest of this section presents some examples of the graphics that you can use to get the information across to everyone who you want to see the fruits of your fiscal labors. Figure 2.1 illustrates the Cash Flow Forecaster's comparison of income and expense.

As you can see, the picture of income and expense provides a great deal of information in a compact and easily accessible form. For example, the graph makes

FIGURE 2.1. CASH FLOW FORECASTER: INCOME AND EXPENSE GRAPHS.

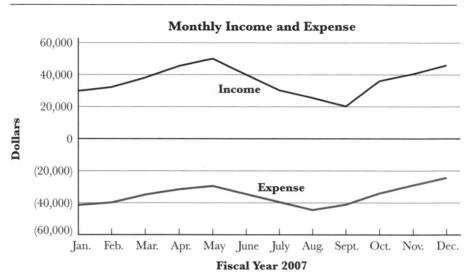

it clear that both income and expense fluctuate in a relatively narrow band, with no big peaks and valleys in either category.

When income and expense are merged as in Figure 2.2, it's easy to see that the institution is running with a major spike in income in May, then a slow summer that gradually resolves itself as fall and winter figures begin to reflect the growing income during these seasons. For much of the year, the institution has negative numbers on a monthly basis.

The graph of cash flow and accumulated cash or debt in Figure 2.3 looks very similar to the graph in Figure 2.2, because we intentionally specified no surplus or shortfall at the end of the prior year. The graph would look very different with a starting surplus or shortfall.

For example, if the organization had started the year with $50,000 in the bank, the graphic image for accumulated cash or debt would look like the one in Figure 2.4.

Notice that the shape of the curve remains the same, but the curve is elevated above the zero line that differentiates positive numbers from negative numbers. The new position makes it clear that no months are spent in a deficit position.

FIGURE 2.2. CASH FLOW FORECASTER: COMBINED INCOME AND EXPENSE GRAPH.

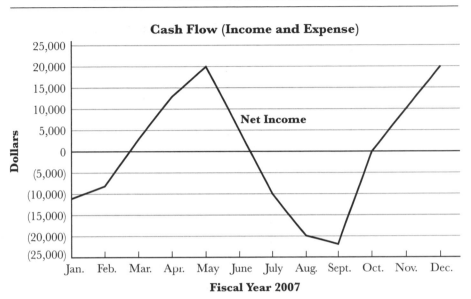

Cash Flow (Income and Expense)

Fiscal Year 2007

FIGURE 2.3. CASH FLOW FORECASTER: ACCUMULATION FROM ZERO BALANCE.

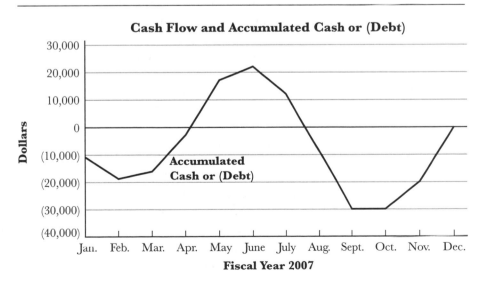

Cash Flow and Accumulated Cash or (Debt)

Fiscal Year 2007

**FIGURE 2.4. CASH FLOW FORECASTER:
ACCUMULATION FROM $50,000 STARTING BALANCE.**

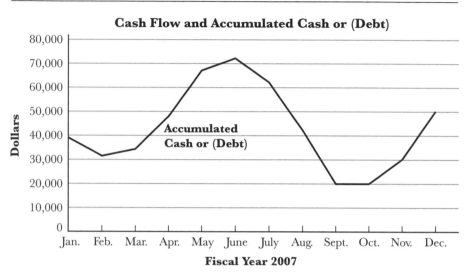

Uses of Cash Flow Budgeting

Here is an example of the implications of budget formats in practice. Not so long ago, a new client called us with an old problem. As her nonprofit institution's chief financial officer, Alice was frustrated at the behavior of the board. In her opinion, they refused to see a serious financial problem that the organization was facing.

At the last board meeting one of the first items on the agenda was monitoring the budget. With one exception, members of the board appeared completely disengaged from the topic. Body language and random comments reinforced the notion that the majority of the board members were simply not interested in talking about the year-to-date figures. Instead, the standing boardroom joke was once again repeated: "Let's ask Don to tell us what all this means and then we can get on with our business."

As usual, Don, an executive at a local corporation, looked up from the budget report and cheerfully commented, "Everything looks pretty good to me: we have cash in the bank; our endowment is earning reasonable interest, and our expenses appear to be in check." With a collective sigh of relief the conversation turned to the next item on the agenda.

Alice had wanted her report to light a fire under the board—to get them to see the serious cash crisis that was looming just ahead. Instead, she had been rebuffed by a board that seemed unable or unwilling to confront the crisis she saw coming.

When asked, Alice agreed to send us a copy of the budget she had just issued to the board. Here is a copy of the budget format that she sent to us (Exhibit 2.4).

The forecast in this budget for the year ahead clearly showed that projected expenses would exceed projected income. Of course, the funds carried over from the preceding year would help out, but not enough to balance the budget. We

EXHIBIT 2.4. ALICE'S ANNUAL SUMMARY BUDGET.

INCOME		
	1. Grants	451,773
	2. Donations	31,293
	3. Gifts	21,236
	4. Earned Income	89,442
	5. Special Events	4,000
	6. Interest Income	1,093
	7. Board Contributions	5,578
	8. Publication Sales	22,180
	Total Income	626,595
EXPENSES		
	9. Salaries	243,487
	10. Fringe Benefits	64,728
	11. Part-Time Wages	162,262
	12. Consulting Fees	94,340
	13. Rent	41,600
	14. Utilities	10,259
	15. Legal and Accounting Fees	19,000
	16. Supplies	15,469
	17. Printing	68,408
	18. Insurance	3,900
	19. Special Events	3,589
	20. Space Management	12,100
	21. Retreat Sessions	4,500
	22. Travel	24,070
	Total Expenses	767,712
	Subtotal	(141,117)
	Carryover from Preceding Year	105,446
	GRAND TOTAL	(35,671)

glanced at the budget and asked Alice via telephone to tell us what she saw as the problem.

Alice told us that the board acknowledged that there might be a shortfall, but still they saw little reason for concern. They were accusing her of being pessimistic, of not having faith that things would turn out just fine. She said that they believed that the situation could be resolved easily with a little cost cutting in the last quarter of the year. But to Alice, the problem was much more serious.

At this point, we asked Alice to insert her numbers into the Cash Flow Forecaster. We discuss the Cash Flow Forecaster at length in Chapter Four, but for now it's enough to take a look at the type of information it generates and the very different perspective it offers.

Alice complied with our request, and later that same day we looked at the documents produced by the software. At this point, we asked Alice to turn to the cash flow budget that she had generated using the Cash Flow Forecaster (Exhibit 2.5). As we talked by phone about how the cash flow budget revealed a host of problems, it suddenly became clear to us that Alice was seeing something very different in the organization's numbers than her board members were. Even using the Cash Flow Forecaster, while the evidence was clearly right in front of us, somehow the board members were not perceiving the dangers that we saw.

What was apparent to us was that the board members, who might have quickly glanced at the summary budget or even the twelve-month cash flow budget, could be missing the boat. If a board member's eye dropped down to the cumulative total line, the starting balance of over $100,000 was obscuring the negative numbers that the running total reflected. In other words, the casual eye was fooled into seeing the positive numbers along the bottom line until November, when the problem appears to pop up.

Exhibit 2.6 takes the information from the Cash Flow Forecaster in Exhibit 2.5 and compresses it to the absolute basics. It reveals the starting balance and the monthly projections for income and expense. Again, a quick glance at the figures in the accumulated cash column suggests that same problem. The carryover funds are being spent down each month, until they are exhausted in November.

But what about Don, the financial go-to guy on the board? Surely, he saw the problem as clearly as Alice. Well, it turns out that Don, with his corporate background, was concentrating on the interest earnings from the endowment and was making a very understandable error. As a businessman, Don was accustomed to looking at the world in terms of assets and liabilities, or profits and losses. He was keeping his eye on the budget, but he was also referencing the institution's balance sheet. The balance sheet recorded the endowment as an asset, so that's how he saw it. Even though he had been informed that the endowment was an irrevocable

EXHIBIT 2.5. ALICE'S CASH FLOW BUDGET.

1. Month to begin analysis (use 1–12, e.g., March = 3)   Start Month: 1

2. Year to begin analysis (e.g., 2002)   Start Year: 2006

3. Cash on hand at beginning of analysis: Beginning Cash: $105,446
(If debt, enter as a negative amount)

Make any necessary notes to the data provided (click): Footnotes

Income 06

	Jan.	Feb.	Mar.	Apr.	May	June	July	Aug.	Sept.	Oct.	Nov.	Dec.	TOTAL
1. Grants	$13,484	$18,215	$25,000	$131,000	$17,000	$15,500	$192,500	$3,574	$15,000	$5,500	$4,500	$10,500	$451,773
2. Donations	$12,715	$1,440	$787	$7,734	$567	$0	$1,000	$500	$2,000	$1,050	$2,500	$1,000	$31,293
3. Gifts	$0	$2,375	$0	$2,017	$1,033	$553	$4,000	$2,926	$1,000	$3,000	$1,332	$3,000	$21,236
4. Earned Income	$4,346	$4,448	$4,007	$633	$11,231	$4,432	$5,000	$15,000	$2,000	$15,000	$14,000	$9,345	$89,442
5. Special Events	$0	$0	$0	$0	$0	$4,000	$0	$0	$0	$0	$0	$0	$4,000
6. Interest Income	$0	$0	$358	$0	$0	$362	$0	$0	$373	$0	$0	$0	$1,093
7. Board Contributions	$2,000	$2,000	$500	$578	$0	$0	$0	$0	$0	$0	$500	$0	$5,578
8. Pub. Sales	$0	$798	$2,135	$4,850	$1,629	$538	$235	$785	$2,462	$2,235	$4,553	$1,960	$22,180
Total Income	$32,545	$29,276	$32,787	$148,812	$31,460	$25,385	$202,735	$22,785	$22,835	$26,785	$27,385	$25,805	$626,595

EXHIBIT 2.5. ALICE'S CASH FLOW BUDGET, *continued*.

Expenses 06	Jan.	Feb.	Mar.	Apr.	May	June	July	Aug.	Sept.	Oct.	Nov.	Dec.	TOTAL
9. Salaries	$19,565	$19,762	$20,416	$20,416	$20,416	$20,416	$20,416	$20,416	$20,416	$20,416	$20,416	$20,416	$243,487
10. Fringe Benefits	$5,126	$5,734	$4,491	$5,553	$5,478	$5,478	$5,478	$5,478	$5,478	$5,478	$5,478	$5,478	$64,728
11. Part-Time Wages	$5,000	$7,050	$6,074	$50,417	$11,874	$7,790	$9,466	$7,711	$9,887	$12,418	$16,786	$17,789	$162,262
12. Consulting Fees	$4,500	$2,035	$9,659	$23,544	$9,874	$5,645	$2,750	$5,455	$7,500	$9,900	$4,553	$8,925	$94,340
13. Rent	$3,500	$3,500	$3,500	$3,500	$3,500	$3,500	$3,500	$3,500	$3,500	$3,500	$3,500	$3,100	$41,600
14. Utilities	$408	$500	$1,174	$1,006	$907	$879	$997	$788	$889	$500	$1,088	$1,123	$10,259
15. Legal/Actg.	$1,500	$1,500	$2,500	$1,500	$1,500	$1,500	$1,500	$1,500	$1,500	$1,500	$1,500	$1,500	$19,000
16. Supplies	$2,093	$2,064	$1,093	$1,093	$593	$3,475	$1,093	$1,093	$1,093	$1,093	$593	$93	$15,469
17. Printing	$3,000	$4,084	$10,323	$3,000	$4,501	$6,000	$11,000	$13,000	$7,500	$5,000	$1,000	$0	$68,408
18. Insurance	$975	$0	$0	$975	$0	$0	$975	$0	$0	$975	$0	$0	$3,900
19. Special Events	$0	$0	$0	$0	$0	$3,589	$0	$0	$0	$0	$0	$0	$3,589
20. Space Mgt.	$1,100	$1,100	$1,100	$1,100	$0	$1,100	$1,100	$1,100	$1,100	$1,100	$1,100	$1,100	$12,100
21. Retreat Sessions	$2,000	$0	$0	$0	$0	$0	$0	$2,500	$0	$0	$0	$0	$4,500
22. Travel	$2,032	$2,706	$1,957	$5,574	$2,048	$895	$3,650	$822	$335	$1,500	$2,151	$400	$24,070
Total Expense	$50,799	$50,035	$62,287	$117,678	$60,691	$60,267	$61,925	$63,363	$59,198	$63,380	$58,165	$59,924	$767,712
Running Total	(18,254)	(20,759)	(29,500)	29,134	(29,211)	(34,882)	140,810	(40,578)	(36,363)	(36,696)	(30,780)	(34,119)	(141,117)
											Beginning Cash	$105,446	
												Overall	($35,671)
Cumulative Total	$87,192	$86,433	$36,933	$66,087	$36,838	$1,954	$142,764	$102,186	$65,823	$29,228	$(1,552)	$(35,671)	

EXHIBIT 2.6. CASH FLOW FORECASTER:
COMPRESSED CASH FLOW BUDGET.

1. Month to begin analysis (use 1–12, e.g., March = 3) Start Month: [1]
2. Year to begin analysis (e.g., 2002) Start Year: [2006]
3. Cash on hand at beginning of analysis Beginning Cash: [$105,446]
   (If debt, enter as a negative amount)
4. Enter first-year monthly Income and
   Expenses in the table:

	Income	Expenses
January-06	$ 32,545	$ 50,799
February-06	$ 29,276	$ 50,035
March-06	$ 32,787	$ 62,287
April-06	$ 146,812	$ 117,678
May-06	$ 31,460	$ 60,691
June-06	$ 25,385	$ 60,267
July-06	$ 202,735	$ 61,925
August-06	$ 22,785	$ 63,363
September-06	$ 22,835	$ 59,198
October-06	$ 26,785	$ 63,380
November-06	$ 27,385	$ 58,165
December-06	$ 25,805	$ 59,924

trust—with principal that could not be spent—on some deeper level, he continued to believe that in a pinch the institution could tap the endowment.

Money in the business world is money. If you have it, you can spend it. The notion of restricted funds just had not fully sunk in for Don. He saw the erosion of the carryover funds during the year, just as Alice did, but instead of pushing for immediate action, he was comfortable with the idea that the endowment could serve as a safety net if things turned sour. In our interview, Don maintained this notion, even when confronted with evidence of nonprofit institutions that have declared bankruptcy and had their endowments transferred intact to other institutions, leaving the creditors high and dry.

Because Alice believed that the numbers in the budgets were so clear, she had not given the graphics produced by the Cash Flow Forecaster to us. But after some gentle urging, Alice ran out the graphics and sent them to us via e-mail. As soon as we saw the printout, the answer to the problem was crystal clear.

When the graphic images of monthly income and expense are charted out as in Figure 2.5, a couple of disturbing qualities immediately become apparent. The

FIGURE 2.5. CASH FLOW FORECASTER:
ALICE'S MONTHLY INCOME AND EXPENSE GRAPHS.

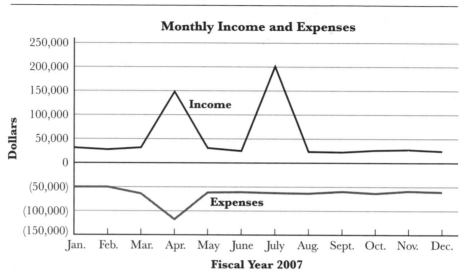

organization achieves a substantial spike in income during the month of April, after three months of losses, but just as quickly significant expenses during the same month wipe out any hope of getting ahead. After that, expenses stay flat, as does income with the exception of a major spike in income in July.

The cash flow graphic in Figure 2.6 makes it obvious why Alice was having a fit. The organization runs with negative numbers during close to ten months out of the year. The numbers are mitigated by the starting balance for the year, but just barely, as Figure 2.6 shows. The trajectory of the institution's finances is downward until June. Income shoots up in July, but it is all downhill from then. Alice was completely correct, the problem was not one that could be addressed at the end of the year. Serious measures needed to be taken as the year began, either by cutting expenses or increasing income, and those measures might be required throughout the year.

Alice saw all this simply by looking at the numbers on her budget sheet. In her mind the numbers quickly translated into an image that flashed danger to her. Why didn't the board members see the figures the same way? Why do so many organizations sail blithely into similarly troubled waters? One explanation is that many or, in this case, all the members of the board simply cannot rapidly convert figures into mental pictures that alert them to a possible problem. A second explanation is that people are not always accustomed to linking money with time,

FIGURE 2.6. CASH FLOW FORECASTER: ALICE'S COMBINED CASH FLOW GRAPH.

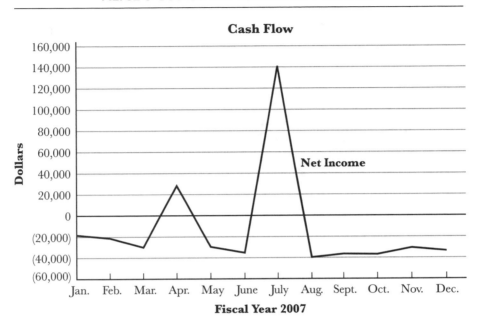

Cash Flow

Net Income

Fiscal Year 2007

and yet, as the graphs reveal, it is the relationship of money to time in this case that tells the complete story. A third possibility is that board members simply abdicate their responsibility for the fiscal side of the institution to whichever board member appears to have the most financial background.

It is not surprising that people can look at the same set of numbers and draw different conclusions. However, anyone who sees cash flow output like Figure 2.7 can instantly identify the problem, while many of those who are confronted with the evidence in the form of columns of numbers fail to grasp the significance of what they see.

After Alice agreed to let the board see the pictures that the Cash Flow Forecaster automatically generates, her report from the next meeting was much different. With these graphics, the board was, indeed, able to see the problem, and to put together a plan to address it.

Alice might have used one more tool to make the case for the financial crisis that was looming ahead. In Chapter Three we discuss a remarkably simple approach that can pay significant dividends with the addition to the budget of a few words. Hard to believe? Turn the page and see how footnotes can make a cash flow budget shine.

FIGURE 2.7. CASH FLOW FORECASTER: ALICE'S PROJECTED PRECIPICE.

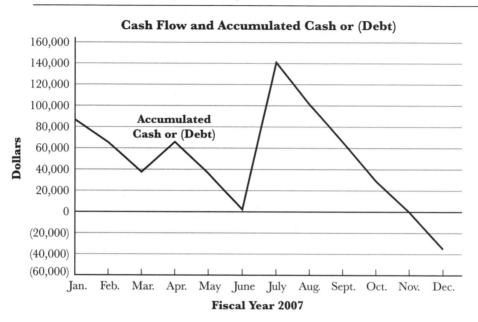

CHAPTER THREE

HOW FOOTNOTES MAKE THE CASH FLOW BUDGET EVEN MORE USEFUL

Perhaps you have had an experience similar to this: The board's treasurer hands out copies of the monthly financial report, and (while everyone is juggling the papers in front of them) the executive director begins an oral report on the budget. People listen, read, shift back and forth in their chairs, and all too often miss the salient points in the report or being made by the director. Too much is going on for any serious analysis to take place in the heat of the moment.

Cash flow budgets that are accompanied by footnotes can make a remarkable difference in the degree to which everyone understands your budget. The cash flow budgets by themselves are a boon to comprehension, but the addition of detailed footnotes can assist even the most fiscally challenged board member.

Despite the benefits footnotes confer, whenever we first propose their use, our clients' questions are always the same: Why do we need footnotes for our budget? Can't they just see the numbers? Don't the numbers speak for themselves? And our answer is always the same, too: The numbers do not speak clearly to all the people reading your budget, so you need to use words to convey the meaning you wish to express. Reading budgets and financial reports for nonprofit organizations should not be a comprehension test. Nor should understanding the fiscal position of an organization be the exclusive domain of a small group of individuals with specialized skills in financial management. Instead, the ideas, assumptions, hypotheses, notations, comments, and biases reflected in a budget or a report should be shared with everyone.

In this chapter we discuss footnotes for every item in our cash flow budget. If you have had painful experiences with footnotes in school, rest assured, our approach painlessly makes the cash flow budget much more informative. Footnotes accompanying a cash flow budget provide a running commentary on each item. They expand the cash flow budget's usefulness by giving the story behind each item of income and expense. Your readers have the information needed to understand the budget on a deeper level before the meeting, and they still have the option of asking for more once you get together.

Footnotes clarify the logic of the budget. If you are assuming that a particular item will have an impact on the strategy the budget represents, this is the correct time to lay the information in front of the reader. Certain assumptions that condition the figures are opaque unless explicitly stated in words. Formulas that generate items of income or expense can be shared. If you have a preference for direct action in one area and for caution in another area, you can express yourself in the footnotes.

Why Footnotes

Footnotes can help focus your reports on the issues behind the numbers. Although footnotes are not a cure-all, a few well-chosen words certainly can bring the budget or report to life.

Here are the footnotes that are included in the cash flow budget we presented in Exhibit 2.2, the sample cash flow budget in Chapter Two:

1. *Grants.* The total amount of grants anticipated this year is $120,000. Of this amount, $50,000 has been secured as part of a multiyear grant from the state. Another $40,000 is highly probable, since we are asking for funds from agencies and foundations that have demonstrated a strong interest in our activities or have shown a historical interest in funding our programs. This leaves $30,000 that is speculative. By the end of the first quarter, we will have proposals pending at five new foundations and six corporations.

2. *Donations* received as part of our annual auction and year-round volunteer telemarketing campaign. Last year the auction raised $15,000. It should do that well or better this year. Consequently, we are forecasting that the auction will raise $20,000 this year.

The telemarketing program has generated a fairly consistent $2,000 to $3,000 per month, with the exception of a sharp dip in midsummer and with some higher numbers in October, November, and December. We believe that at least $20,000 can be considered highly probable from this source.

The balance of the $50,000 scheduled for donations is speculative. We believe that the auction and the telemarketing will deliver these funds above and beyond our estimates, but we cannot be certain of achieving this goal. To increase our chances of reaching our mark, we will be using more part-time helpers for the auction this year, and we will be placing the emphasis on obtaining more items and greater attendance at the event.

3.   *Gifts.* We differentiate between *donations,* which are contributions made as a result of direct solicitation through telemarketing or as income from our annual auction, and *gifts,* which are contributions that come directly from friends or associates of the organization. Most of our gifts come from planned giving. Although it is difficult for us to estimate the arrival of funds, our experience indicates that roughly $25,000 per year will come from this source. The balance of the $35,000 allocated to this category, while speculative, is a reasonable estimate of the performance of a program initiated last year. By asking board and staff to secure matching funds for their gifts to the organization, we are confident that we will obtain $10,000.

4.   *Earned Revenue* from the services we provide is a constant source of cash.

5.   *Salaries* are provided for members of the staff. The breakdown by position:

• Executive Director	$40,000
• Assistant Director	$35,000
• Clinical Supervisor	$25,000
• Development Director	$20,000
• Two Clerical Staff at $16,500 each	$33,000
• Four Field Workers at $23,000 each	$92,000
Total Salaries	$245,000

6.   *Fringe Benefits* are calculated at 22% of base salary. They include our health plan through Group Health, the pension plan we offer through Cosmopolitan Life, and the portion of Social Security paid by the organization ($245,000 × .22 = $53,900). Divided by 12, the annual amount of $53,900 equals $4,491.66 per month.

7.   *Part-Time Wages* are projected for assistance with our annual auction. This year, we estimate that we will require up to 1,500 hours of effort. Based on an average cost of $10 per hour for this help, we have budgeted $15,000 to be spent between January and March (1,500 × $10 = $15,000).

8.   *Consulting Fees.* Our strategic plan is being developed by a planning and consulting firm that will work for a total of 50 hours on this project (50 hours × $150 per hour = $7,500).

9.   *Rent* has been budgeted for eleven months this year. In December we will be moving into a rent-free space that has been promised to us by a local real estate developer who has room opening up in one of his buildings. We can use the space for two years. At the end of this period, we will be asked to pay market-value rent.

10.   *Utilities* have also been budgeted on an eleven-month basis. The new space will be provided to us without utility charges for the first year.

11.   *Legal and Accounting* services are higher than usual this year. We will be audited for the first time and will incur higher fees during the first three months of the year. Our normal legal retainer is $500 per month, and this year an additional $500 has been included for accounting services during the months of September, October, and November. No payments are scheduled for December.

12.   *Supplies* have always been an important expense for us. The supplies are vital to the service we perform. With the exception of January, which is usually a costly month, our normal monthly cost is $1,093. During May, November, and December, our inventory of supplies is always allowed to decline.

13.   *Printing* continues to be a major expense item because our publications are in considerable demand. Printing schedules are timed to coincide with our major program activities.

◆ ◆ ◆

Your footnotes can illuminate important concepts that would otherwise be hidden in the numbers. For example, when developing the income side of your cash flow budget, clearly differentiate the funds that you anticipate receiving, according to at least three categories:

- *Secured funds:* Money already in the bank, part of a multiyear grant, or backed by contracts or collectible pledges.
- *Highly probable funds:* Funds that you can historically count on coming in from major contributors or agencies with which you have long-standing relationships.
- *Speculative funds:* Proposals pending, or projected income from a campaign that is planned but not yet implemented.

You can use your footnotes to indicate in which category the anticipated funds currently fall. This will enable you to gauge the relative strength of your position. For example, you might note that 30 percent of your funds are secured, 50 percent are highly probable, and 20 percent are speculative. In this case, you are in a relatively strong financial position. On the other hand, if 75 percent of your budget is speculative, you may want to be very careful about your expenses during the first two quarters of the year.

Information on the current status of your efforts to obtain funds—or for that matter to incur expenses—can be illustrated easily with the text of your footnotes. By using the footnotes as a commentary on the budget, you are enriching the experience of the reader, and you are also making sure that your intent is clearly understood by all readers of the budget.

How to Set Up Footnotes

We are not talking about the kinds of footnotes that you had to do for those papers in school. That may have seemed like running over broken glass in your bare feet. These are just notes that anticipate and explain what each item in the budget means and how your institution goes about handling it.

Start by creating headers for each item in your budget. Items such as grants, donations, and earned revenue are listed under the general heading of income. If you have an item in your chart of accounts for fringe benefits, use the same term in your cash flow budget.

Avoid using account numbers. Most of the people reading this budget will be baffled by them. If you wish to refer to these account numbers, simply run off a separate budget sheet for staff that includes them, but leave them off for the rest of the world.

Number each item in your budget, starting with the first line item as number 1. Item-by-item numbers will serve as indicators of the specific footnotes that you will be including to amplify the numbers in each line item. For example, using the sample cash flow budget items that follow, the information relevant to each item would be shown on a page of footnotes, each corresponding to the number of the item on the budget page:

5. Salaries	$244,992.00
6. Fringe Benefits	$53,892.00
7. Part-Time Wages	$15,000.00
8. Consulting Fees	$7,500.00

On the footnote page, provide the reader with the formula, the specifics, and all the relevant information needed to understand your budget. This is particularly helpful to those unaccustomed to reading financial statements or reports. It is also very useful to someone at a distance from your organization, perhaps a foundation program officer or a government agency reviewer who is reading your budget and trying to visualize how you operate your programs. Footnotes may actually help you to get that grant or contract—assuming your financial picture warrants the award; the more people who can comprehend your financial materials, the better your chances of winning it.

How Footnotes Help

Financial reporting in the nonprofit sector is not as standardized as you might think. Exotic and creative terms, as well as interesting and sometimes arcane concepts, seep into even the most conventional fiscal documents and therefore into people's thinking about your budget. Since your board may have better things to do with their lives than learn a new financial language, it makes sense to use footnotes to spell out exactly what the numbers mean and the logic that informs them. This lends considerable clarity to budgets, and it also helps illuminate shaky assumptions that may need to be challenged before things get out of hand.

For your board, the benefit of reviewing financial footnotes is that they tell the story behind each number. In a matter of moments, board members can have their questions answered about the various assumptions and details that the numbers reflect. Given a cash flow budget—with accompanying footnotes—in advance of the board meeting, they can quickly and easily prepare themselves for the more fruitful financial discussions that will occur.

From your perspective as an administrator, preparing the footnotes for the cash flow budget provides an opportunity to amplify the meaning of individual items in the budget. The formulas and assumptions used to develop specific income or expense projections can be illustrated through the footnotes. Your institution's game plan can be illuminated both in prose and in the numerical items presented as part of the cash flow budget. If you have ever faced tough financial questions during a board meeting, you can appreciate the value of prefiguring what is being conveyed by your cash flow budget. You will reap substantial benefits by anticipating questions from board members and then recording your answers in the footnote section of your cash flow budget. They will see that you want to convey more information to them—and they may appreciate that when your performance review comes around.

Better information, in terms of both the operations of your institution and the greater clarity afforded by footnotes, can enhance the understanding of every board and staff member. And that positive feeling will be elevated further if you adopt a critical strategy in dealing with the future, the use of cash flow forecasting to anticipate a range of possible futures, which we cover in the next chapter.

CHAPTER FOUR

FORECASTING IN A FRACTION OF TIME

A s the size and complexity of a nonprofit institution increases, the amount of time devoted to planning and budgeting usually increases. Some of this effort is naturally directed toward making financial forecasts. Since none of us can know the future with certainty, this raises the fundamental question of whether all the effort spent in trying to interpret the future might be better spent on other activities.

In this chapter we propose a new method for forecasting that requires minimal inputs of information. Using cash flow principles, these forecasts produce graphic images of alternative scenarios that enable board and staff members to move into the future with constantly updated information. We examine forecasting as a strategic tool for nonprofit institutions and, since forecasting and risk management are often linked, we explore the relationship between predictions and risk.

Any forecast has two dimensions. It must incorporate preparation for the future and acknowledgment of the need to be ready to adapt in the face of uncertainty. The Cash Flow Forecaster included with this book can be used to enhance forecasts, and this chapter discusses why less is sometimes more when preparing forecasts.

Forecasting the Future

Can you can tell the future? Or do you know someone who can? If so, don't waste your time holding fundraising events. Pick winning lottery numbers, or head to the racetrack and use those sure-fire predictions to buy tickets for long odds on the ponies.

For the rest of us, forecasting future events in complex systems such as nonprofit organizations is rather more challenging. As you might expect by now, we believe the key to forecasting is working within a cash flow framework.

The benefits of cash flow forecasting are many. It will save a lot of time in preparing financial reports for board meetings. Board members will have early warning of times when they will need to use a line of credit or dip into reserves. Cash flow projections can be generated quickly for discussions with bankers and others. A comparison of options based on different scenarios is readily available. Thus the board and staff will have useful, accessible information for making decisions for the organization.

A cash flow forecast is a strategic tool. To understand this, it helps to think about strategy for a moment. Strategy is all about direction. You can advance, hold still, or retreat in the face of any possible situation. The art in strategy is to both prepare for the future and adapt your response as required by changing circumstances. Forecasting provides an opportunity to imagine the future as a form of preparation. It also creates the basis for adaptation, or modifying your approach to fit new or changing circumstances.

Strategy has a directional aspect. The decision to wait until next year before buying a house can be considered strategic if holding off includes waiting for more information, for example, a pay raise or lower interest rates, or a change in the real estate market. Strategic thinking merges two behaviors: preparation or planning or even imaging done prior to acting, in this case selecting a direction to follow, and being prepared to alter or modify the action or direction if circumstances change.

Some organizations develop careful plans and then follow them without regard for changes in their environment. Some organizations do not develop meaningful plans and are constantly altering course based solely on the circumstances they encounter. Neither approach can alter the course of future events. And neither balances the demands of the environment with the dictates of the program adopted by the organization.

Forecasting involves making a prediction that something will happen. Often that requires visualizing many possible alternatives. So a forecast can include multiple predictions. It can also include an understanding that as you move toward the future, you may be required to switch quickly from one alternative to another.

The organization that is locked into a plan has made a forecast and will not deviate from it come hell or high water. The organization with no plan is not attempting to forecast at all; instead, it is purely adapting to its environment. Forecasting that is strategic is forecasting that takes both preparation and adaptation into account.

A cash flow forecast is an organizational strategy expressed in numbers. It gives heft to the goals and objectives that the organization adopts and creates measures that can be independently weighed by others. By projecting cash flow into the future, an organization can forecast its intent in a concrete manner. The forecast provides a fiscal platform for its plans. Forecasts also create a sense of the direction the organization is heading. And speaking of direction, it has been our experience that one of the principal reasons that forecasting is viewed as a once-a-year event is that the time and effort necessary to prepare forecasts demand too much of the staff. Our approach supplies a solution to the problem of tedious preparation.

Cash Flow Curves

As promised, the Cash Flow Forecaster takes some of the hard work out of imagining the future. The Forecaster software contains a critical hypothesis that stems directly from our experience of working with clients over many years. As we assisted institutions in creating cash flow budgets, we noticed a pattern with clients that we worked with year after year. At first it was subtle, but quickly it became apparent to us that the shape of the cash flow curve for any given institution was essentially the same from year to year. As Figure 4.1 and Figure 4.2 demonstrate, the shape of the cash flow curve is similar from one year to the next.

If you stop and think about it, this makes sense. Despite the apparent randomness of grants from donors and foundations, the annual life of a nonprofit institution typically has a seasonal pattern. For example, a school collects tuition for the fall semester during August and September, which results in a spike in income during those months. In May, the big fundraising event brings another surge of income as partygoers dance the night away for goodness knows how much per ticket. The summer is slow, both in income and expense, and then the cycle starts up again. People in the performing arts will recognize the seasonality of subscription campaigns and fund drives at other times.

Just looking at the shape of the annual cash flow curve—with income and expense dancing around the intersection of plus and minus numbers—provides

FIGURE 4.1. CASH FLOW FORECASTER: ONE-YEAR CURVE.

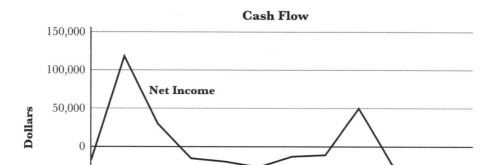

important information that links time and money, but it does not tell the whole story. The information that is not included, unless you compare one year's cash flow curve to another year's cash flow curve, is the amplitude of the curve, the degree to which income and expense increase or decrease during any given financial period.

Amplitude in this case means the extreme range of a fluctuating quantity, so if last year your school earned $100,000 during the annual fundraising auction, the income curve would have reflected that amount of revenue. If this year the school had lousy attendance at the auction and only raised $50,000, the general shape of the curve in time would be the same. It would occur, as before, during the month of the auction, but the amplitude—or the height of the curve—would be half the size of the prior year, since $50,000 is half of $100,000.

In other words, our hypothesis simply says seasonal or recurring activities will be reflected in the same general time frame as the income and expense curves that characterize a specific institution. What may vary is the size of the curve, based on the actual income or expense obtained. Most forecasting systems focus on the amount of increase or decrease that will occur from year to year. We leave that to the manager to estimate using the Cash Flow Forecaster. However, the built-in algorithms allocate the estimated increases or decreases along a curve that is

FIGURE 4.2. CASH FLOW FORECASTER: THREE-YEAR CURVE.

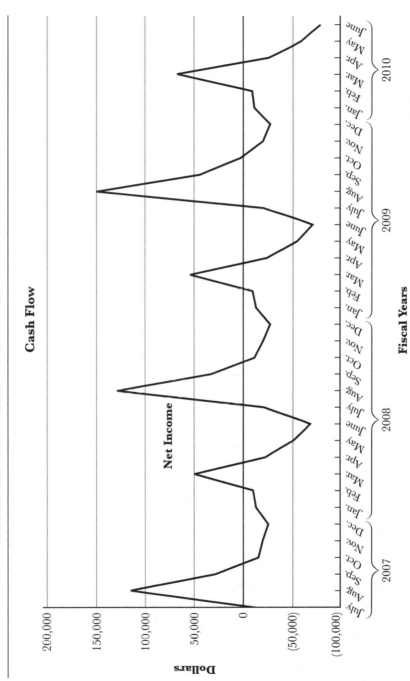

generated in the base year, and those algorithms control the shape of the curve in coming years. So even if the anonymous donation last year and the sudden increase in heating oil costs were not anticipated, the overall shape of the curve might seem pretty constant from one year to the next. As a result, the cash flow curve can become an important tool for forecasting.

Preparation and Adaptability

Cash flow forecasting has been around for a long time. Staff members of your institution may already be using a cash flow spreadsheet to project the numbers for future budgets. Cash flow spreadsheets enable you to manipulate and calculate the rows and columns within a budget projection. If you want to explore different projections of income and expense, individual calculations must be performed to see how they unfold over the course of the fiscal year.

The Cash Flow Forecaster is different from conventional spreadsheets, because it contains algorithms that provide an allocation formula based on our hypothesis about the similarity of the shape of your institution's cash flow curve from year to year. This means that when you introduce assumptions into the Cash Flow Forecaster, the entire budget is revised, and the graphics enable you to see the impact of your judgment at once.

For example, say that you want to see a scenario in which earned income for next year will increase by 5 percent and that all expenses, including inflation, will increase by 7 percent. You have already filled out an item-by-item cash flow budget, or you have simply taken the monthly totals for income and expense for the preceding year and introduced them into the three-year table in the Cash Flow Forecaster. You have put in a date for the starting month of your fiscal year, a date for the preceding year, a starting balance—either plus or minus—and then twenty-four numbers reflecting actual income and expense for each month in the prior year. You are then asked to drop in the assumptions from your scenario, in the form of percentages of increasing or decreasing value, into the appropriate cells, and the rest is figured for you. The effect of your assumed scenario on the institution's budget is instantly available in both numerical and graphic formats.

Given the ease of testing different assumptions, it is feasible to generate many different scenarios, one after another. You have more choices this way, and since each assumption represents a potential future path, if you monitor your progress through the year, you can assess the impact of your assumptions and the accuracy of your financial predictions.

The Cash Flow Forecaster enables you to prepare for and adapt in the face of an unknowable future. In this context, preparation is the process of gathering and analyzing financial data to formulate budgets and projections. Adaptation is the process of generating alternative scenarios, some of which may be used to accommodate the institution's strategy to changing circumstances.

Preparation: The Classic Approach

In classic financial management systems, the emphasis is on preparation. If you believe that past performance has a powerful influence on future results, then it makes perfect sense to concentrate your efforts on careful preparation. You are betting that the more precise and comprehensive your preparation, the greater control you may exert on the future. We believe just the opposite is true. While the past is helpful to review, it is really much more useful to focus on the possibilities that may emerge in an unknowable future. Within our approach, the emphasis is on adaptability by the generation of alternative scenarios or possibilities that can be matched up quickly with changing circumstances that unfold as the year progresses.

The classic approach to forecasting normally compiles lots of historical information during the budget development process. The implicit goal of all those late-night meetings and earnest roundtable discussions is to muster the intellectual resources of the institution in an attempt to obtain precision in forecasting. Yet when you review most of the texts in the field, you find the authors still advocate having credit or a cash reserve in place to cover shortfalls and unexpected drops in income or increases in expenses. In other words, good risk management still calls for hedging your bets, regardless of the effort that went into the forecasts.

Our approach leads to exactly the same place: the use of credit to respond to the unexpected. The difference is that we consciously avoid the mustering of significant institutional resources in the form of endless meetings, the late-night budgetary preparation sessions, the staff time to aggregate all this information, and the administrative time spent trying to make a coherent case to the board for forecasts that rarely work in the end.

Instead we urge our clients to rely on the pattern or curve created by actual income and expense figures from the prior year. From our point of view, the ease of using the prior year's actuals and not the prior year's budgeted numbers helps to create a realistic platform of what actually happened last year from which to move into the future.

Adaptability: The Current Requirement

As an example of the need for institutional adaptation, consider the changes that will need to take place at the Bill and Melinda Gates Foundation now that Warren Buffet has decided to donate approximately $1.5 billion a year, to be spent within each year the gift is received. The BMG Foundation will have to seriously adapt itself to handle the doubling of grant volumes anticipated from Buffet's largesse. At almost every level, the foundation will need to modify and adapt its policies and procedures to handle the larger volume of grant making required by the gift.

Another example is reflected in our work with a client a number of years ago. We consulted with a theater that had just discovered a major deficit, which the business manager had hidden by some creative accounting and persuaded an unsuspecting auditor to approve. To save the institution, we helped them to institute a creditholder program to generate collateral, which meant they could then borrow from their bank. (We discuss the creditholder concept in detail in Chapter Nine.) A fully secured term loan from the bank quickly got them back up to speed. Then this tiny theater suddenly had first one, then two, and finally three hit shows in succession. Because the shows were each so successful, we urged them to rent additional venues and continue to take in the income instead of terminating each show at the end of its scheduled subscription run. During a nine-month period, this small theater had three shows playing to standing-room-only houses, all at the same time. It was, for that moment, the second-largest employer of Equity Actors outside New York City. Talk about the need to make some major adaptations, and quickly.

Here is another example of the difference between the classic approach to forecasting and our approach. Imagine that you could observe all the administrative personnel at a major educational institution, hard at work on their annual planning endeavor. You might see that they were using a planning and budgeting process that was lengthy and time-consuming. When the effort was over, they would undoubtedly have produced a well-informed document allocating resources effectively for the coming year. But would these planning and budgeting efforts be adequate for forecasting?

If you believe that forecasting is largely about preparation, then it is likely that you would believe that these efforts will be rewarded. In effect, you are betting on past performance and good planning to prepare for the future. But what really happens?

In a three-year period Stanford University, despite its excellent budgetary planning process and long history of effective fundraising, experienced a series of unanticipated circumstances that in the 2001 fiscal year resulted in the receipt of $120 million less in gifts and grants than in the year 2000—a 26 percent drop in contributions. During the same three-year period Stanford's endowment, one of the largest in the country, took major hits in a sour market, which significantly decreased the amount of investment income available. In 2003, the institution suffered a $20 million deficit, which prompted it to freeze faculty and staff salaries for the coming year.[1]

Knowing all this, suppose you tried to predict the cash flow balance at the end of the year in Stanford's budget three years hence. You would want to know something about the recent income and expense figures from the institution, perhaps from last year. You also might like some information about the characteristic pattern of income and expense in relation to time that constitutes Stanford's cash flow.

This is a function that the Cash Flow Forecaster serves. It automatically supplies an allocation formula for the likely cycle of income and expense over time that characterizes the University, based on last year's actual income and expense. Because it does this with much less input, the Cash Flow Forecaster allows you to keep advancing your forecast on a daily, weekly, monthly, or quarterly basis. Since you can easily feed in new information, you are likely to be highly adaptive as conditions change from month to month. In the case of Stanford, the use of a rolling forecast might have allowed the institution to avoid some of the difficulties that it ran into when its budgetary process failed to mirror the rapid changes in its environment.

Stanford University is hardly a target for criticism. Rather, its experience, which incidentally is mirrored by many other organizations across the nation in the past few years, may be helpful and instructive.

This example demonstrates the difference between the conventional approach to forecasting—which calls for a considerable amount of time and energy and tends to lock the institution into a game plan—and our method. By making the process itself simpler and easier through the judicious use of automation and some mathematical concepts, our hope is that institutions can be more adaptable and responsive to changing conditions.

What this means for administrators is that the Cash Flow Forecaster enables people with diverse levels of skill in financial management to grasp the notion that it is possible to keep advancing their forecasts and to generate new scenarios as a way to be both prepared and adaptable. In this way, the Cash Flow Forecaster opens the door to rolling forecasts, within which actual income and expense figures can be tracked on a monthly basis and changes made strategically.

Rolling Forecasts as an Alternative to Static Predictions

We advocate a different process of forecasting from the one currently used by many institutions. That is, we recommend rolling forecasts rather than static predictions—prompt and nimble course corrections based on live data. In *Beyond Budgeting,* Jeremy Hope and Robin Fraser discuss the concept of businesses moving away from the fixed targets and performance-oriented incentives imposed by the strictures of current budgetary approaches.[2] They discuss the importance of rolling forecasts as a means to update estimates that are made about the future financial position of an organization.

The notion of checking and interpreting the resulting information in short intervals is sometimes difficult for people who are wedded to the idea of following the game plan, no matter what. We have sat in boardrooms where the call to stay the course was an emotional rallying cry. Yet reacting and responding to change, being adaptable and responsive to the environment, also has its advocates. The issue is not which posture is more emotionally satisfying, but rather how the leadership can use the financial data to gauge the momentum of an institution in light of its missions and its environment. Fiscal information can serve as a guide to the fit between the institution and its environment. It can reveal the need for financial resources, and it can also reveal the need to examine whether the institution is still fulfilling its mission.

Rolling forecasts should not open the door to micromanagement by board members. The broader picture that leadership is required to consider in the financial arena should not become the excuse for backseat driving on the part of the board. Monthly monitoring should not be used as an opportunity by the board to tell you and your staff that your allocations were wrong. It is the job of the board to provide coherence, which means a clear sense of the institution's direction and a moral sense of what is correct or incorrect practice. That does not mean meddling in day-to-day operations. Rolling forecasts can be useful to both board and staff as a means to arrive at decisions that are strategically sound for the institution in relation to a changing environment.

Getting Started with the Cash Flow Forecaster

This is the perfect time to open the Cash Flow Forecaster and take a look at how it works. First you need to click the "Quick Instruction" tab and read the instructions—which you can follow even if you don't have a solid grounding in information technology. They will get you started—and if you want to dive right in and start using the program, check out the more detailed info on the "Instructional Guide" tab.

Here are two rules to follow. First, use cash-basis accounting concepts rather than accrual accounting concepts when you fill out the Cash Flow Forecaster. Since most nonprofit institutions that have been audited use accrual accounting, you will want to reach instead for your checkbook and the petty cash account. Only money that has been received and deposited counts in our system. So if you collected money at the annual auction, you can count that as revenue, but if someone promised to pay next week, you should make a note and leave it off the system until the money is received. The same is true for credit card expenses. Yes, you swiped your card for those office supplies in October, but you actually wrote the check to the bank in November. Account for those charges in November. To make this simple, think bookkeeper, think checkbook, and consider letting the accountant play golf on the day that you introduce last year's actual income and expenses into the Forecaster.

In the accrual method of accounting, both income and expense are shown as soon as they have been earned or owed, even if they have not been received or paid out in cash. In this virtual world, you are tagging and accounting for items of income and expense before they are received and paid. There are perfectly good reasons to do this, and your accountant will be more than happy to explain them to you before teeing off, but for the time being remember, only cash counts when filling out the Cash Flow Forecaster.

The second rule is that you should not include depreciation or amortization expenses in your forecasting. Neither amortization and depreciation are cash expenses; you don't actually pay them to someone else. So, for the purposes of the Forecaster, leave them aside.

With these two rules in mind, sit down at the computer by yourself—or with your bookkeeper, if you have one. The first question is the month that your fiscal year starts. With this information the program automatically shuffles the template to suit your calendar, and then recommends that you be granted a gold star for following directions.

The software will begin by asking you to fill in the date for the last year in which you have actual income and expense figures by category and by month.

Make sure you have the institution's checkbook nearby, with its monthly totals for income and expense for last year, because you are also asked for a closing cash balance from the prior year (the money in the bank or the amount owed at the end of the last year).

You then post the actual income and expense figures from last year into the budget format, and as you might suspect by now, we have included a special area for footnotes to jot down any notes for each category of items. So, for example, if heating oil was especially expensive last year, you should make a note that it was higher than usual.

Once the prior year's actuals have been used to compose a cash flow budget for the year, and with detailed footnotes in hand, the algorithms that drive the Forecaster are ready to help explore the shape of things to come. The program quickly creates a cash flow curve. It shows income graphically as one line, expense as another line. It shows cash flow during the year, and it shows the accumulated financial position of the institution. This is your base year, and it really does not matter if it is representative or not. It is just the starting point for the forecasting process.

As soon as you move beyond Year One, the Forecaster has fields for making predictions based on the percentage of increase or decrease in income and expense anticipated for the coming year. Having recorded your actuals for the past year, now you have to come up with the percentage of increase or decrease in total income and expense. If you check out the Three Year segment of the Cash Flow Forecaster, you will see the fields that call for your assessment of the percentage increase or decrease in income and expense. Some administrators have a finger on the pulse of their institution and can rapidly come up with an estimate of possible increases or decreases in income and expense. Others may want to use a more analytical process.

Using the Cash Flow Forecaster: A Hospital Example

Creating effective operating strategies, for some of our clients, begins by identifying those components of income and expense that have the greatest impact on their budget. The chief fiscal officer of one hospital we have worked with identified three variables as most likely to influence the hospital's income: the number of patients served and the amount of insurance each had, the grants the institution might obtain from donors, and the institution's annual fundraising efforts. In the expense column, the CFO chose medical and administrative expenses, costs for facilities and equipment, and the debt service incurred as the hospital borrowed to encourage rapid growth in a highly competitive environment.

Looking at the base year, from the original income and expense numbers, the CFO was able to see what percentage each of these variables contributed to the overall budget. Armed with this information, he was in a position to calculate percentage increases or decreases in each of the variables and to create a weighted average so that all the numbers could be compressed into a single percentage increase or decrease for the entire fiscal year.

The logic used in coming up with a percentage figure for the income from the number of patients was straightforward. He multiplied the current projection for the number of patients, in this case 11,000, by the amount of medical services paid by insurance, plus any payments that were made out of pocket by patients. This produced a number that revealed the average payment per patient. He then projected an increase from 11,000 to 14,000 patients. He factored in the 9 percent increase in service fees planned, and this gave him a second number that established a new average rate of income. By dividing the old rate by the new rate, he obtained the percentage increase between one year and the next.

Our hospital administrator then performed the same operations for the increasing or decreasing projection for grants and for fundraising. When he had the amount, an increase in this case, he weighted the averages to reflect their overall role in the annual budget and saw that his income projection for the next year was close to 15 percent. This is the figure that he plugged into the second-year cell of the Cash Flow Forecaster in the screen for five-year budget projections. He did the same calculations for the three key variables for expense and placed the overall percentage—in this case, just under 13 percent—in the second-year cell. Following the same approach, he was able to derive percentages for each of the next four years.

Once the baseline calculations were done, it was easy to experiment with a number of different scenarios. The Cash Flow Forecaster adjusts to a change in the annual percentage figure in a nanosecond, and the CFO had six different scenarios in graphic form in a matter of moments. One final step remained: to assess each variable according to its sensitivity to direct action by the board of trustees and administrative staff. This allowed the CFO to identify which future scenarios could be most powerfully influenced by the efforts of the institution's trustees and staff.

This is the information, along with the various scenarios, that the CFO presented to the administrative director and the trustees at the next meeting. The participants of the meeting immediately saw that certain variables were outside their immediate influence, for example, the number of grant requests actually accepted by foundations, or the proceeds from fundraising efforts. They could speculate on these numbers, and they could, of course, instruct the Development Department to be more aggressive in submitting proposals or inviting aging donors to lunch, but beyond these actions, the probability of dramatic increases or decreases in gifts and grants seemed unlikely.

However, in examining the expense variables, they saw one item that was very sensitive to their direct action. The long-term borrowing that the institution had done in years past to fund new facilities and equipment was a fixed cost on the budget. Over time it had gradually slipped out of everyone's awareness. While playing with the Cash Flow Forecaster, the CFO had plugged in some numbers that reflected a lower interest rate and shorter term for the debt. With the immediate cost of refinancing, the impact of these changes was not particularly impressive, but gradually, over a number of years these costs could have a measurable and positive impact on the bottom line. Loans had been obtained at a time when interest rates were relatively high and their terms were not particularly favorable to the hospital. By consolidating the loans and refinancing the loan package, the hospital might achieve savings that would significantly reduce costs.

In addition, once the idea of refinancing was raised, several trustees who had strongly advocated developing and sustaining a cash reserve started to reconsider their support for that plan. A few calculations were enough to convince them that tapping into the cash reserve to reduce the level of debt might be productive. The transfer of funds did not pose any immediate risk to the institution, and the savings on debt service were actually greater than the earnings being generated by the reserves in an unsettled market.

Trustees and staff decided to talk to their bank about the cash flow numbers generated by the scenarios to see if an optimal basis for refinancing and reducing their cash reserve could be reached that would be acceptable to both parties. This proved to be a very critical decision; it turned out that the bank was willing to see the cash reserve diminish as a potential source of collateral in light of the lower interest rates the institution was requesting.

Granting that the forecast itself was fuzzy, the course of action to be pursued was anything but vague. It pointed toward a strategy that board and staff members could undertake at once, with a favorable impact on the institution. By directing their attention and energies to this one variable, the board and staff were able to quickly and positively influence the financial outlook of the hospital for several years to come.

Using the Cash Flow Forecaster: An Education Example

Exhibit 4.1 is an example from an educational institution that used a very simple method to weight the averages of different variables and come up with one percentage figure for income and another figure for expense.

EXHIBIT 4.1. SIMPLIFIED WEIGHTING STRATEGY FOR DETERMINING OVERALL PERCENTAGE OF CHANGE: AN EDUCATION EXAMPLE.

For Income (or Expense):

1. Determine the major income (expense) items.

2. Determine the percentage contribution of each of these items to the total income.

3. Using past trends or other data, estimate next year's percentage increase for each major item.

4. Multiply the percentage contribution of each item by its associated percentage increase.

5. Total the products to find the overall percentage.

Income Example:

1. Determine the major income items.
   Total income   1,477,472
   Tuition income   945,582
   Fundraising income   356,000
   Other revenue   175,890

2. Determine the percentage contribution of each major item.
   Tuition income   945,582   64%
   Fundraising income   356,000   24%

3. Using past trends, estimate next year's percentage increase for each major
   item.
   Tuition income   23%
   Fundraising income   5%

4. Multiply the percentage contribution of each item by its associated
   percentage increase.
   Tuition income (64% contribution by tuition x 23% increase)   15%
   Fundraising income (24% x 5%)   1%

5. Total the products to find the overall percentage
   Tuition income (64% x contribution x 23% increase)   15%
   Fundraising income (24% x 5%)   1%

   Overall Percentage Increase for Income   16%

A cash flow forecast links future plans with numbers. This helps to focus every-one's attention on strategy—the direction that can be taken to accomplish a change. The strategy is different from the forecast in the sense that it evolves out of the possibilities multiple forecasts provide. The Cash Flow Forecaster is crucial in making the task of forecasting less cumbersome. The benefit is that more time is available to think about the implications of the future and to imagine actions that may be more effective in the present.

Clearly, working out all the calculations before dropping them into the Cash Flow Forecaster is not an easy task, but with a little practice, you can get pretty good at imagining the possibilities or creating templates for varying your assumptions. Or you may want to try out a number of scenarios just to see what might happen. For example, you might try a high-income, low-expense prediction, or a high-expense, low-income one. Are you still curious? Then key in a scenario in which income and expense do not change a great deal, a more moderate scenario. These are simply guesses that establish a range of possibilities that you can use to compare and contrast your progress on a month-by-month basis as the year proceeds.

These scenarios give you a sense of what might happen, but—as you know—they don't tell you what will happen. Instead, by tracking your monthly progress through the year, using each month's actuals as they occur, you and your board can see if you need to make adjustments or to anticipate changes in your actions. If all this sounds strangely strategic, it is. Your scenarios provide a range of options, and since all strategy devolves to a decision to advance, retreat, or hold still, your actions on any given financial front will be subject to the test of strategy. To wit, did it work? And can you do it again?

Remember, being strategic is more than a once-a-year activity. Using the Cash Flow Forecaster to both forecast and monitor your results will enable you to be strategic on an ongoing basis. And speaking of strategy, here is a little tip on thinking strategically: try to look at information without assigning a moral value to it. The wise strategist knows that what appears to be favorable one moment may be unfavorable the next. It is useful to contemplate or appreciate the information before deciding whether it is good or bad news. When people talk about turning a lemon into lemonade, they are expressing a truism about finding a way to adapt to bad news and turn it into good news.

Adapting means paying special attention to the changing environment surrounding your institution. To forecast effectively, you need to read the feedback provided by the environment in which you operate. You have to try the models or scenarios out, see how well their predictions work in the real world, and, if need be, adjust the models to do better the next time. All adaptive agents such as administrators or board members have to be able to take advantage of what the world is trying to tell them.

With the Cash Flow Forecaster, we are simply shortening the cycle from the more typical annual planning and prediction function to one that can be viewed twelve times or fifty-two times or more in a year. By making the inputs to the system simple and easy, or at least painless and inexpensive, you increase the opportunity to generate, test, and adapt your scenarios. This will allow you to be better prepared for the uncertainty of the future and more effective in trying to adapt to circumstances as they arise.

Dealing with Unusual Events

How about taking the past three years and averaging the figures before dropping them into the Cash Flow Forecaster?

If last year was lousy or absolutely terrific, it may not seem to be at all representative. Yet trying to establish a representative year is actually much more difficult than it seems. Oh, the math is easy—that's not the problem. The difficulty comes in making a determination of what is representative. Attempting to average the past years will really confuse the situation. Remember, the shape of the curve is probably going to be the same, but the amplitude will have changed, and that is based on actuals. It is much better to footnote the differences and then go with what actually happened, since there is no way of knowing if this will be repeated in the coming year.

Here's a concrete example. Say a social service agency has an annual contract with the state to provide services. This contract is a major portion of the agency's income, only supplemented by some special fundraising appeals. If the state is late one year with its payment, the income side of the curve will be depressed, while the expense side of the curve may remain fairly constant. Will the agency throw out this year because the interruption in funding is an unusual event that may not be repeated in the future? Or say oil prices go through the roof one year and heating costs go up crushingly. Does that make the year invalid?

It is easy to imagine that looking back at three to five years of actuals would suggest that such events are anomalies. But what if something is not a one-time occurrence? Should you discount it because it does not average out over time? Our suggestion is that you use the actuals from last year, and then watch the monthly actuals carefully as the year progresses. In this way you are not betting that the past will average out anytime soon.

In the world of commercial investment, the ill-fated hedge fund Long-Term Capital Management counted some of the brightest minds of the economic world on its staff and board. In its financial practices it consistently bet heavily that its investments would "regress to the mean," which is another way of saying that they would average out over time. This did not happen in a timely fashion, and the bailout of the fund cost billions. Roger Lowenstein's *When Genius Failed: The Rise and Fall of Long-Term Capital Management* documents the tragic consequences to U.S. financial institutions of this meltdown.[3] The lesson here is to be careful about relying too much on the past to shape your decisions about the present and the future.

Long-Range Forecasts

Long-range forecasts are really tough. Who predicted the breakup of the Soviet Union, or the presidential election results of 2000, which brought us the second Bush administration? Nevertheless, you actually can try to make predictions for multiple years. Just remember that the further out you forecast, the less likely you are to be very accurate. What is most important is to start thinking in terms of cash flow and to make sure that you have a warning of any potholes ahead in the road.

The Forecaster can be used to run out to twenty years. We built this feature because we were interested in helping organizations not only conceptualize their cash flow, but also develop a revolving line of credit and term debt to manage their cash flow. For now, those long-term forecasts may not be meaningful, but if you ever need them, they are nice to have, in much the same way this knowledge is useful when you have a long-term mortgage.

Imagine for a moment that an organization ended last year with an unexpectedly high deficit. After checking to make sure that the deficit was really an anomaly, the executive director and the board might consider dealing with the shortfall by taking out a five-year term loan. (A term loan is a multiple-year loan that has a fixed monthly payment for interest and principal.) The Forecaster can help the board to see under what conditions the loan can be repaid and how much still needs to be raised to sustain operations.

Figure 4.3 is an example of a seven-year cash flow forecast that a small private mental health clinic called Salud Mental used to address its financial circumstances. It turns out that even a peek at possible futures can be helpful to board members.

In this seven-year forecast, the organization was anticipating a slight decline in income in the second year and higher expenses the following year. Then, as the number of clients got closer to capacity, the increases in income and expense would stabilize. What makes this projection valuable is not the accuracy of the numbers but the way it allows the board and staff to quickly see the impact of slight variations in the enrollment of clients and in their ability to address midyear increases in heating oil expenses, in relationship to the entire annual budget. The shape of the curve remains constant in this seven-year projection; after all, it was generated using the starting year's numbers as a base. However, as the annual income and expense assumptions were introduced, they showed a definite upward trend. This is the key to using the forecast. On an overall level the pattern plus the assumptions reveal a trend that is instantly apparent.

It is useful to note that the clinic was able to meet its seven-year projections during a period that was remarkably turbulent for the economy, when many nonprofit organizations suffered. By using cash flow as a basic budgetary instrument and the Cash Flow Forecaster as a source of guidance, the institution kept itself in good shape.

Here is how it worked out. Salud Mental grew rapidly in its first year and then saw its income decline. By the end of 2002, the effect of a two-year downturn in the local economy made the current level of costs a challenge for many patients. Looking ahead, the board feared that income could decline for the first time in the next year. Despite some state aid and new insurance plans, there was just not

FIGURE 4.3. CASH FLOW FORECASTER: SEVEN-YEAR PROJECTION.

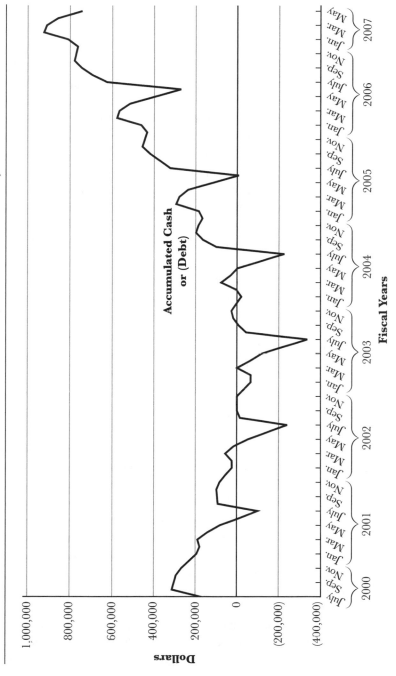

enough income to provide the supplements needed to attract many new clients. Matching the actuals on a month-by-month basis with the projected income and expense in a cash flow framework, the board was able to see that early in 2003 corrective action would need to be taken to deal with future events.

Using the Cash Flow Forecaster, the board and staff of Salud Mental examined their assumptions with regard to the preceding years. By concentrating on the overall picture, they were reminded of a recurring pattern of interest by clients who could almost, but not quite, afford the current level of fees. These clients earned too much to qualify for state aid and yet not enough to pay the total fees. Playing with the Forecaster's capacity to quickly generate scenarios, the board found that changing the percentage of income by a few points indicated that a change in the fee policy might be worthwhile. This is a common phenomenon; the figures in various cash flow scenarios often trigger tactical ideas such as these.

In a meeting that took place in November 2002, the board decided to adopt three measures to compensate for an early indication of declining revenue:

- An analysis of fees was undertaken, and a decision was made to reduce them by 20 percent for 2003 as a means to increase the number of clients, after it was determined that caseloads could increase at least that much without a loss of quality service.
- A review of the budget indicated that total expenses could be reduced only by 10 percent. The clinic was running about as lean as could be imagined.
- Given a heads-up, Salud Mental alerted its bank that early indications were that income would be down and, despite some cuts in expenses, the deficit for the year was likely to be slightly higher than originally budgeted.

These measures had an immediate effect. The reduction in fees did result in higher enrollments of clients for 2003, which allowed the program to come within 2 percent of its income goals for the year. The cuts in expenses covered a percentage of the shortfall, and the bank, having been given an early warning, increased the credit available to the program for the year by 15 percent.

What does all this information mean for the future prospects of Salud Mental? By staying on top of cash flow and by trying different forecast scenarios, the clinic was able to respond quickly to a downturn in clients; its staff were able to take three significant corrective actions, and these actions had a positive financial effect on the bottom line.

The cash flow budget and the Cash Flow Forecaster allowed board and staff members to manage fiscal risk more effectively. It did this by identifying points along the year when there was a high probability that some form of precautionary action might be necessary. With a heads-up provided by the Forecaster, the board and staff of the institution saw when it needed to borrow using the institution's fully secured line of credit to bridge the temporary shortfall.

Strategy and Cash Flow Forecasting, Together At Last

The Cash Flow Forecaster allows both large and small organizations to project their cash flow. It creates a "fuzzy forecast," one that is useful for dealing with future events. The conventional approach creates what appears to be a precise forecast, yet, in truth, any forecast is subject to the uncertain nature of the future.

Our intent when forecasting is not to be seduced by the appearance of precision but rather to become comfortable with the hazy, uncertain nature of the forecast itself. It is essential to remember, as Peter L. Bernstein reminds us: "Anything can happen. We do not and cannot know the future."[4] Yet, as Bernstein also reminds us, "Whether you should take a risk depends not just on the probability that you are right, but also on the consequences if you are wrong." It is the willingness to pose these consequences to ourselves and to the board that makes the job of administration so vital in looking ahead.

Clearly the Cash Flow Forecaster is not a substitute for human judgment within your organization. But it will increase the financial comprehension of your decision makers by making the modeling of future scenarios very easy. It is a tool that provides decision makers with a clear overview of the cash flow of an institution. It also encourages effective risk management by alerting managers and board members to unanticipated financial problems. Finally, the act of reviewing possibilities will often stimulate new and strategic thoughts about how to solve these problems.

These thoughts should help to set your mind at ease about whether the Cash Flow Forecaster will pinpoint your exact financial position two years out, to the penny. It won't. What it will do is to enable you to recast your forecasts and see their implications at once. As a consequence, you will be able to identify things that lend themselves to direct action and others that require patience and watchful attention. Focused strategic action is the adaptive component that allows you to change with regard to your environment. By placing special emphasis on the adaptive component of forecasting, we are urging you to consider using your forecasts as a vehicle for moving into the future.

Forecasting of cash flow is important because it requires a comprehensive understanding of all the strategic elements confronting a nonprofit institution. The administrator must be able to assess the strengths and weaknesses of the organization, and also the opportunities and obstacles posed by the environment. If securing profitability is a classic test for the CEO of a commercial enterprise, then accurately forecasting the cash flow of a nonprofit institution is a comparable skill in the nonprofit world.

A corollary to this skill is the ability to manage the risks forecasting illuminates. Because there will always be unknowns that impact their endeavors, managers need to hedge by making provision for an unexpected outcome. Managers who do so are acknowledging that even the best forecasts can be altered by circumstances beyond the institution's control.

If the goal of financial forecasting is perfection, then a lot of fiscal sages are in serious trouble. Our advice is to prepare adequately, use the Cash Flow Forecaster to speed up your work, and then be willing to adapt to changing circumstances, whether in or out of your control. The goal, as we see it, is to be able to forecast in a way that is ordinary, and good enough to help you and your board to move your institution in the right direction.

This advice is also our way of moving you toward the next chapter, which is on fiscal monitoring using cash flow. Paying attention is the key word for monitoring, and that is the way that you take the right steps to get from point A to your desired point B.

CHAPTER FIVE

MONITORING

A Key Element in Developing Financial Strategies

To govern and administer a nonprofit wisely, you have to monitor its financial information. That is, the leadership of a nonprofit organization should be constantly focused on the question of whether or not the financial data indicates any changes in the external environment or within the institution. By monitoring the financial progress of the institution through the year, decision makers establish the basis for acting strategically as circumstances allow.

Ready access to financial information that is readily understood—and forecasts that can be easily converted into alternative scenarios—enhances the strategic capacity of the leaders of an institution. It makes adaptability more likely, and it certainly makes for more vibrant reports from the treasurer.

In this chapter we explore some very basic terminology, starting with the term *monitoring* as it relates first to strategy in general and then to financial strategy in particular. We present our cash flow–based approach to financial monitoring and contrast it with other methods of monitoring that are currently used by the field. In the course of this examination we take a hard look at the issue of whether past performance helps anyone understand and predict future results.

An issue that arises again and again in nonprofit boardrooms is whether or not the carefully prepared financial reports—crafted at such expense in terms of staff time and energy—are useful to board members in making fiscal decisions. We suggest that the process of generating financial reports needs to be greatly simplified, and at the same time the reports that are being monitored need to be much more meaningful to board members and managers when formulating institutional strategy. In this chapter we demonstrate an approach that reduces the volume of information that board members are required to review and at the same time decreases the time spent by administrators preparing financial reports—and still provides a net increase in useful information transferred.

Because monitoring is such a basic component in the formulation of strategy, it is useful to define the function that monitoring serves in the nonprofit organization. *Monitoring,* according to the dictionary, stems from a Latin word meaning "to warn." And it is precisely the cautionary aspect of monitoring that differentiates it from the notion of simply observing phenomena or circumstances. As a manager or as a board member you are monitoring your organization with the intent of warning yourself and others when things are not going in what you believe is the right direction.

Monitoring as Assessment

When you monitor the financial reports of your institution, you are conducting a form of organizational assessment. You are looking for evidence of organizational strengths and weaknesses. Monitoring cash flow income and expense can also gauge the impact of the environment on your institution. In this sense, it is a form of external assessment, as you try to spot opportunities that may arise within the environment or obstacles that may impede your progress.

What are we looking for when we monitor financial reports?

Before the next financial report from your institution lands in your hands, it is helpful to pause and consider your own ideas about what you are about to observe. Observation is never a completely neutral activity. All observers bring ideas to the process that can alter their perception of what they see and what it means.

Monitoring incorporates several considerations—some inherently pragmatic and others ultimately philosophical. For example, on a pragmatic level, you might be interested in seeing in the financial report an indication of how the institution is performing as it attempts to cut costs. Conversely, on a more philosophical level you might look for indications that your approach to something, let's say some of the services you are providing, is affirmed or contradicted by the fiscal information. On this level, the financial reports can help you to glimpse whether you are using the right strategy to accomplish your goals. Understanding what you are trying to learn from the available information is the first practical consideration when dealing with monitoring.

Once you have ascertained what the focus of your monitoring should be, the next practical consideration is: Who needs to know what? Or, how can you divide the labor of monitoring between board and staff to create the greatest useful understanding of the institution's financial position?

On the more philosophical side, as Peter Bernstein points out in *Against the Gods*, "[There is] a persistent tension between those who assert that the best decisions are based on quantification and numbers, determined by the patterns of the past, and those who base their decisions on more subjective degrees of belief about the uncertain future."[1] This debate boils down to one's view about the extent to which the past determines the future. And the issue of reliance on the past to predict the future has a profound bearing on the approach to monitoring adopted by managers and board members of a nonprofit institution.

How do we sort out the most meaningful fiscal information for our organization?

From a business perspective, the bottom line involves the assets minus liabilities that constitute a company's profit at the end of the year. Monitoring in business does track cash flow, recognizing that it is the lifeblood of the enterprise, but the real focus for the shareholders is seeing how much the company nets when the fiscal year ends. And, of course, how much they stand to gain as investors.

In the mission-oriented nonprofit sector, we believe that the key to effective monitoring is to concentrate on actual income and expense in relation to time. Of course, everyone on staff and on the board waits breathlessly for the auditor's final report that declares how the assets and liabilities balance out. But at meetings during the year, the importance of cash flow in dictating strategy should be clear. Your cash flow will serve as an indicator that your strategy is working the way that you imagined it, or it may show you that it is not working as you had hoped. Cash flow reports can signal that it is time to change direction—or that it makes sense to stay the course, at least until the next report.

An organization's cash flow is the key to providing information that is critical in establishing the basis for an ongoing financial strategy. Therefore, it logically follows that looking at income and expense on a monthly basis will be the most meaningful way to proceed. This is easily accomplished by having the bookkeeper place the most current monthly totals for income and expense into the Cash Flow Forecaster at the end of each month. You can instantly see the status of your organization and compare it with two different sets of numbers. By simply looking at the graphic images for last year's actuals and then by looking at the current actuals for this month you can see the difference between your income and expense from last year and the monthly totals for income and expense for this year. This comparison is quite concrete. You will see actual-to-actual results by month over the period of a year. If income was higher last March than it is this March, you will instantly see the difference and its implications for the coming months.

Figure 5.1 illustrates this. The graph lines reveal the difference for those who are less inclined to spot the numerical differences.

FIGURE 5.1. CASH FLOW COMPARISON (INCOME AND EXPENSE): 2005 AND 2006, AS OF MARCH 2006.

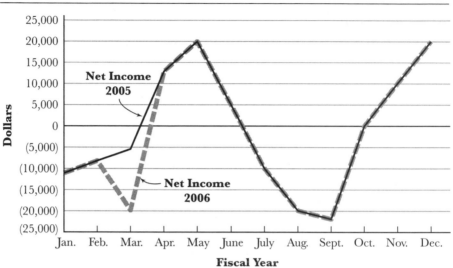

What you are seeing is a direct comparison between the actual figures for the month of March in one year and actual figures for the next year. There was a significant drop in income, from $34,158 in the first year to $17,500 in the next year. Expenses dropped modestly from $39,594 to $36,482, but the overall impact on the institution was substantial.

Unless more income is anticipated that will help to compensate for this drop, it is likely that the administration and the board will need to quickly decide whether to reduce expenses, if that is an option, or to redouble efforts to gain additional resources, or to call the bank and make sure the fully secured line of credit is available for the months ahead. In this case, the information signals the need for some action.

However, if the forecast generated near the end of the last year had projected a likelihood that March might be a month with less income and slightly less expense, the differences could be much smaller, and you might proceed with a sense that your forecasts were moving into the future with some confidence. For example, if the forecast had projected a drop in income to approximately $20,000, given a shift in funding for a grant from a local foundation, the difference between that figure and the actual income number of $17,500 would be far less surprising—and less depressing.

When you compare your forecast for income and expense with the actual amounts for the most recent month, this information serves to let you know how close your estimates were to the actual income and expense ultimately registered in your accounts.

When you are using your forecast as the base, the Cash Flow Forecaster has a built-in program that automatically calculates how your advancing numbers may play out until the end of the year. The consequences of the actual-to-actual income and expense, or the forecast-to-actual income and expense, will be presented by the software both numerically and graphically.

Allocating Monitoring Responsibilities

It is axiomatic that for financial management to be successful, someone has to pay attention to the details. Counting the beans is after all a large part of what taking care of business is all about. But do board members always have to be the ones counting, or is this a case where a division of labor might be a benefit to everyone?

The answer, we believe, is that board members need to see the big picture, the general direction in which the institution is heading. Boards are asked to make policy, not to mull over every detail in the ledger. Pointing the way for the institution to proceed should not mean weighing each item on a long budget form against its historical or forecast counterpart.

Board members need to see whether the institution's monthly income and expenses are significantly different this year from what they were last year. Differences in these overall numbers should then be discussed in the boardroom and decisions made to effect a shift in plans or policies if called for by circumstances. Strategy is very much the responsibility of the board, in concert with administrators. Tactical shifts, on the other hand, should be left to staff, since they are normally tasked with implementing strategy within fairly broad parameters established by the board.

On the other hand, administrators and their professional financial advisers must pay careful attention to the details, the item-by-item issues that have an immediate impact on operations. If the price of heating oil has suddenly climbed but the price of paper has dropped, the staff is meant to assess the impact of these numbers on operations and to make adjustments, in some cases on a weekly basis. The item-by-item approach is a tool for linking actual figures from the past to current figures and taking action where needed.

This differentiation between what the administration needs to know and what the board needs to know may seem uncomfortable to some. However, is it any more uncomfortable than sitting at a meeting at which a board member spends an hour pressing the executive director for an item-by-item explanation for why office supplies are more expensive than last year? Or watching the entire board engaged in a discussion over a category that makes up less than .005 percent of the total budget?

We believe that it is also much more important for senior administrators to act strategically in the financial realm. It is their job to find the best fit between the strengths and weaknesses that characterize your institution and the obstacles and opportunities that your environment offers you.

Administrators do need access to the details. But, just like the board members, they also need to see the big picture. Rather than sweating the variance between an item-by-item analysis of this year's actuals for income and expense and your budgeted figures, we suggest cutting to the chase. Use the Cash Flow Forecaster to report the total monthly changes that occur between the figures based on last year's actual income and expense and this year's actual monthly income and expense figures. And then plug in the numbers for the projected income and expense and compare those figures to the actual monthly totals. The Cash Flow Forecaster instantly reveals the implications of these numbers for the rest of the year. For the majority of board members and senior administrators who are monitoring an organization's fiscal affairs, the actual-to-actual and the actual-to-projected figures are enough to work with, when they can see them in the context of the entire fiscal year's cash flow. And the amount of information they need to review is much more manageable.

In other words, using a larger palette allows both the administration and the board to see if things are moving in the right direction. Remember, all the detail is there. Nothing has been lost by using cash flow or focusing on larger-scale movements in fiscal terms. Those who want detail, the nuts-and-bolts types, can have it with a brief telephone call to the bookkeeper or the individual vested with responsibility for keeping the records.

Monitoring and Financial Strategy

We have provided some criteria for deciding where to direct your monitoring, and we have proposed that the tasks be divided up so that both board and staff members can focus on information that is most meaningful for their role. Before comparing our approach to monitoring with the conventional method for monitoring, let's clarify what we mean by the term *financial strategy*.

Financial Strategy

"Stay with the game plan" may be satisfying as a cliché, but it is rarely strategic to insist on following a given course of action unless a continual stream of information informs this choice.

Faced with impenetrable thickets of data, nonprofits tend to choose among several bread-and-butter strategies. For example, some managers attempt to organize their affairs so that their institution will always have a balanced budget at year's end. The value placed on balancing the budget is powerful enough to override pursuing opportunities that suddenly arise, or it might engender an obsessive accumulation of cash reserves to avoid having to face the consequences of a shortfall. Rather than take a risk that might generate new income, the balanced-budget advocates may neglect an opportunity that might threaten the bottom line. Similarly, some administrators fight to protect their cash reserve at high levels even at the expense of operating demands. So the college administrator who insists on retaining a cash reserve equal to one full year's income is hoarding money that might be used for programs or scholarships on the notion that a drought may cut off all sources of income for the institution—a rather unlikely scenario.

Some organizations refuse to borrow, and instead adopt an implicit fiscal strategy of using their vendors or staff as their bankers when funds are not in hand. Anyone who has worked for an organization that held paychecks or bill payments until money was actually in the bank knows that the people in charge made a choice to not pay staff or vendors on time so as to avoid having to borrow. The institution's administrators or board members clearly were unconcerned with sustaining goodwill in the community or among the staff when they decided to follow this strategy.

We have worked with managers and board members who routinely cast their institutions' financial fates to the winds as a strategy, usually in the firmly held belief that they would be bailed out by supportive donors regardless of their financial misdeeds. When problems emerge the usual tactic is to blame external events such as stock market volatility, a natural disaster, or a range of rising costs for siphoning off contributions. The people responsible for the fiscal health of the organization carefully distance themselves from managing risks that have materialized, instead of handling them with a little monitoring and perhaps some short-range planning.

Then there are institutions that publicly avoid any appearance of financial difficulty by issuing statements touting their solvency, when in fact they need serious help. In these cases, the cover-up is usually seen as a way to persuade donors to continue their support of a winner rather than appeal for help and be perceived as a loser.

Not all financial strategies rely on effective monitoring. Some financial strategies are based more on ideology than on observation. Failed hedge fund Long-Term Capital Management appears to have cultivated a financial strategy that relied on the mathematical notion that market events always return to the mean within a normal distribution. Anyone who follows baseball will be familiar with this old canard. Here's an example that demonstrates that blindly following a mathematical concept may not be the best way to evoke fiscal strategy.

Long-Term Capital Management had two Nobel Prize–winning economists on its board, and that may have helped persuade investors that the idea of regression to the mean, wrapped up in financial terminology, was an adequate justification for their investment in risky derivatives and other exotic investment instruments. But as Benoit Mandelbrot, Roger Lowenstein, and others have noted, the overarching problem was a lack of an ongoing awareness that their model was not an accurate portrait of the volatility of real markets. Placing their faith in the math, the traders at LTCM failed to observe carefully the signs that might have warned them that their model was not always correct.[2]

Financial strategy in some organizations is simply to adopt a policy that mandates cuts in expenses in the face of shortfalls in income. In extreme cases, the institution may be placing a higher value on balancing its budget than on fulfilling its mission. In contrast, some board and staff members are always willing to take risks rather than cut services. This is a policy that persists even on the edge of fiscal ruin.

Strategic Monitoring

We believe that such off-the-shelf financial strategies are simply too mechanical and inflexible to address the complexity of nonprofit organizations in these economically and socially turbulent times. Instead, financial strategy should be viewed as those policies and procedures that reflect an ongoing and sometimes changing view about finding the best fit between the institution's internal conditions (its strengths and weaknesses) and its external environment (the opportunities and obstacles that are present).

The method of monitoring that we propose and use with our clients is quite different from the method they are currently using, so it makes sense to discuss it here and then to contrast it with the practices in use in most institutions.

Peering over the shoulder of Sherry, one of our clients' fiscal officers, provides some insights into how monitoring is accomplished using the Cash Flow Forecaster. At the end of each month Sherry sits down at her computer and drops two numbers into the Cash Flow Forecaster. These numbers represent the total for all income received in the past month and the total of all expenses paid during the same period. These two numbers are posted each month until the end of the fiscal year. Sherry can compare the actual totals for income and expense for the month with the previous year's totals. The Cash Flow Forecaster can easily generate graphics and numerical cash flows for each year in a matter of seconds.

What Sherry is seeing on the screen is the direct comparison of actual income and actual expense by month from last year to this year. She can immediately see changes that may require her to watch out for consequences, or that things seem pretty much as usual, in which case she may choose to simply watch the numbers and wait to see if changes occur in the next month. In other words, the financial information suggests whether the organization can stay the course or should interpret the change as a signal to action.

In establishing a base year, using actual figures for income and expense, the Cash Flow Forecaster sets a point of departure. It allows for comparison of past months with present figures. Sherry reports these figures to her boss, Susanna, the president of the college, who then asks her to quickly compare the actual figures for income and expense for this year to the projected numbers that were embedded in the budget that the board passed at the beginning of the fiscal year. Susanna has a different agenda when she asks for a comparison of these figures. Her interest in monitoring the difference between the projections in the budget and this year's actual income and expense total is to see if alternatives need to be considered in light of changes that may be occurring. Her decision to adopt a new set of fiscal alternatives, made in consultation with the board, is consistent with the use of a rolling or moving forecast to allow the organization to be adaptable. She and the board are trying to anticipate whether the institution will have a surplus or a deficit and then to take immediate action to keep things on course.

Since the Cash Flow Forecaster has a provision for calculating percentage increases or decreases for income and expense, the figures are instantly available to Susanna. She is able to see where the forecasts for income and expense differ from this year's actual income and expense numbers. The differences in total figures for income and expense are an effective measure of the degree to which the forecast was accurate. So if the actual income and expense numbers are close to the forecast, Susanna might assume that things are financially on track and there is no need to consider alternative measures. On the other hand, if the actual income and expense figures are quite different from the forecast, Susanna might be inclined to dig a little deeper into the specific items that contributed to the difference. She and Sherry can easily review the accounts in the accounting software package that they use, and together they can spot the increases or decreases in specific areas.

If the forecast calls for income that did not arrive in the past month, or if expenses were much higher than the projected figures, Susanna can call the board president, Cynthia, and ask her to chat with the members of the Executive Committee about this circumstance.

In this example, the board approved the college's budget last year based on the strong possibility of a large grant arriving from the XYZ Foundation. However, recent communications from the foundation suggest that the grant may be delayed beyond the term of this fiscal year. To accommodate this recent development, Susanna alerts Cynthia. After reviewing the numbers and glancing at the graphic images from the Cash Flow Forecaster sent to her via e-mail, Cynthia is in a position to decide if the board needs to consider some of the alternative scenarios that were developed at the board budget session at the start of the fiscal year.

During the planning session, one board member urged everyone to consider the possibility that the anticipated large grant might not come through. At the time this seemed unlikely, but the board was willing to go along with the request because it took just seconds to see the scenario using the Cash Flow Forecaster. As a result, an alternative scenario has already been developed based on this grant's failure to arrive on time. Cynthia and Susanna are now in a position to look at the immediate implications of that alternative. In concert with the board members at the next meeting, a decision might be made to adopt the alternative scenario as the new forecast. In this case, board and staff members could look at the Cash Flow Forecaster on Cynthia's laptop computer and instantly see the financial implications of the new scenario.

By having timely information, Sherry, Susanna, and the board are able to shift gears and adjust to the changing circumstance. Similarly, if a surprise gift from a donor suddenly appears in the coffers, the board and staff can see the positive fiscal implications as they enjoy a brief celebratory moment.

Monitoring as a Form of Navigation

Our approach to monitoring financial reports is akin to the art of navigation, which keeps ships and aircraft on course—or at least on track—as they proceed. Today, the link to navigation is amplified by the contemporary use of electronic devices to assist us in knowing where we are. Cash flow–based tools can greatly reduce the time and energy required to monitor the financial status of a nonprofit institution. In this sense, the Cash Flow Forecaster is the electronic equivalent of a Global Positioning System (GPS) unit in nonprofit institutional fiscal monitoring.

Our approach for using the cash flow budget and the Cash Flow Forecaster to analyze information is similar to the one used aboard sailing ships. Using a nautical chart, the navigator plots a compass course from point A to point B as a straight line. The nautical term for this is *Rhumb line,* pronounced just like *rum.* The Rhumb line is the most direct route between two points that maintains a constant compass direction. It establishes a baseline against which course changes can be compared. On sailing vessels that must tack back and forth in relation to the wind, this method of navigation is very important (see Figure 5.2)..

The important thing to grasp in this analogy is that the wind and sea are constantly changing (landlocked readers: think of the water in the birdbath on a windy

FIGURE 5.2. RHUMB LINE AND COURSE CORRECTIONS.

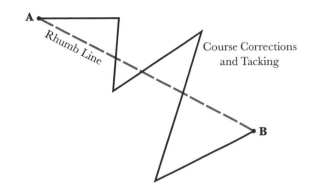

afternoon), but the position of the vessel can be estimated by reference to the speed and direction of each tack or change of direction in relation to the line established for the most direct course.

By monitoring actual income and expense in relation to the projected income and expense in the budget, our nonprofit navigator can see where things are on course or are heading off. The curve generated by the Cash Flow Forecaster's algorithms provides a basis for comparison on a monthly, weekly, or in some cases daily basis.

In the past, navigation was a process that required considerable effort, and it is still a challenge when using the ancient, time-honored tools of the trade. But with the advent of GPS units, which use satellite signals to instantly locate themselves anywhere on earth, the difficulty of navigation has been radically reduced. In a similar way, the use of the Cash Flow Forecaster can assist managers who want to track their institutional progress electronically. This is so because fresh data—namely the actuals from the prior month—act as a signal alerting administrators and board members to take corrective action or to stay the course if things are progressing nicely. To our way of thinking, this type of monitoring requires keeping careful track of where you are and where you want to be, and then using this information to make decisions about how best to get there. In the nonprofit environment rather than in the seaway, the goal is often to come close to your projected figures for income and expense. You may not hit the mark precisely, but getting close to the figure you penciled in earlier in the year is very gratifying. Having a bit more income than expense is also a definite bonus.

Staying briefly with the nautical analogy, at least with regard to monitoring, the true test of navigation is landfall—bringing the vessel safely into the harbor that is your target. The passage may have been a bit stormy and the course may have deviated from the ideal, but if you can arrive at your destination safely and can still make it to the waterfront bar for a cold one, then you have done an ordinary, good-enough job of navigating.

The Limited Power of the Past

Many methods of monitoring financial reports rely heavily on a technique called *historical variance analysis*. Virtually every piece of financial software used by nonprofit organizations includes a reporting function that allows you to compare each item of income and expense from last year with your budgeted figures for this year. The comparison is expressed as a percentage, either positive or negative. Fiscal reports that use historical variance analysis display columns of numbers that show changes between last year and this year on an item-by-item basis.

Implicit in the use of historical variance analysis is the belief that past performance has something important to tell us about future outcomes. Yet, as noted, it is important to be very cautious when relying on the past for clear insights into an uncertain future. Monitoring is about trying to spot change, some variation in the condition of the environment or in the institution. For change to be noticed, it must be observed in relation to something else. This is the reason that financial reports typically compare actual figures for income and expense from a prior period, say last year, with the actual figures for this year. Or they compare the budgeted figures with this year's actuals.

The challenge is knowing just how much information is necessary to reflect a meaningful change that calls for action. Conventional financial reports using historical variance analysis often present information at the level of item-by-item detail. This means that decision makers are confronted with relatively large volumes of information when comparing last year with this year. Is there meaning in knowing that heating oil is much more expensive than last year and that the variance is 7.93 percent? There may well be, but before we attempt to answer this question it is helpful to look at an alternative.

Monitoring using our approach always starts with larger numbers, such as the actual income and expense figures for this year and last year, or the monthly totals for last year's actual income and expense in relationship to the budgeted figures for this year. When glancing at these overall numbers, we look to see if the organization's annual income and expense projections are between plus 3 percent and minus 3 percent of the actual figures for income and expense. If the numbers fall within this range, which is a fairly generous 6 percent, then it is likely that the organization is on the right course. In other words, if an overall margin for error of 6 percent is applied to the entire fiscal year budget but not to individual categories of income and expense or to each month's totals, we can get a quick reading of whether the institution is hitting or missing its predictions.

Since the Cash Flow Forecaster looks at the entire fiscal year, each time we introduce new numbers, the program recalculates the progress of the institution through the end of the year. If the budget as forecast was balanced, a sudden decline in income in February or any other month will show up in the year-end total column as a number that can be easily converted into a percentage change. Looking at that percentage is one way to quickly see the implications of present circumstances on the institution's forecast future.

Balancing all the factors that go into making up the annual cash flow cycle of an institution is complex work. Budget projections that come within the range of plus or minus 3 percent should receive high marks for accuracy, even though precision is not something that forecasting is really all about.

A glance at software used to report on a nonprofit institution's fiscal position reveals that variance analysis is a commonly used tool, and it certainly appears on most of the financial reports we have observed over the years. When we ask new clients how relevant this monitoring technique is to formulating strategy for their institution, we are often greeted by blank stares, so it's worth taking a look at this question.

If heating oil cost $1,500 per month last year, for example, and the staff projected this year's cost at $1,600, these two figures can be compared. The percentage change or variance would be reported as 6.25 percent. But suppose that the cost this year is not $1,600 per month. Instead it is $2,100 per month. Then the variance would be closer to 28.5 percent. For the numerically inclined, all this detail may be interesting or even amusing, but how does it enable administrators and board members to act strategically?

Should the staff have hedged their bets on heating oil by installing a new electric heating system? Perhaps, in hindsight, that might have made sense, but what if the price of heating oil had declined, as it sometimes does? Would the installation costs have been a justifiable expense? Or, even more important, how much time and energy (pardon the pun) should the staff have devoted to this one item in a budget with many variables, all competing in some way for attention? Clearly, the answer is not too much time.

To manage risk and fulfill their role as stewards of the financial health of your organization, board members need to see a bigger picture of the institution in relationship to its environment. In this context, how many times have you sat in a board meeting and watched the executive director being quizzed by a trustee as to why this year's winter fundraising auction generated less money than last year's? And while this is going on, everyone on the board is ignoring the role of inflation on the institution's budget, or a national survey that demonstrates that contributions are 3 percent lower this year than last, or the local corporate donor that now out-sources most of its work to goodness knows where and no longer cares much about its neighborhood.

Explaining the margin of error between this year's actuals and last year's per-formance has become a standard item in every executive director's repertoire. So, rather than pressing for better analytical measures, board members—and also many managers and some foundation officials—spend time trying to establish a correlation between variance in individual items on the budgets presented to them. Often these highly speculative explanations for increases or decreases become the focus for discussion and decision making.

Without getting too technical about the sensitivity of the process to small dif-ferences in estimated inputs, it seems clear that all too often administrators and board members use historical variance analysis as an arithmetic stand-in for more substantive measures and strategies for weighing and addressing uncertainty in the nonprofit sector.

Because we are skeptical of the predictive power of the past, we advise our clients to focus on developing alternative plans or scenarios in the face of an un-certain future. Formulating financial strategies to include lots of contingency plans and being nimble enough to deploy them if warranted seems to us like a better way to deal with changing circumstances.

Monitoring is a key element in formulating financial strategy because it is the process by which information is used to warn board and staff that change is tak-ing place. If the change spotted by the monitors is deemed to be significant, then leadership can explore options that will respond to the change.

In Chapter Six we look at the opportunities that cash flow thinking creates for answering some of the perennial questions that have emerged in the nonprofit world. If you are interested in research, we warn you that this chapter will be hard to put down.

CHAPTER SIX

CASH FLOW ANALYSIS AS A STRATEGIC TOOL

Information conveys a strategic advantage to those who obtain it. Cash flow analysis confers benefits on institutions whose administrators use it, while also offering the opportunity to compare and contrast the performance of a wide range of institutions within the nonprofit sector.

Cash flow analysis opens the door to understanding three key factors in nonprofit financial management:

- The relative cost of funds raised, earned, and borrowed
- The role of inflation on budgets
- The importance of time and timing in nonprofit financial governance

In this chapter, we examine how these three concepts will help shape your thinking about strategic issues that emerge all the time in the boardroom.

The Relative Cost of Capital

Paying careful attention to cash flow introduces the concept of the cost of capital into your financial thinking. In business, the variable cost of money is a primary consideration in many financial decisions. In the nonprofit world, the costs of raising a dollar, earning a dollar, or borrowing a dollar are often ignored. Cash flow analysis enables the board to make decisions about which type of capital to use in specific situations. Each dollar, whether raised, earned, or borrowed, costs something to acquire, and the costs usually differ. Good cash flow management allows the institution to make an informed judgment in its own best interest.

The three types of money available to a nonprofit—funds raised, earned revenue, and the judicious use of credit—all work together, like the three legs of a stool. Take away one and you have an unstable financial platform. Together, the use of gifts and grants, retained earnings, and credit helps your institution to deal with the often chaotic financial environment nonprofits confront. The wise use of all three approaches can bring remarkable stability to your organization. That means three costs—raising money, earning money, and borrowing money—should always be considered when financial decisions are made by the board and staff of nonprofit organizations.

Fundraising

The first consideration for every nonprofit should be the cost of raising money. While there is considerable speculation within the nonprofit sector about the actual costs of raising funds, the Association for Health Care Philanthropy, which has studied the issue for years, has clearly identified these costs.[1] Among its member institutions, those that have been raising money for more than five years spend a median (half above and half below) of 28 cents to raise a dollar, while those that have been at it for less than five years spend a median of 33 cents to raise a dollar. However, within the group that has been at it for less than five years, the range of expense to raise a dollar is quite dramatic. The top quartile spends 71 cents to raise a dollar. And that means that about 12 percent of all institutions less than five years old spend even more than this to raise a dollar, leaving many of them with less than a quarter on the dollar to spend on their programs. By contrast, the third quartile spends 19 cents to raise a dollar. And the bottom quartile—25 percent of all institutions less than five years old—spends less than this amount. A major variable in this survey was differentiation by length of time the development program has been in existence, even within the first five years.

This actually makes sense. Think about the funding pyramid in which organizations slowly sift and sort through the pool of potential donors to reach that 20 percent of donors who actually give 80 percent of the money.[2] All this effort requires time and money. Gradually, as more large donors are identified, the costs of raising funds from them should decline, since they are a much more targeted audience for fundraising appeals.

It is perhaps noteworthy that the Association of Health Care Philanthropy reported that among the organizations surveyed in 2005, the median costs for raising a dollar had increased by 15 percent from 2004 to 2005, pegging it at the highest rate in three years.[3]

In professional development work, the real costs of conducting a long-term campaign, with an annual component, special fund features, and an occasional capital requirement, all have to be accounted for somewhere.

Program-Related Income

The second consideration for every nonprofit should be the cost of earning money. Just as it costs money to raise money, it also costs money to earn money. In general, we advise our clients to estimate that they will spend between ninety and ninety-nine cents to earn a dollar, and that is qualified by the fact that for some, the costs may be much higher.

By way of example, most U.S. businesses operate with relatively small profit margins. Supermarkets, for example, can spend as much as ninety-eight cents to raise one dollar from their customers. Now think about the theater you attend—and that note it prints at the bottom of the program for the play: "Your ticket pays for one half of our annual costs." Which is another way of saying, "We just spent $2 to get your $1 admission." Although that may sound much like saying, "We lose a bit on each piece but make it up on the volume"—which would be ridiculous for a business—it's not necessarily a bad deal for the theater. Foundations, corporations, government agencies, and individual donors are all solicited to make up the balance of the costs through their gifts and grants, and do so to promote the theater's efforts and to associate themselves with its role in the community.

Loans

The third consideration is the cost of borrowing. Borrowing, particularly if it is fully secured by collateral made up of cash or a cash equivalent, is very inexpensive. Many bankers are willing to lend at or below prime for fully secured nonprofit organizations.

Deciding What Money to Use

So money costs money, and different types of money—the dollar you raise from gifts and grants, the dollar you earn from sales or services, and the dollar you borrow from a bank—all have different costs. The key to effective money management in the nonprofit world is to know which dollar is most cost-effective for which situation.

Cash flow thinking reminds us that costs have a real impact on the money that comes in and the checks that go out. Seeing a shortfall down the road provides administrators with an opportunity to select—from the different types of capital— the one that will best solve the problem. If you anticipate a shortfall next month, and your earned revenue stream is projected to be lower, and the grant from the XYZ Foundation has not yet arrived, it may make sense to fill the gap by using your fully secured line of credit rather than by tapping your cash reserve, which was raised at considerable expense in years past.

Cash flow thinking also provides greater sensitivity to the impact of inflation. You will see that your expenses are increasing if inflation is rising, and that information allows you to take corrective action. You may not be able to resist the forces that drive inflation, but with an awareness of its impact you can make adjustments in your expenditures to compensate for its effect on your organization.

The Impact of Inflation

Inflation—the increasing price of goods and services that causes a decline in purchasing power—is a fact of life in the twenty-first century. Although the U.S. inflation rate is currently moderate (it was 3.5 percent in early 2007), it still must figure into any nonprofit's fiscal thinking.

Inflation is frequently understated in the nonprofit sector. The staff may slip a fudge factor for cost of living into the salary and fringe benefits column in the budget, but across-the-board inflation factors of 5.5 percent or 6.5 percent, the actual rate for nonprofits, are rarely factored in. Nonprofit inflation rates are higher than the rates reported in the morning newspaper for three reasons: the nonprofit sector is more labor intensive, it makes less use of economies of scale, and it has no incentive to invest in advanced technologies.

One easy way to see the impact of inflation on your institution is to place your best estimate of inflation into the Cash Flow Forecaster under the Three Year tab. If you start with last year's actual figures for income and expense and then project your best estimate of the percentage of inflation for the coming years, the program will project your estimated inflation rate across your budget.

It only takes a second to do this. And seeing the percentage of inflation allocated across the entire budget will provide your board with a new sense of the importance of inflationary trends. Inflation exists, so don't ignore it for a moment. When estimating future expense, calculating investment income, and comparing and contrasting the cost of different dollars, inflation must be factored into the equation.

During the latter half of the 1980s, at a time when inflation was hovering around 6.5 percent, a number of major nonprofit institutions began to run significant annual deficits. At the time, all sorts of explanations were given by pundits and professors to explain these almost catastrophic shortfalls. Administrators were blamed for failing to anticipate the problem, board members were roasted for not making adequate provision for reserve funds, and the public was castigated for not providing enough emergency relief. While it is impossible to know if this widespread rash of deficits was caused by these specific factors, another explanation is worth tossing into the mix. Nonprofit inflation rates tend to run 2 full percentage points higher than those of the for-profit economy, which would have resulted in an 8.5 percent impact on institutional budgets. At that rate, left unnoticed for a couple of years, the effect of inflation on the institutions would surely have been enough to register on the panic meter. While this is a shameless instance of Monday morning quarterbacking, the role of inflation, particularly if unacknowledged, ought to be on everyone's mind as they review their cash flow budgets.

The Impact of Time

Time poses a special problem in the nonprofit sector. The funding environment seems chaotic in part because none of the funding sources, including foundations, corporations, government agencies, or individual donors, coordinate their deadlines or grant periods. Moreover, none of them typically ask for cash flow budgets, which integrate money and time. Instead, they ask for balance sheets that provide a fiscal snapshot, or annual budgets that compress an entire year into a single income and expense projection.

Getting funders to align their deadlines and grant periods is about as likely as getting them to accept snapshots of your office décor as proof that their money is well spent. And it may be a while before funders wake up to the benefits of asking for cash flow budgets instead of measures of financial solvency, such as audits and balance sheets. Despite this oversight, decision makers in nonprofit organizations can still use cash flow techniques to defend themselves against the vagaries of the world. All we are suggesting is that you reintroduce the element of time into the nonprofit equation.

That the present value of money in the future is less than its face value explains why a nominal $1,000,000 lottery win—paid at $50,000 per year for the next twenty years—is worth considerably less than $1,000,000. As the mathematician John Allen Paulos reminds us, figured at an interest rate of 10 percent, the $1,000,000 has a present value of only about $426,000.[4] You can obtain this value from tables and from financial calculators. As you might imagine, sophisticated investors are keenly interested in the net present value of money. Yet in the nonprofit sector, there appears to be some confusion when bequests, for example, are made that require incremental payouts over time. Just like that million-dollar lottery award, the actual amount of spendable income—the cash flow—may be considerably less, once the impact of time on the money is part of the picture.

Failing to acknowledge the role of time often leads to financial mismanagement of nonprofit organizations. Timing issues—such as not having enough cash on hand to meet payroll when the check from the foundation has not arrived—are frequently defined as fiscal problems in the nonprofit world. Cash flow analysis offers a remedy for this. In case after case, we have found that by using cash flow budgets and forecasts, financial problems can be anticipated and solved quickly. Deficits can be systematically erased and institutional finances stabilized.

We have looked at the differential costs of money, gazed at the impact of inflation, and tossed in time as a factor to be considered. Now, it makes sense to consider these three concepts in relation to your institution's real fiscal—and social—health.

Cash Flow Principles and the Bottom Line

A business has one bottom line. It is either fiscally solvent or it is on the way to being out of business. At least in theory, decisions can be focused on that one bottom line, letting the chips fall where they may.

All nonprofits have two bottom lines: the immediate pursuit of their social or artistic purpose, and long-term fiscal solvency. Social purpose distinguishes nonprofit organizations from commercial entities. In this way, nonprofits are profoundly different from businesses that focus exclusively on trying to be fiscally solvent.

Years ago, a management guru and serious thinker named Geoffrey Vickers, who was later knighted for his insights, proposed that every human decision has two ingredients or components.[5] The first is a qualitative, emotional, holistic, feeling about something, which Vickers called a "judgment." Think about feeling hungry for a moment and you will capture a sense of what he is talking about. You feel hungry and that feeling sets you up for the second component of the decision-making process.

Vickers called this part of decision making the realm of "choices." So you feel hungry, and if you decide to satisfy this feeling, you can choose to go to the refrigerator for a snack, or you might choose to go to a restaurant. If you select the latter course of action, you then might choose whether to travel a long distance or a short distance, or you might select a Chinese, Italian, French, or American menu, an expensive place or cheap one, whether you wish to dress up or go casual, and so on and so forth. In the rational, linear realm of choice, you are driven by a series of options that you can select in order to gratify your original judgment that you felt hungry.

The link between Vickers's decision-making analogy and the challenge for nonprofit administrators and board members is clear. With two bottom lines, one related to social, cultural, or aesthetic values and the other tied to financial welfare, decision makers are called upon to articulate their values, in essence their *judgment*, about almost any item under consideration. Then they are asked to make choices, or at least to hand off the chore to someone who will make them and report back. It is in the territory of choices in the nonprofit arena that our three concepts about the cost of money, the role of inflation, and the impact of time and timing come directly to bear on strategy.

In the nonprofit sector, both bottom lines command attention, and they often compete. When the artistic director comes in with a proposal for truly grand costumes for the show, the theater board may be torn between the budget and the aesthetic vision of the production. Business sense might urge them to pare back the production costs, but their artistic sensibilities may wholeheartedly support the concept of making an opulent statement. This happens all the time in nonprofit organizations, particularly in cultural institutions, and demonstrates the tension between fulfilling the social or artistic mission of the organization and keeping the budget in balance.

Another example is the decision to own or rent their premises that confronts nonprofit organizations all the time. Ownership may satisfy a deeply held feeling for security on the part of decision makers. But with the costs of a capital campaign, the impact of inflation on the budget, and the time necessary to amass all the capital required to own or buy, the choices may be less than heartwarming. Cash flow thinking introduces these variables into the decision-making process in a very concrete way. Your cash flow budgets, forecasts, and monitoring help decision makers shape their choices, sometimes contrary to their feelings but ultimately for the good of the institution.

Making financial decisions in an environment where two bottom lines need to be balanced poses a special challenge for decision makers. Part of the difficulty is that administrators and board members currently lack reference points within the nonprofit sector that can be used to assess fiscal policies. In the commercial world, a number of key indicators help people see the consequences of their financial policies. Beyond profitability, they can use numerous markers, including market share, to judge their financial decisions. Industrywide statistics allow for comparison. Analysts study trends and patterns, and then report on their findings. Data from credit and other services helps them define levels of performance. They have a wealth of information to use in comparing and contrasting fiscal performance.

Unfortunately, the data on financial performance available to the non-profit sector is limited. Attempts over the years—by motivated consultants, well-intentioned university professors, and large accounting firms—to establish meaningful ratios and other indicators of performance have met with less than satisfactory results.

The use of different terms and definitions has often made attempts to compare and contrast information from multiple institutions difficult. Funders have been asking applicants for annualized summary budgets (the conventional budget format that you probably use) for more than three-quarters of a century, but the amount of financial information that can be correlated is remarkably scant. Budget size is usually the one major differentiation that can be made from a system that focuses on assets and liabilities.

While many nonprofit associations and some field-related publications attempt to monitor the financial well-being of nonprofit organizations, the basis for comparison is often unavailable. If on the operational level people use financial terms in different ways, despite the Federal Accounting Standards Board recommendations, analysis will be difficult.

Attempts to use ratio analysis in the 1980s to provide risk management benchmarks for nonprofit organizations proved problematical. Ratios developed by field—for example, education, health care, or social service—stumbled when confronted with the diversity of financial reports in the nonprofit world. The ratios could be established; that wasn't the problem. The problem came when attempts were made to interpret the numbers. Without comparisons to establish a baseline for understanding the value of the ratios, the meaning that could be derived from them was limited. For example, liquidity ratios (weighing the liquid assets of an organization against its liabilities) lend themselves to widely differing interpretations of sufficiency. Should the institution have cash reserves equal to three months' worth of income or three years' income?

Ratios are at their best when compared to something else. Unfortunately, two major difficulties confront users of ratio analysis in the nonprofit field. One is the lack of standard definitions for the various financial terms just discussed. The second is a lack of comparable data that makes it difficult to apply industry standards when trying to decide whether to ramp up your capacity with substantial investment or to rein in the budget.[6] As a consequence of this confusion over the meaning of ratios, historical variance analysis has been left as one of the few tools available to a nonprofit organization trying to understand its financial situation.

Cash flow analysis, on the other hand, can provide some concrete answers to very important operational questions. When you forecast your institution's cash flow, you have a tool that, while admittedly fuzzy, can still cue decision makers to possible windfalls or shortfalls down the road. If your cash flow monitoring reveals that one month is off the charts compared to last year's numbers, you can quickly decide whether or not to take corrective action.

Reserve or Borrow

Cash flow analysis answers the question of whether it's better to have a cash reserve or a line of credit. That is, perhaps the most basic example of how cash flow can assist decision makers is applying cash flow thinking to the question of whether to solicit funds for a cash reserve or set up a line of credit to serve as a reserve fund.

Cash reserves or rainy-day funds always seem like a wonderful idea. The thought of having a little extra cash tucked away for a cold and blustery budgetary lapse seems so cozy and warm. And, frankly, it is nice to have some cushion in reserve. But does it make sense to have much cash—cash that was expensive to raise and will produce very low rates of return, given its liquidity—lying around waiting for a rainy day that may never come? Credit serves exactly the same function for a nonprofit organization, and it allows you to use your hard-earned dollars in service of your mission whenever you have a need.

Still unconvinced about the question of cash reserves versus a fully secured line of credit with your bank? Here are some numbers to consider.

The cash flow cost comparison chart indicates that setting up a fully secured line of credit is barely a tenth the cost of establishing a cash reserve. This cash flow analysis uses all three principles cited earlier: money costs money, inflation is a significant consideration, and time and timing are critically important in nonprofit financial management. The application of these principles, along with some assumptions about earnings and interest, provide valuable insight in the question of which is more cost effective, a cash reserve or a line of credit.

In calculating the cost of this cash reserve, we used the figure of twenty-five cents to raise one dollar. Obviously this assumption can be adjusted in specific cases. On this basis, it cost $7,500 to raise the reserve. During the year the cash reserve earned $963 in interest, making the net cost $6,537. In contrast, the line of credit carries an annual fee of 5 percent or $150 per year. Interest costs for the use of credit equals $738 and interest earned from surpluses equal $185 for a net interest cost of $553, or—adding the fee—a total cost of $703.

The cash reserve costs much more than the line of credit by the end of the year. The math in Exhibit 6.1 for the cost of the cash reserve is ($7,500 − $963 = $6,537) versus the cost for the line of credit, which is ($150 + $553 = $703). To assess the difference in percentage terms we divide 6,537 by 703 to come up with 9.3, or not quite 10 percent.

EXHIBIT 6.1. COST COMPARISON OF A $30,000 CASH RESERVE AND A $30,000 LINE OF CREDIT
(Figures in Whole Dollars).

Cash reserve

Initial cost (prior year)									(7,500)
Interest earned	67	38	49	95	166	184	146	77	0	0	35	106	963*
Net cost									(6,537)

Line of credit

Initial cost (this year)									(150)
Interest earned					66	77	42						185
Interest paid	59	102	86	16	0	0	0	43	162	162	108	0	(738)
Net cost									(703)*

Notes: The cash reserve was raised the prior year at a cost of .25 per dollar = $7,500.

A fee for the line of credit costs .5% or $150 per year.

Line of credit is fully secured by creditholders and carries an interest rate of 6.5% per year.

Surplus funds each month are invested at 4.25% or .00354% per month.

Cash reserve = $30,000 invested at 4.25% or .00354% per month.

* All fractions of a dollar have been removed to make the table easier to read.

And the cost picture is actually worse than what Exhibit 6.1 presents. Non-profit inflation erodes the value of the cash reserve. If that inflation is 4 percent in the national economy, and two full points higher in the nonprofit sphere, inflation will cut into the value of the cash reserve by 6 percent per year. An amount equal to this must be placed back into the cash reserve to preserve the buying power or net value of the fund—in newly raised dollars (at twenty-five cents apiece). To the extent that interest earnings on the principal do not cover the 6 percent required to sustain the fund, more costly money must be raised. If this is not done, the cash reserve becomes a sinking fund and will have lost half its current value in fifteen years. Without cash flow analysis it is difficult to make this type of comparison. This may explain why cash reserves enjoy such popularity in the nonprofit sector and lines of credit are underutilized.

The value of cash flow analysis is further underscored by the problem of standard definitions for fiscal terms within the nonprofit sector. An example of this problem was brought to light in 2004, when the *Chronicle of Philanthropy* attempted to define the term "endowments" for a study on that topic. Complaints were heard from a number of institutions that the definition was too loose or not applicable and therefore they refused to participate in the study.[7]

The lack of comparable data can make it difficult to apply field-related standards—say, when that theater company's board is trying to decide whether to go for the expensive production or to rein in the budget. Attempts have been made (to developed standards in the absence of comparable data), particularly by folks interested in risk management. *Managing Risk in Nonprofit Organizations: A Comprehensive Guide* contains a wealth of information and lots of scary stories about all the things that can go bump in the bank for nonprofits. Yet in the section on financial analysis the authors offer prescriptions, rather than backing up their arguments with the figures that demonstrate the basis for their suggestions.[8]

Cash flow thinking can provide you with vital insight into how your institution operates. Cash flow budgets reveal the internal workings of your institution. This information allows you to establish the norms that will characterize your annual cash flow. The establishment of fieldwide standards represents a challenge that the funding community may eventually address, but it will not happen until these grant-making institutions are willing to shift their analytical focus in the direction of cash flow concepts and embrace quantitative statistical techniques. Institutions (within and across fields) and the agencies that fund them may someday create broad guidelines or standards that can be applied to the field. Until this happens, you might be wise to keep your own counsel and carefully consider interpreting your own cash flow data.

The Pennsylvania Council on the Arts is a leader in its field in the area of grant-making innovation. While providing funds to cultural institutions in many different artistic disciplines, the Council employs a system of peer review that completely avoids asking panelists to make judgments about grant amounts. Instead, three areas of review, starting with last year's actual income and expense, the artistic quality of the institution, and the degree to which it engages the community are all weighted and given a score. These scores are then normalized using standard deviation techniques, and grants are awarded within the parameters of the agency budget. The funding formula variables allow the Council to distribute limited resources over a large number of grantees and make adjustments gradually in relation to past funding levels. Policy decisions are therefore solely made by the PCA's governing council and can be uniformly applied.

Using this approach, the Pennsylvania Council on the Arts has conducted research that demonstrates that the decisions made by its panels show no statistically significant variance when viewed over many years, and by artistic discipline. This may be the first empirical demonstration of the effectiveness of peer review panels' operating within a clearly defined and annually consistent structure.

The relevance of the Pennsylvania Council on the Arts story is that it reflects a shift that is gradually taking place in the entire economy and also within portions of the nonprofit sector. The use of increasingly sophisticated statistical techniques, of improved forms of data collection and data manipulation, and of fiscal measurement signals a sea change in the way we see economic behavior.

As Kevin Phillips reminds us, more and more of the emphasis within our economy is being placed on financial thinking. Phillips's term for this trend is the "financialization" of decision making within contemporary society.[9]

While much of the fiscal reporting in the nonprofit sector is directed to the institution's board and staff, another audience also has considerable consequence. The donors, foundation officials, corporate giving staff, and the personnel of government agencies all ask for financial materials. Curiously, almost none of them ask for cash flow reports. And, as the next chapter outlines, the analysis of financial information in the nonprofit world may actually be hampered by the attitude of many funding authorities.

CHAPTER SEVEN

CASH FLOW ANALYSIS FROM THE FUNDING COMMUNITY'S PERSPECTIVE

The analysis of financial information has another side that we would be remiss to pass over without some mention. While much of the fiscal reporting in the nonprofit sector is directed to the institution's board and staff, donors, foundation officials, corporate giving staff, and the personnel of government agencies all ask for financial materials, and they cannot be denied.

What's Wrong with the Current Situation

Since most nonprofit institutions rely on donors for a significant portion of their revenues, any discussion of financial matters needs to include a reference to the climate or culture of fiscal sophistication evident in the funding community. For example, many donors, both individual and institutional, base their giving on an assessment of the mission and reputation of their applicants, rather than on a careful analysis of their track record of successful financial management.

For the leaders of nonprofit institutions, the management implications of this donor tendency go far beyond a concern with marketing. As many observers in the nonprofit sector have noted, the credibility of a nonprofit institution is likely to be damaged by adverse disclosures of any kind.

If your institution has experienced a recent shortfall, or if you have conducted a capital campaign that did not succeed in reaching its goals, or if any hint of impropriety is circulating in the community, donors may react by withholding funds. As a consequence, nonprofit institutions have a powerful incentive to conceal financial bad news from their supporters. And this makes the issue of clear, accurate reporting something of a paradox for institutions that are releasing their financial reports to donors and institutional grant makers.

Are the consequences of telling the truth about the fiscal position of the institution worth the risks of incurring a funder's punishing indictment in the event of troubling news? This circumstance is particularly relevant in the nonprofit sector, since unlike the commercial world, the number of potential sources of funding is much smaller than that of potential investors in the general public, and the people who fund organizations often talk to each other. Once tainted, a nonprofit organization is unlikely to enjoy the opportunity to recapture the funding community's favor. This disturbing situation leads to a further complication, namely the potential for misunderstanding built into the methods foundations and other funders use to collect financial information from nonprofit institutions.

Perhaps the best indication of the impact of the methodology used to collect information is seen when nonprofit institutions are asked to fill out application forms for funders. The quality of data contained in the application forms nonprofit institutions fill out merits a careful and critical look.

Living in U.S. society, with its mania for testing and forms, no one who has taken the College Boards or filled out an insurance or mortgage application will be surprised to hear that forms can be complicated and painful. So it may seem natural that many funders use application forms loaded with questions requesting lots and lots of information. Whether that information will be particularly valuable is not so clear.

Asking people for information without hypotheses in place to examine the responses is like casting a big net and then seeing what, if anything, gets pulled in. Over the past seventy-five years, in all too many cases, too little of value has emerged from the big nets used by foundations and other funding authorities. As a consequence, ex post facto research is a major industry in the nonprofit world—a process a little like calling to invite friends to a celebration dinner and then raiding the refrigerator after they arrive to make a meal out of whatever is there. It would be far better to plan ahead and shop for fresh ingredients for that special gathering.

This is where cash flow budgeting and some rigorous testing can make a valuable contribution in the future, if funders are willing to ask for cash flow information from applicants.

We see a significant disconnect between the value of the information requested by funders and the utility of the information provided by applicants. In our experience, the information that comes in on application forms and in the budgets filled out by applicants holds up very poorly to rigorous analysis. So, instead of reaping a gold mine of practical information, many funders simply accumulate tons of data that they carefully file and forget.

We suspect that problems arise from the tremendous variation in definitions used by nonprofits when filling in the budgets and by the lack of a common basis for making comparisons. The solution (you'll be unsurprised to hear from us) is the use of cash flow budgeting, which provides a clear picture of the dynamics of the funds moving through an institution each year and also lends itself to comparative analysis and better research. Because all financial transactions can be resolved to cash, either as income or as expense, the categories open the door to some comparison that is currently not possible.

For example, while you can compare budget size among a group of nonprofit institutions, the dynamics of financial affairs during the course of any given year are difficult, if not impossible, to ascertain using the methods in place today. If donors and funders used cash flow budgets, the variations in income and expense not just by institution but also across institutions could be directly compared. Regional or local impacts on different types of institutions could be measured. The seasonality of fiscal matters could be contrasted. A better understanding would be gained of the importance of operational dollars—the working capital—required to run a nonprofit institution.

The impact of inflation, the differential cost of money, and the role of time and timing would be clear to donors and their institutional counterparts. All this information can be derived from cash flow analysis, and it is particularly important if the health and well-being of nonprofit organizations is high on your list of priorities.

Cash Flow Analysis and What Funders Want

When you come right down to it, we believe that funders want to know if your institution has the capacity to accomplish the project proposed in the application. This is one of many questions that funders ask themselves as they stare at the financial documents arrayed on the table before them. Curiously, these are often the same questions administrators need to ask themselves before leaping into the fray with an application.

One response to the question of what funders want is to ask how they can expect us to accomplish the project proposed in the application when they are unable or unwilling to provide us with the working capital that we need. In other words, if they do not help us to obtain operational dollars, the basic overhead resources that we need, how can we succeed?

And if the working capital requirement of nonprofit institutions is not to be completely ignored by the funding community, then we contend that funders need to ask for cash flow budgets when they evaluate proposals for grants or gifts.

Funders is a currently fashionable term applied to those folks who supply money to nonprofit institutions, and *applicants* is the term used to define those who apply for funds. In the usual configuration, the funders sit on one side of the desk and applicants sit on the other side. We believe that funders and applicants should be on the same side of the desk, metaphorically as well as literally. If you are both trying to address a social, cultural, or environmental issue, doesn't it make sense to be working together as partners, rather than as grantors and supplicants? This does not mean that every application can or should be funded. What we are advocating is a shift in thinking from the inception of the application process until a final decision is made.

As we've noted, many board members of nonprofit institutions cannot fully comprehend the financial statements presented to them. The same can usually be said of the staff of foundations, government agencies, and institutional and in-dividual donors, all of whom are requesting budgets from applicants. Since each funding source has its own idea of what constitutes a budget appropriate to its needs, the requests are rarely consistent. Even when a common data form has been developed, the interpretation of financial information—or a fatigue factor based on the inevitable size of these forms—may prevent anyone from getting a clear picture of the financial position of the applicant.

What is worse, a surprisingly large number of the individuals who review these applications, either on staff or on panels, do not know how to read the financial statements presented to them. Audits are often used as the only measure of sol-vency or acceptable practice. This lends only partial credence to the application and is potentially unhelpful to a funder seeking to gauge the impact of its grant on the institution or its ability to implement effective programming to address a priority concern.

The confusions surrounding financial statements generally lead funders to focus on after-the-fact evaluation rather than address the issue of performance up front. Clearly it is time for a change in the budget forms that funders insist that applicants fill out. Both the applicant and the funders would benefit from the greater accuracy and understandability of cash flow–based financial reports.

Surely it will not come as a total surprise to you that we believe it is time for institutions and funders to adopt cash flow budgets for fiscal reporting. A simple cash flow budget provides an accurate picture of the month-by-month financial position of the institution. Moreover, it enables all parties to understand clearly what money is available for spending and what expenses are being incurred. Funders and applicants need to understand the fiscal condition of those who are carrying out the work at hand. It is not enough to just shovel money at organizations, although most would be happy to be the recipients of such largesse. Both partners need to see what is going on, and cash flow budgeting is the way for that to happen.

Using cash flow budgeting also opens the door to analysis that is not possible with the diverse and largely incompatible budgetary forms currently in use. It introduces the importance of time and timing in the management of funds in the nonprofit environment. It enables policymakers to weigh the relative advantages of different strategies, such as whether to create a cash reserve or endowment or to purchase or renovate a building. It demonstrates the impact of inflation on organizations, and it provides a basis for fieldwide comparison.

The Cash Flow Forecaster is a tool that can greatly assist the funding community. It makes it possible to compare and contrast the budgeting and forecasting ability of one institution in relation to other institutions that share the same environment. This can be done by establishing the mean (the average) for a range of institutions, and then performing standard deviation analysis (a statistical technique that measures the variability within a frequency distribution).

By using a common standard, in this case cash, and by eliminating all other variables, it is possible to compare and contrast the financial experience of many different organizations. Not only that, it is possible to address one of the toughest assessment issues all funders face: How can we be sure that our applicants have the managerial sophistication needed to use our funds wisely to fulfill their—and indirectly our—mission?

When all the organizations in a sample are using a universal standard of cash, it is possible to determine the relative status of any given institution by tracking cash flow budgets and forecasts for income and expense. Cash flow analysis makes it possible to compare an individual institution's results with the track record of all the other organizations either in a given field or across the fields. Trying to do this with the current system of financial statements poses serious problems with the comparability of the data.

Using the Cash Flow Forecaster as a basic budgeting requirement has another advantage. Funding agencies that use online applications—something more and more are doing—can use the software as a simple way for institutions to submit their figures. We suggest to funding agencies that they ask for the last year of actual income and expense figures, rather than projections into an unknowable future. Moreover, we urge the institutional funders to stress how important footnotes are as a means to convey more information about the applicant organization and its administrative and programmatic strategies.

Finally, we suggest that institutional funders point out to applicants that the opportunity to fill out the Cash Flow Forecaster is a special treat. Applicants receive a built-in reward for submitting their proposal: a useful tool that can be used on an ongoing basis to budget, forecast, and monitor their own fiscal position. Wouldn't it be lovely to get a useful and enduring gift just for applying? It might make the pain of rejection sting less, knowing that the funding agency was at least thinking about your long-term financial welfare, even if the check is not going to be in the mail.

The Cash Flow Forecaster can be used by all parties in the nonprofit sector to accomplish a number of tasks:

- Providing easily understood fiscal reports based on a cash flow budget
- Graphically portraying fiscal information to make it clear to administrators and board members
- Identifying the specific periods when an institution should plan to borrow or use reserves to stabilize cash flow
- Quickly generating forecasts that reflect different scenarios to enable administrators and their board members to explore options based on changes in income and expense
- Assisting administrators and board members, as well as funders, in determining the organization's precision in forecasting
- Reconciling multiple uses of borrowing, such as lines of credit and term debt, with the institution's cash flow budget.

With these benefits to consider, funders might be well served to use the Cash Flow Forecaster in new and creative ways. Or just as a way to say thank-you to all the wonderful applicants who applied, whether or not they received funding.

This chapter concludes Part One of the book, which addresses and answers two key issues in nonprofit financial management: why so many people seem to struggle with their current approach to budgeting and reporting, and how current approaches to forecasting and reporting, which consume significant amounts of staff time and energy, can fail to produce genuinely meaningful results. In both cases, we have tried to demonstrate, as we have with our clients over the years, that cash flow concepts and tools can answer these questions and more.

In Part Two, we discuss what administrators and their boards can do with the increased information available from cash flow thinking. We also address the heightened efficiency and effectiveness of forecasting and reporting.

PART TWO

ESTABLISHING FINANCIAL SECURITY

The cash flow tools and techniques discussed in Part One set the stage for more effective strategy. Our approach builds step by step, so mastering cash flow thinking and using the tools we presented in earlier chapters set the stage for establishing greater financial security.

Cash flow thinking creates new choices for decision makers to obtain working capital on the local level. Access to operational dollars means that institutions can be more self-reliant. Armed with information on cash flow, decision makers can use their own knowledge and local resources to create financial security for their institution. With this goal in mind, we are ready to address two more overarching issues.

• *Ensuring financial security for nonprofit institutions in an uncertain environment poses a difficult challenge to administrators.*

Cash flow thinking opens the door to a new resource for addressing financial security. It allows administrators to gain access to working capital from local institutions in a timely and cost-effective manner.

Administrators and their board members tend to be very focused on obtaining more money for their nonprofit institution, but resources are scarce and very unequally distributed. Combining environmental constraints with the restrictive nature of many gifts and grants, institutions must constantly struggle to obtain enough money to fulfill their mission. Our assessment of the fiscal needs of the vast majority of nonprofit organizations is that their single most important priority should be access to working capital.

Nonprofit organizations need to learn how to borrow working capital from their local bank to ensure their financial stability. To borrow, one must have collateral.

A concept that we have used effectively with our clients is to develop a category of new volunteers in the nonprofit sector. These volunteers are called *creditholders,* a term that we coined years ago. Along with cash flow budgeting, forecasting, and monitoring, creditholders are the key to gaining local access to working capital.

Once institutions have established creditholder programs and learned to engage in fully secured borrowing, the use of credit to provide working capital can be extended as a financial strategy. We will show you how credit can be used to deal with shortfalls and as a means to stabilize the financial position of nonprofit institutions. We will also show you how to start and maintain a creditholder program for your institution.

The use of cash flow budgets, forecasts, and reports is linked in our approach to the use of fully collateralized credit. The use of credit to fill gaps in income is made clear by cash flow analysis. However, fully secured credit can also be used to deal with surpluses. Which leads us to the next issue.

•   *Cash reserves, endowments, and other forms of capital accumulation often do not enhance a nonprofit's ability to fulfill its mission.*

The role that surpluses and capital accumulation play in the financial life of nonprofit institutions is a problem for only a small percentage of the nonprofit field. Nonetheless, the amount of attention that is devoted to capital accumulation strategies by nonprofit institutions is disproportionate to its value. We propose that nonprofit institutions use credit and credit-related tools as an alternative to cash reserves, endowments, and ownership of buildings and equipment.

Of all the questions in the nonprofit world that trigger intense emotions, few can rival the issue of ownership of facilities and equipment. Given the passions associated with these issues, we provide a series of recommendations and some cash flow–based software that makes comparison of different strategies much simpler and easier.

CHAPTER EIGHT

CASH FLOW STRATEGIES IN TODAY'S ENVIRONMENT

Strategy is a balancing act in which an institution's strengths and weaknesses are weighed by decision makers and then matched up with the opportunities and obstacles their environment presents. Effective strategies represent the conscious attempt to act in ways that maximize strengths in relation to opportunities presented by the environment, and to minimize weaknesses in the face of obstacles.

Through the cash flow concepts and tools discussed in Part One, administrators and their boards can identify the fiscal strengths and weaknesses of their institution. The information derived from cash flow analysis provides a powerful lens for seeing the financial circumstances of an organization. To round out the picture, it is equally important to turn a cash flow–oriented lens on the environment to see what possibilities and threats are out there to challenge your strategies.

These are troubled times in the tax-exempt world. Nonprofit organizations and their institutional supporters are being asked to do more and more with less and less. The economy is up and down, the market is wobbling, corporations are altering their donations in the face of globalization and the constant requirement for elevated compensation for the CEO. At the same time that middle-class salaries are stagnating, skyrocketing federal expenses for foreign wars and tax cuts for the ultra-wealthy are pillaging the federal budget. The media have discovered that they can evoke huge amounts of heartfelt and impulsive donations by showcasing natural disasters. Financial service firms have created new products to lure families into donor-advised funds. The Internet has spawned an entirely new way of giving for the electronically savvy. New categories of nonprofit organizations are increasingly being added to the mix. What is happening with the federal government at all levels hardly bears mentioning. Trillions in deficits can do that to you.

And all this is in the context of a very significant foreign ownership of our public debt, ownership that may not be willing to invest in the United States forever. Let's not even talk about escalating health care costs or aging Baby Boomers. All these factors and more are pointing to some serious weather in the landscape of the nonprofit sector.

But before we get all wrapped up in the worldly woes that beset the nonprofit field, it is perhaps advisable to take a closer look at how nonprofit organizations are managing their own fiscal affairs.

Capital Accumulation in the Nonprofit Sector

Capital accumulation is the name of the game in U.S. fundraising circles today. So even while nonprofit organizations with modest budgets toil away at the annual fund drive, many of their board and staff members lust after the cash reserves, endowments, and capital building campaigns that the larger nonprofit institutions are pursuing. No doubt some of this passion is inflamed by publications in the field, which often feature mega gifts for endowments or buildings that fan a perception that donors are keenly interested in making just these types of gifts.

But like the grapes hanging on the trellis in Aesop's classic fable about the fox, these acquired funds often remain tantalizingly out of reach for day-to-day operations. The balance sheet may look good, but the actual cash available for running the organization is often surprisingly low.

Despite the popularity of capital accumulation more and more evidence supports our assertion that the use of this practice by nonprofit organizations is harmful for individual institutions, the constituencies they serve, the local community, and ultimately the entire nonprofit sector.[1] While larger institutions worry about having adequate resources, their handling of the money they do acquire is often very inefficient. As a consequence, these institutions offer less service relative to their resource base than many smaller institutions manage to provide. At the same time, the larger institutions' need for more money—in the face of a relatively inelastic pool of funds—squeezes the smaller institutions and makes it more difficult for them to provide services at all.

Capital accumulation is a standard approach to money management among nonprofit institutions, just as it is in the wider U.S. society. It is part of the increasing financialization of our contemporary world, as Kevin Phillips has noted in his book *Wealth and Democracy*.[2] The number of nonprofits invested in Wall Street and the recent emergence of donor-directed funds managed by financial service organizations are both excellent examples of Phillips's point.

Americans have always accumulated capital. Why should nonprofits be any different? To answer this question, let us begin with what we call "The Parable of the Pond."

The Parable of the Pond

At night all the animals in the jungle come down to the waterhole to drink. Cool, clear water flows into the pool from three nearby springs. When one spring slows, another always seems to increase, and so the volume of water is pretty much the same from year to year. A keen-eyed observer might note a very slight increase in the amount of water each year, but the animals hardly notice. They are thirsty from the heat and efforts of the day.

Over the past seventy-five years, the behavior of some of the animals has changed. First one elephant, then another, and another have been taking water from the pool and dumping it into a large cistern next to the pond. The elephants seem to delight in removing water from the pool with their powerful trunks and spraying it into the open cistern. With their strong and clever trunks, these massive pachyderms are the only animals who can open a small spout at the base of the cistern and withdraw a tiny amount of water. But the small amount of water coming through the spout hardly satisfies the elephants, and they continue to drink their fill from the pond.

This odd behavior is having a serious effect on the smaller animals. Since the pond gets only so much water each day, and since the largest animals drink the most water, there has always been a competition among the smaller creatures for adequate water. This competition continues to this day, but with a different consequence.

Because the elephants are accumulating water in the cistern and are only able to withdraw a tiny amount, they are still thirsty and they make their presence at the pool felt by all the smaller animals by continuing to drink most of the precious water. Slowly, it is becoming apparent that the combination of daily consumption by the elephants and their hoarding of an increasingly large amount of water in the cistern is depriving the smaller animals of water.

In essence, the same thing is happening in the nonprofit sector in this country. The larger institutions are rapidly depleting the resource of available money given each year, a resource that is fairly constant. And because much of this money is invested in endowments and buildings—both very inefficient uses of capital—the volume of available funds is dramatically declining for smaller institutions.

Like the water trickling from the spout in the cistern, the resources available from endowments are tiny in comparison to the needs of the large institutions. Therefore, they return again and again to the pool for operational funds or capital campaigns, in effect double and triple dipping.

Just like the three streams in our parable, the three funding streams—individual contributions, foundation and institution grants, and government funding—all supply support. When one source is higher, say individual donations, another source may be lower, and the net effect is a fairly constant resource pool—which is then inequitably distributed.

In our story, the smaller animals are in serious trouble, and a case might be made that smaller institutions in the nonprofit sector are also in danger because of these practices. However, before leaping to any conclusions, it makes sense to examine some data from a very reliable source.

Evidence Accumulation

By comparing two sets of figures reported by the Internal Revenue Service (IRS) over a thirty-year period, we can see both a pattern of capital accumulation in the nonprofit sector and the significant growth that has occurred in the past ten years.

A 1998 report issued by the IRS Statistics of Income Division examines the income and asset allocation in the nonprofit sector over the previous two decades.[3] The study shows that although the number of nonprofits has grown dramatically, the pool of all gifts and grants has remained relatively constant.

Using 1992 constant dollars, the report demonstrated the following data points:

- The number of nonprofits filing tax returns with the government (contributions and earnings of more than $25,000 per year) rose from 82,048 in 1975 to 180,931 in 1995.
- Contributions from all sources to nonprofit organizations were relatively inelastic, increasing roughly 6 percent a year over the twenty-year period, less than the rate of inflation in the nonprofit sector during this same period.
- Total revenues increased from $129 billion to $617 billion in 1995, due in part to increases in health care and private school tuition.
- The total book value of assets controlled by nonprofit organizations increased from $258 billion in 1975 to $1,063 billion in 1995. This quadrupling is a clear indication of the accumulation of capital by larger nonprofits over this period.
- Two-thirds of the returns filed by section 501(c)(3) organizations were filed by institutions with assets of less than $500,000. These organizations held only

1 percent of the total assets and obtained 4 percent of the revenue of the sector. Meanwhile, organizations with assets of $10 million or more represented only 5 percent of the returns filed, but they accounted for nearly 89 percent of the total asset holdings and 80 percent of the total revenue reported.

- In 1975, with assets of $66.3 billion, 26,889 foundations granted $5.1 billion dollars, or roughly 7.7 percent of their total assets. In 1995, 47,983 foundations held assets of $245 billion and granted $11.9 billion, or slightly less than 5 percent.

Using the earlier study as a baseline, it is instructive to see the recent growth in the nonprofit sector. According to Paul Arnsberger, Melissa Ludlum, and Margaret Riley of the IRS, the aggregate book value of assets, as reported by nonprofit organizations that filed IRS information returns for tax year 2002, was $2.1 trillion.[4] In real terms, this amount was 66 percent larger than the aggregated book value of assets held by nonprofit organizations for tax year 1993.

The same study revealed figures that indicate that nonprofit organizations earned 41 percent more in revenue for tax year 2002 than they had earned for tax year 1993. Total charitable expenditures reported by nonprofit organizations for tax year 2002 were 50 percent larger than those reported for tax year 1993.

These statistics provide an overview of the system of income and asset allocation in the nonprofit world over the past thirty years. The numbers help give us a context for many of the ideas expressed in this book. The figures demonstrate that the pool of gifts and grants remained relatively inelastic for the twenty years studied. It has not grown as fast as the number of organizations competing for the funds.

The statistics also reveal that financial assets in the nonprofit sector are, to a remarkable degree, being accumulated rather than spent on mission. The increase in the book value of assets is a telling sign of this accumulation. In some fields, such as education and health care, revenues have increased dramatically over two decades, but in other sectors, such as social service and the arts and humanities, revenues have not increased nearly as much. Even with the excesses in gains and losses in the years since the IRS study, the trend is upward. In other words, more money is being accumulated in the nonprofit sector.

There is an obvious skew in the size of nonprofits and the assets they hold. If the largest organizations—5 percent of all nonprofits—hold 89 percent of the assets of the sector and derive 80 percent of the total income each year, that leaves 20 percent for the remaining 95 percent of organizations.

Finally, although foundation assets have increased dramatically, the actual percentage of grants as a function of total assets has declined significantly. More money is being held, less is being granted.

Recently, Lucy Bernholz assessed the capital markets in the philanthropic world. She reported that in 2002 the roughly 62,000 foundations in the United States managed more than $476 billion dollars in assets and made more than $30 billion in grants, an expenditure of 6 percent (which overstates actual foundation giving, as administrative costs and money management fees are included in this number). Total giving is, of course, much higher. Estimates cited by Bernholz peg the total number for the year 2002 as more than $240 billion, with 76 percent coming from individuals, 7.6 percent from bequests, and some as-yet-unknown percentage from donor-advised funds. Bernholz noted that there are currently more than 70,000 donor-advised funds, so these funds now outnumber foundations.[5] An article in the *Chronicle of Philanthropy* points out that accurate figures for neither the assets nor the total gifts from donor-advised funds are available.[6]

Where Does the Money Go?

How do members of the Association for Health Care Philanthropy allocate their fundraising proceeds? Children's hospitals, health care systems, and academic institutions allocated the highest percentages of funds raised to construction and renovation (29.0 percent, 27.2 percent, and 26.9 percent, respectively). Nonprofit health care entities and their public counterparts spent between 30 percent and 35 percent for community benefit programs and 25.3 percent for general operations, and public entities spent 39.8 percent of their funds for equipment. Long-term care organizations applied the most to endowment (28.2 percent).[7]

The Association for Health Care Philanthropy is one of a few organizations in the nonprofit world that systematically survey their members about the costs of raising funds and about fund allocation. The 2003 report indicates that significant sums being raised each year are devoted to buildings, equipment, and endowments. The 2005 report from the association indicates a slight decline in spending for endowments, but the largest expense line items for all institutions were still construction and renovation, accounting for 23.9 percent, and another 18.8 percent was spent on equipment.[8]

The information from the Internal Revenue Service, from the Association of Health Care Philanthropy, and from other sources in the field indicates that it is not just the institutional givers who are accumulating funds; the largest nonprofit institutions are also helping to create a climate of scarcity through their accumulation of wealth.

In Chapter Fifteen we examine how funds that are currently being used for capital projects might be treated differently if society provided greater incentives for socially oriented investors to assume ownership of the physical plant of the nonprofit sector. Meanwhile, many nonprofit institutions will continue to spend a major portion of their revenues on buildings and equipment.

U.S. philanthropy might be characterized as divided into the haves, the have mores, and all the rest. All the rest includes at least two-thirds of the institutions in the nonprofit sector, and all the small to medium-sized institutions that are struggling to compete for the crumbs of the pie.

For a sector of the economy charged with addressing social, cultural, and environmental concerns, the enormous discrepancies in financial assets between large and small institutions may seem like a paradox. After all, aren't philanthropy and charity linked in the common goal of easing social suffering and bettering mankind's lot? The emergence of contemporary philanthropy as a corporate form of giving has set the stage for some of the remarkable differences in income distribution now found in the nonprofit sector.

Looking at the investment policies and practices of foundations, endowments, and the financial service businesses that manage donor-directed funds, it seems likely that the process of investment is the major problem behind the growing gap between rich and poor institutions. By applying very narrow investment goals to obtain returns and by using the available investment opportunities, the effects we experience in philanthropy can be explained. In other words, the increasing preoccupation with finance in the world of philanthropy has resulted in funding decisions and portfolio investments that encourage capital accumulation. This in turn creates a lack of access to working capital for most nonprofit institutions, since money that might otherwise be available to them is invested in Wall Street and beyond.

The remarkable divide that has occurred between those with and those without money can be explained in a variety of other ways. One explanation comes to us from the desktop. Computer simulation of game theory concepts opens the door to understanding the rules that societies generate that enable the rich to get richer, even when the rich are little computer-generated dots, not humans with all the drive, initiative, and resources that *Forbes Magazine* normally attributes to successful wealth creation in this country.

Vilfredo Pareto, an Italian industrialist, economist, and sociologist who worked around the beginning of the twentieth century, described the power laws that govern the distribution of wealth in societies. Pareto's wealth distribution curves, dating from 1909, demonstrate that in every society studied a tiny portion of the population has immense wealth. In the broad middle of the curve, Pareto shows us all the people actively striving in a rising and falling struggle to move up, and at the bottom of the wealth curve, men and women starve and children die young. In other words, a pattern or rule emerges that concentrates wealth in a very few hands.[9]

If you pay careful attention to the practices that operate in the philanthropic world, you will see that many behaviors do act like rules influencing who is advantaged and who is disadvantaged. You might note that wealthy people often provide the lion's share of their support to institutions that are already well heeled—the same institutions that provide services to those with wealth.[10] Federal tax policy allowing for the same deduction, regardless of the giver's income, also tends to skew things in the favor of institutions that benefit the rich.

The punch line here is clear: nonprofit organizations that are not part of the upper 5 percent will have to compete for the 20 percent of the pool of revenues and gifts and grants that are left each year by their wealthy cousins. And the competition is bound to get tougher. Does this mean that all nonprofits that are not big and rich are doomed to be small and poor? Not necessarily.

We believe that institutions that are not part of the top 5 percent can change the impact of the rules of the game on themselves by using cash flow budgets and forecasts, by learning to safely use fully secured credit, and by being advocates for changes in the way all that hoarded money is allocated.

We are reasonably optimistic that our approach to money will assist the majority of nonprofit organizations that can't or don't hoard capital. Our method offers these lean-running nonprofit organizations ready access to working capital from a source outside the usual pool of philanthropy or the rapidly emptying government troughs. In Chapter Nine, we open the door to a new resource for your organization, one that is outside the rules of philanthropy.

CHAPTER NINE

CASH FLOW OPENS THE DOOR TO A NEW RESOURCE

If capital accumulation by the larger nonprofits is the current trend, small and middle-sized organizations need access to a new resource for their working capital. At the same time, large institutions need help in using their resources more efficiently—both to better serve their constituents and to avoid inflicting hardship on their colleagues and their communities.

Just like the water hole described in Chapter Eight, the modern nonprofit sector is a competitive environment, and one where survival demands that the smaller players look beyond the traditional pool—in this case one made up of raised and earned income. Cash flow budgets, particularly multiple-year cash flow budgets and cash flow forecasts, open the door to a new resource in the use of credit and to a new form of collateral.

In this chapter we take you through each of the steps necessary to achieve financial stability without large cash reserves or emergency fundraising campaigns. We discuss cash reserves and endowments later, but for now, our focus is on defining a resource for you to use so that borrowing can be an important part of your overall financial strategy.

A key premise of this book is that if you understand your institution's cash flow, you can convert that understanding into a line of credit with your local bank. Preparing to borrow requires all the skills necessary to prepare clear and understandable financial statements, to project your cash flow, to forge a working understanding of credit with your board of directors, and to create a community-based creditholder group. It also involves selling the organization and its fiscal prospects to a possibly reluctant banker.

Key Questions

As disciples of debt we talk frankly about borrowing that is safe and sane. That requires us to introduce and define a number of terms that relate to your use of credit. We also introduce the concept of a creditholder group and explain how creditholders can be a vital asset to your institution, to say nothing of opening the door to the prudent use of credit.

What is the relationship between working capital and a line of credit?

Working capital, according to the second edition of the *Random House Dictionary of the English Language,* is the amount of capital needed to carry on a business. Accountants use the term to refer to current assets minus current liabilities. A third definition is liquid assets, as distinguished from fixed capital assets. We think of working capital as the money that nonprofits need to conduct their operations.

We believe that it is the lack of access to working capital that poses the greatest obstacle to success in the nonprofit sector. Since individual and institutional donors, foundations, and government agencies continue to resist paying their full share of the operational costs of nonprofit institutions, we urge our clients to take matters into their own hands. By adopting our cash flow approach to budgeting, forecasting, and monitoring, by forming a creditholder group, and then by heading to the bank, these organizations can obtain working capital without having to accumulate vast reserves. In combination with raised and earned revenues, borrowed dollars can be used when they are most needed.

Bank loans come in different forms. Rather than granting a series of operating loans related to specific transactions, the bank may set up a *line of credit.* In this arrangement, the nonprofit is allowed a bit more freedom, since a set sum has been placed at its disposal on an annual basis. This means that the institution does not have to relate each borrowing effort to a single specific purpose, but may use the funds for general, short-term operational needs. Lines of credit come as secured and unsecured agreements.

We advocate that nonprofit organizations provide security for their lines of credit in the form of collateral from creditholders. Typically, the line of credit must be repaid for at least thirty days during the yearlong cycle. This means that the line of credit *revolves,* or is paid off at specific intervals during the course of the year. In this regard, a line of credit is different from other banking tools, such as a term loan that runs for a predetermined period (or *term,* as it is called) before it needs to be paid off. By borrowing and repaying during the course of the year, your institution is demonstrating that it is using the line of credit exactly as it is meant to be used, to obtain short-term funds when you need them and repaying these funds when you don't.

Who are creditholders and why are they important to your institution?

To borrow, you need collateral. That's a basic fact of life in the real world. Collateral is something that most nonprofit organizations seem to have in short supply, so we focus on your developing a new category of volunteer, a group of supporters known as *creditholders*—a term we coined in an article in the July 1992 issue of *Practical Philanthropist*.

All nonprofit organizations need a creditholder group. Creditholders are the people who love you. They are the people you will grow to love. They support your mission. In some cases they may be the people you serve, or perhaps their parents or grandparents. Creditholders are friends, associates, supporters, family members, staff members, alumni, former patients, ex-addicts who have gone on to be rock stars or motivational speakers, or almost any other type of constituent. Creditholders are individuals or institutions that support the mission of a non-profit organization by providing collateral to a bank that requires fully secured borrowing. Often the amounts deposited are relatively small, but with enough creditholders in place, a sizable volume of a very liquid asset can be mobilized. We cover how to approach potential creditholders in Chapter Ten.

Usually, creditholders provide funds that are used to purchase a certificate of deposit. The money in the account is pledged to the bank as collateral for borrowing by the nonprofit. But the creditholders still own the money, and they receive interest based on the amount they deposit. Interest is paid out annually or rolled over into the account.

Some creditholders have stocks or bonds that they use in place of cash. In this case the bank holds the certificates, often discounting the total value of the stocks, since bankers recognize that stocks fall as well as rise, even if other people don't always believe this is true.

The creditholders' funds—either as cash that is used to purchase a certificate of deposit at the bank or as stocks and bonds—are pledged as a source of repayment for either a line of credit or a term loan. To reiterate a point that is sometimes difficult to grasp at first, creditholders retain ownership of their assets but make them available to assist the institution. Unlike cosigners, who guarantee repayment of a loan through a promissory note, creditholders are prepared to place a liquid asset in the hands of the bank to serve as collateral.

With a creditholder group, your organization gains a stable resource that can be used to mobilize credit whenever it can be shown that other sources of revenue will repay the loan. Interest charged by banks for lines of credit secured by creditholders' certificates of deposit are typically a point or two above the interest paid by the bank for the certificates of deposit. This is often below the prime rate.

Borrowing at a lower rate enables nonprofits to pay their vendors quickly, gain discounts, and avoid late-payment penalties. When vendors are asked to provide donations rather than discounts for fast payment, their response is usually to contribute slightly more, often offsetting the interest costs of borrowing.

Creditholders gain an opportunity to provide invaluable assistance to a nonprofit organization they believe in, without cost to themselves. And the bank gains the collateral it needs to justify a loan to the organization.

Terms of the Trade

Since knowing what terms mean is important to both borrowers and lenders, we take some care in the coming paragraphs to define various terms and concepts clearly.

For example, borrowing that is completely backed by an asset that the banker can readily convert to cash is sometimes referred to as *fully secured borrowing. Collateral* is the asset that is used to offset the liability taken by a lender. Collateral comes in various forms, but for our purposes we are talking about collateral as cash or cash equivalents. Collateral is normally required until a loan is repaid. In the event of default, the lender has a legal right to claim the collateral as payment of the loan.

There is a slight difference between the collateral that is offered by the creditholders and collateral that accompanies a conventional commercial loan. Typically, when participants in a commercial loan place their assets in the hands of the bank to secure a loan, they have an expectation that they will profit from the business transaction. Creditholders do not have a direct stake in the nonprofit institution that they support. They will not receive any financial reward from the operations of the nonprofit as payment for their participation, apart from the interest they earn.

The technical term for the creditholders' participation is *hypothecation,* which means pledging an asset to a lender but not relinquishing control over that asset. So a creditholder hypothecates an asset by buying a certificate of deposit or pledging a stock or bond as collateral. The collateral allows your nonprofit institution to borrow. Again, the key point is that the creditholders do not lose control over their assets; everything still belongs to them, unless the nonprofit defaults on its obligation. In practice, creditholders have provided funds for all sorts of borrowing, including lines of credit, *bridge loans* designed to span the gap between a project and its eventual funding, and term loans.

A *term loan* has a maturity in excess of one year. Term loans offer some advantages to the borrower. The installment repayment schedule and the amount of payment are usually tailored to fit the borrower's financial activities. In the nonprofit sector, fully secured term loans can be used to address deficits. The length of time needed to repay the loan gives the institution an opportunity to slowly and with luck even gracefully meet its obligations.

Purposes of Borrowing

With these definitions in mind, addressing the challenge of financial stability is simple, particularly once you have mastered cash flow budgeting, monitoring, and forecasting. So the next group of questions are those that emerge when we suggest that borrowing might be the way to go for a new nonprofit client.

Why go through all this bother? Why not just ask for donations, create a cash reserve, and call it a day?

Whenever we talk about borrowing to nonprofit board and staff members, at least one person will always ask why they should go to the trouble of assembling creditholders. This is a valid question. But before we answer it, here is a quick definition of *cash reserves:* sums of money, usually called profits in the commercial sector, that are dedicated to the purpose of meeting current and future obligations. Cash reserves are similar to savings accounts in the sense that, since they are often needed on short notice, they are highly *liquid* (meaning they can be quickly converted into cash), as in a bank savings account or a mutual fund that allows for easy withdrawal. Normally cash reserves earn low rates of interest, given their low risk and high liquidity.

So when asked whether a cash reserve might be easier to use than a line of credit, we reply that while donations are still important and will be gratefully accepted, your organization may have ongoing cash flow requirements that still need to be addressed. At current levels of fundraising, and with earned revenue that may just be able to support the existing operations, stabilizing cash flow through the use of credit is an essential component of good management. Placing money in the creditholder pool will help ensure the long-term survival of the institution by enabling it to handle its current obligations immediately and still present excellent programs or services. After all, money always costs money—that's a basic principle—and the cost to your institution of creating a cash reserve is also a factor that must be considered.

How can cash flow lead to new choices?

Once you have an annual cash flow budget, you can see income and expense in relation to time. You know when you need to secure additional funds and when you have surpluses. Using the Cash Flow Forecaster, you also have a sense of what the future might bring. The next step is to match up your new information with the opportunity and obstacle cards that your environment has dealt you. Remember, on a national level the pool of available resources is relatively constant, and a great many institutions are vying for the dollars in the pool.

Why not use some basic cash flow thinking to look outside the resource pool for the working capital that you need. And the most widely available and accessible source for working capital is probably right in your own community. To get the working capital that you need, it's time to explore the use of credit as a financial resource for your organization.

The Value of Credit

At its most rudimentary level, credit—the ability to borrow from a financial institution—is about time. For example, if you as a manager find yourself in the position of needing to make payroll, and the check from the foundation that you were counting on has not arrived, you have three choices:

- You can delay your payments, using your vendors and your staff as a substitute for your bank.
- You can draw on a cash reserve built up in the past to use at such times—if you have one.
- You can draw on a line of credit with your bank to provide low-cost funds that will be paid back when the check arrives. Again, you can draw on a line of credit only if you have one, and the time you need it most is not the best time to establish it.

Problems of goodwill arise when you choose the first option, not paying your staff or vendors. In addition, in the case of the vendors, you lose the opportunity for early-payment discounts, and you incur any penalties for late payment the vendors may choose to impose. If you might have received a 2 percent discount for early payment and instead rack up some 1.5 percent per month late charges, your annual costs for this behavior can be a staggering 20 percent or more.

If you have set aside a sum of money for a cash reserve, the second option, you need to be able to put your hands on it quickly. That means that you will have gained very small amounts of interest on the money, since it is highly liquid. In many recent years mutual funds have not returned enough to investors to compensate for the annual rate of inflation.

On an intuitive level, having a cash reserve to use at such times seems to make sense. You get some interest when you are not using the reserve, and you avoid interest charges when you do use it. Unfortunately, the original cost of the funds, the low interest rates obtained, the marginal interest avoided, and the inevitable effect of inflation on money held by nonprofits add up to make retaining a cash reserve a very costly option. Using the same cash flow budget and the same assumptions, as sketched in Chapter Six, a cash reserve can cost ten times as much as a fully secured line of credit, or more.

Which brings us to the third option: to obtain a fully secured line of credit with your bank, meaning that your creditholders will place a dollar's worth of collateral in the hands of the bank for every dollar you borrow. This is perhaps the single least understood method for stabilizing the financial situation of a nonprofit, so please forgive us when we keep repeating the point.

The management-by-crisis mode of operation ultimately comes down to not having the funds you need to pay the bills you have at the time you need to pay them. Businesses across the world routinely borrow when they need funds and pay them back when they don't. Yet for many in the nonprofit sector, borrowing carries with it an undeserved stigma and is viewed as a sign of poor management.

Isn't borrowing a sign of poor management?

Borrowing has a terrible reputation in the United States. As people often say, *Americans love credit and hate borrowing.* That is, people love the idea of being creditworthy, of being able to command respect at the bank and the bar. What makes folks nervous is when you actually use your credit to borrow: then you are in debt, and goodness knows what might happen. This is the moment when debt is equated with losing the family farm. It evokes visions of gaunt and ill-clothed homeless people from Oklahoma photographed trying to make their weary way in battered vehicles to the promised land of California.

Yet if you have the ability to establish a line of credit with your bank, then you have the essential financial management skills to ensure your fiscal stability. To have a line of credit with a bank means that you have prepared clear and understandable cash flow statements, projected your cash flow over the coming years, forged a working understanding of your fiscal situation and the uses of credit with your board of directors, and formed a community-based creditholder group to provide you with collateral.

Once a cash flow budget is adopted and a forecast created, the clarity with which each month's income and expense can be charted will be improved. This understanding opens the door to the use of credit as a predictable, inexpensive, safe, and accessible financial solution.

Credit allows you to place your hard-earned dollars into the service of your mission when you have a need. Borrowed dollars are *current* (meaning they are not discounted over time), and they are less expensive to mobilize than other forms of capital.

To efficiently obtain working capital, a nonprofit organization can secure a line of credit and then borrow funds to meet immediate expenses. One rule of thumb is to say that, in general, a line of credit equal to between 10 percent and 20 percent of an organization's annual operating budget is advisable. Institutions using the Cash Flow Forecaster can easily fine-tune their future borrowing needs by simply following the cash flow dips in the graphic presentations.

The length of time most organizations require credit each year is relatively brief. Once a line of credit is established, operating funds will be available as needed. Organizations with access to cash can pay quickly, often negotiating significant discounts from suppliers. Added together, those discounts can translate into savings that may compensate for the cost of the interest on the loans.

Why are time and timing so important when borrowing?

In case you hadn't noticed, people who rent things tend to be very careful about time. Bankers are no exception. It makes perfect sense. In Western culture, we truly believe that time marches on, in a linear, sequential fashion. This means that when all else is in question, at least time can be treated as a constant. Therefore, a line of credit, like all other loans, is meant to be used for a specific period of time. It is designed to stabilize cash flow during a one-year period; it is not designed to address long-term debt or activities that involve ongoing ventures.

A line of credit is an annual instrument. It must be treated that way. As noted earlier, you prove your merit to the bank and your creditholders by paying off the line of credit for at least thirty days during the course of each year.

Can borrowing pose a danger to some nonprofit organizations?

Some nonprofit organizations have gotten into trouble when they used their line of credit to incur debt or to pursue new ventures. The symptoms are always the same. The institution reports that while everything is going along just fine, it will be unable to repay its line of credit this year. The promise of tomorrow is offered as a sure cure, and the debt sits on the line as long as the banker is willing to tolerate the excuses.

When this happens, as we have observed many times over the years, the blame is often directed at the line of credit rather than the financial practices of the institution. The litany goes something like this: *Well, if we had just known that our revenues would be down this year, we never would have borrowed from our credit line. Instead, we would have cut expenses. The problem is that we were tempted into using our credit line. Without credit, we would have imposed serious austerity and we would have been okay.* That's just a variation on "the devil made me do it."

When the discussion reaches this level, it is time to revisit the purpose of credit and the sense of timing that it requires. Credit from a financial institution is obtained when the risk of lending is perceived to be less than the rewards of lending, at least from the banker's point of view. From the institution's point of view, borrowing needs to be carefully integrated into overall plans. Good risk management allows the prudent use of credit, meaning that plans are in place to manage the credit as well as other resources, or better.

Why not cut costs as a sure-fire way to solve financial problems?

Murray Dropkin, one of the pioneers in the field of cash flow management and author of *The Cash Flow Management Book for Nonprofits,* and Peter Drucker, the granddaddy of nonprofit organizational theorists, have a few choice words for the folks who believe that cost cutting is the primary way to go.[1] They point out that in the long run most extreme cost cutting is likely to backfire. As Drucker notes, major cost cutting frequently leads to higher costs in eighteen months or less.

This is the case, Drucker says, because people in the organization figure out how to get around the austerity measures so they can get their job done, or they hire temporary workers, who can ultimately prove to be more expensive than the regular payroll. The key to real cost cutting, Drucker says, is detecting whether your operations are really working or whether they are compromising your efforts. If that is the case, modifying those operations or even eliminating them is a more effective approach.

Doesn't it make good sense to adopt businesslike practices and defer paying our vendors for as long as possible?

The notion of withholding payment of bills makes little sense in the nonprofit sector. Goodwill is important for most nonprofits. They lack the economic muscle to stiff vendors and still keep them coming back for more. The loss of discounts and the assessment of penalties for late payment generally overwhelm the advantages of withholding payment. Organizations that establish a fully secured line of credit will find that they can pay on time, reduce or eliminate penalties, gain valuable discounts, and secure far better terms from vendors.

Some organizations that use a fully secured line of credit to pay quickly even ask their vendors to consider writing a contribution check instead of offering a discount. Since the vendor you pay promptly on delivery loves you better than your dog does, some vendors are willing to make out tax-deductible contribution checks for up to 5 percent of the bill.

Is the use of credit a substitute for fundraising or earned revenue?

The use of credit is not and should not be seen as a substitute for ongoing fundraising activities or for pursuing earned revenue strategies. Credit is a powerful tool for nonprofit organizations. It can be used to provide both short-term and long-term financial stability. The key to using credit safely is having an annual cash flow budget and forecast that shows income and expense through time. The cash flow budget pinpoints, with varying degrees of precision, the times when you need to borrow funds to maintain your operations and the times when you need to pay back the line of credit because you have surplus funds. Without a cash flow budget, you are flying by the seat of your pants—and the ride can get very bumpy. To smooth things out, just remember, there is a powerful link between cash flow and the safe use of credit.

Without a clear sense of cash flow, very costly reserves need to be accumulated to help the organization protect itself from the chaotic and sometimes random nature of the funding environment. Cash flow budgeting and forecasting often signal the potholes in the road ahead, and that should spur organizations to make provision—through a fully secured line of credit at the bank—for the expected and the unexpected events that befall all organizations, large and small. Do this, and if the check from the government agency is late, the market decides to melt down, or the special event is a bust and doesn't provide the projected income, the mission of your organization will not be sacrificed.

The work of setting up a cash flow budget, a four-line summary report, and a game plan for addressing events in the future will go a long way toward eliminating much of the management-by-crisis behavior that all nonprofits experience from time to time.

The bottom line is that you will still have to conduct the annual campaign and earn revenue. Credit can simply enhance the way you go about doing business. And if you do decide to use credit, you will not be alone. Many nonprofit institutions borrow. As Tuckman and Chang pointed out in their journal article on debt in nonprofit organizations, more than 71 percent of all nonprofits hold at least some form of debt.[2] The problem is that borrowing is still widely seen as a sign of poor management by many in the nonprofit world, even though it has proved to be a valuable financial tool in the commercial sector. As youngsters, we are taught that it is better to have money in the bank than to borrow it. Debt of any kind should be avoided, we are told. But for an organization struggling to fulfill its mission and meet immediate needs, establishing and using credit can be a sound and cost-effective financial strategy.

Despite our advocacy, not everyone is comfortable with seeing their nonprofit institution heading down to the bank to borrow. For these skeptics, we recommend reading Lendol Calder. Calder has a simple answer for critics of debt. In *Financing the American Dream: A Cultural History of Consumer Credit,* Calder argues that debt is as American as apple pie and that consumer borrowing has been an important engine of economic growth. And he doesn't stop there. Rather than encouraging profligate behavior, he says, the installment borrowing we use to buy cars and houses forces us to commit to regimens of disciplined financial management.[3]

Nonprofit organizations have many ways to borrow. Foundations and other interested parties have established special loan funds, often with special interest rates. But, in our view, these are just the warm-up act for the big time. In Chapter Ten, we talk more about creditholders, collateral, and borrowing from local commercial institutions, also known as banks.

CHAPTER TEN

BANKS, CREDITHOLDERS, AND CASH FLOW

Your cash flow presentations are good for more than budgeting and forecasting or increasing the comprehension of board members. You can also use your cash flow budgets and forecasts when you go to the bank. If you dread the thought of dealing with your banker, this chapter may change your mind in some very positive ways. We show you how to guarantee that you receive a warm welcome from your banker when you drop by to ask for a loan or a line of credit. And as you may have already surmised, creditholders and collateral play an important role in getting the red carpet rolled out for your visit.

Collateral, Collateral, Who's Got the Collateral?

Bankers cannot lend to you without collateral, except under special circumstances that typically require community service loans to be classified. Nonprofit organizations trying to establish a line of credit discover that banks require two guarantees of repayment—cash from operations and assets to act as collateral—before they are willing to lend. Typically, the primary source of repayment is from a nonprofit's earnings or from grants and gifts. The problem for many institutions is that they lack assets that bankers can easily convert into cash, which means they lack collateral or at least the type of collateral that bankers want. So, without collateral, no borrowing from banks, right?

In truth, we have observed some nonprofit organizations that have been able to borrow small sums without adequate collateral. Usually the local banker is a friend of the board president, or the husband of the richest woman in town is on the board. In every case the banks considered such lending irregular, but they ignored their reservations until a fiscal problem emerged for the nonprofit organization. Then the banker was required to reassert the normal relationship between the bank and its borrowers. Collateral was demanded as coverage for the credit.

The lesson is clear. Get your collateral up front and ready to go before borrowing, and both you and the banker will sleep better at night.

If a nonprofit considers using the closets of old roller skates donated in 1889 for the orphans, or the dozens of boxes of chalk and the cracked blackboards in the old one-room schoolhouse as collateral, then it is in trouble. Very few bankers want reams of used file folders, donated computers that run eight-inch disks, or a performing arts center with a leaking roof and a failing furnace.

As we revealed in Chapter Nine, however, you do have access to a form of collateral that you may not have considered, one that is within your reach and one that bankers worldwide are happy to accept without reservation. After all, bankers have fantasies too. What bankers dream about, when they imagine the most perfect collateral in the world, is cash, plain old-fashioned cold, hard cash. And you have access to cash and very liquid cash equivalents—stocks and bonds—from the people who support your organization. This cash is generated by creditholders and is the collateral that always enables you to borrow.

Reassuring Creditholders

But what about risk for the creditholders? That may seem like an impossible barrier to this course of action.

Any endeavor that involves money involves the risk of loss. Even the most secure investments are not fully bulletproof. However, you can reduce even the admittedly small risks that creditholders face.

To start, by now you have a cash flow budget, or at least the understanding of how to set one up, and you have the Cash Flow Forecaster to act as your slightly cloudy crystal ball. You can see your cash flow, the influx of income and the outflux of expenses. Remember the graphs provided by the Cash Flow Forecaster; they enable you to see the times when you need to borrow and the times when you have the funds to pay back the bank. In other words, you have a reasonably clear sense of when you need help and when you don't.

The line of credit you are planning should be pegged to at least 10 percent of your annual operating budget. Make it more, if you are a high-risk enterprise currently operating without a safety net, perhaps a festival with a three-day business plan or an institution almost solely supported by grants. In these cases, you may want to consider a line of credit equal to 20 percent of your annual operating budget. These are rule-of-thumb numbers. You can determine how much you need monthly by looking at the running total line of your cash flow budget. In practice, your line of credit may be plus or minus a few points depending on the timing of the income and expenses in your monthly income stream. For now, you are borrowing only to stabilize your cash flow, to smooth out those highs and lows, and to avoid those cash-crunching paydays when the grant check is late.

Understanding your cash flow and your limited borrowing requirements will help you cut the risk to the creditholders. However, before soliciting funds from creditholders for a line of credit, it is important that your board establish a policy stating that the line of credit will be used only to cover fluctuations in cash flow, not to address long-term debt or to serve as venture capital. (It can also establish a set of policies for long-term borrowing, but for now, let's just stay with specific use of a line of credit to flatten out your cash flow's peaks and valleys.)

This means that before the creditholders' funds are pledged as collateral, the institution will already have determined its capacity to repay the loan from operational funds. Or, stated in another way, *you know that you have the money to repay your borrowing, and thanks to the creditholders who have provided you with collateral, the bank is going to rent you some of its money for a short time.*

Given this policy, the degree of risk to creditholders is kept very low. You and your board should talk face-to-face with people about becoming creditholders based on your cash flow forecasts. You should explain how their dollars will help you borrow from the bank during those periods when you are low on cash. After you explain the organization's borrowing policy and outline any possible risks, each person can be asked to place a modest sum into a collateral account. Our rule of thumb here is that creditholders should never pledge more cash than they are willing to lose if something untoward happens. For this reason, it typically makes sense to have lots of creditholders who all feel safe and understand that everyone is sharing the risks. Losses happen in an uncertain world, even to the best of people with the best of motives and in the safest of situations.

We are often asked what would happen if the organization failed and the bank wanted to capture the creditholders' funds. Since we have never heard of this happening, our answer is couched in hypothetical terms. The bank would first attach the assets of the organization. If these prove to be insufficient and if the organization could not work out the credit arrangement with the bank, then and only then would a bank have access to the creditholders' pledged funds.

In effect, the nonprofit is the buffer between a creditholder's assets and the bank. This means that by the time the bank called on the creditholders, the organization would be technically bankrupt or at least in the late stages of bankruptcy. We have always urged creditholders to play it safe with the amount they choose to pledge, and we assume that in an extreme case, where the institution was about to default completely, the creditholders and the bank could strike a deal to have the creditholder funds be considered a contribution to the organization rather than to the bank, in which case they would count as a charitable deduction. All theory, up to this point.

The incentive of creditholders to support the organization is hardly financial. After all, people can earn interest with almost complete security in a bank savings account or by buying Treasury Bills. However, by placing their funds in a special account with your organization's bank, they have the chance to help you operate effectively, thus furthering the social purpose of your organization at no cost to themselves. This is particularly true of folks with stocks and bonds.

Is having a creditholder group really legal?

Having creditholders offer cash or cash equivalents to provide the basis for borrowing is legal. Banks have been accepting the pledge of financially valuable items as security without transferring possession or title for a long, long time. *Hypothecation,* the technical term for this activity, may sound unfamiliar, but you'll find it featured in all dictionaries under the letter "H"; it is part of the everyday language of banking.

As a cautionary note, it is always wise to tread carefully before adopting a new financial approach. Having said that (our lawyers can now relax), we need to share with you a little story that is instructive.

One of our clients had a board member, a self-proclaimed expert on non-profits, who raised the question of whether the use of creditholders was legal or a violation of the Internal Revenue Service or Securities and Exchange Commission regulations. The board reacted strongly to this question by asking their attorney, a member of a large law firm, to research this issue for them. Many, many thousands of dollars in legal fees later, the answer came back. The lawyers checked with the IRS and the SEC. Turns out that—as we knew—the use of creditholders poses no legal problems at all. The lawyers concluded therefore that there was no reason that consenting adults who have been properly apprised of the risks associated with being a creditholder would be prevented from participating in the program. The risk, of course, is that the institution that one loves with all one's heart and soul will be unable to meet its obligations and will default. In that case, the bank that has loaned money has every right to collect the dollars or stocks and bonds that creditholders have placed in the bank's vault.

Obviously, it makes sense to check with your state Attorney General's office, but to date, creditholder groups have encountered no legal obstacles that we or our lawyer know about. Our advice is to check out your local situation—just don't spend a fortune doing it.

Creditholder Status

You may be wondering whether creditholders aren't really donors in disguise. Curiously, not all creditholders are donors, although some people combine the roles. It works this way: many of your institution's donors will also consider becoming creditholders. In our experience, people do not stop being donors simply because they have decided to assist the institution by becoming creditholders. The purposes of the two actions are different, and donors and creditholders, even those who are confused about variable annuities and charitable remainder trusts, will know the difference. Your usual contributors will often choose to add creditholding to their support for your organization, and creditholding has another big advantage in that it can draw in people who don't feel they have surplus resources to give away, but who are well disposed toward your institution and willing to put some of their resources at risk to help you operate effectively.

And these new creditholders—people who have formerly not been donors—often become the bottom tier of the organization's fundraising pyramid. (Fundraising pyramids are those multicolored charts always shown at fundraising seminars that show how you have to work your way through the 80 percent of the people who contribute 20 percent to reach the 20 percent of the people who contribute 80 percent of the money.) After participating for a while, they feel a sense of partnership with the organization. Creditholders tend to move beyond helping provide credit; they start to make donations, become advocates for the institution, and bring in other participants as both creditholders and donors.

Many of the organizations we have worked with over the years link their annual fundraising drive with their annual creditholder drive. Imagine asking Mr. Jones for a contribution. If he demurs, saying he loves your institution but that he and his wife are giving to the organization across the street, wouldn't it be nice if you could follow up by asking him to park some money with you as a creditholder. It happens!

This method offers several advantages to all the parties involved. It's worth recounting them again: The organization gains a stable resource that can be used to mobilize credit whenever it can be shown that other sources of revenue will repay the loan. Creditholders gain an opportunity to provide invaluable assistance to a nonprofit organization they believe in, without cost to themselves. The bank gains the collateral it needs to justify a loan to the organization.

Creditholders will often place larger sums in the bank than they will donate to the organization's coffers. We have found that some people who support an institution with a $50 check each year are perfectly willing to place $2,500 in a creditholder's account. In discussions with creditholders over the years, we have been told that they clearly see a difference between "parking funds" with an institution, as some call it, and donating out of their own pocket. The funds that are used by the creditholder to provide ongoing support for an institution are perceived to be deposited temporarily. On the other hand, making an unconditional donation legally constitutes the end of the financial transaction. Perhaps the only exception to this rule is a gift that has strings attached. Normally even these gifts are final, so long as the nonprofit institution fulfills the terms and conditions associated with them. Some creditholders have told us that they view their participation as a form of savings, in the sense that they are helping a nonprofit organization but have every intention of using the funds once they have been released from their time-based certificate of deposit.

It is the sense of helping without incurring an expense that motivates some creditholders to place more funds in a certificate or deposit or to pledge more in stocks and bonds than they might if they were making a donation. This perception frequently means that forming a creditholder group is faster and easier than running a capital campaign or holding an annual fundraising drive.

Getting Started

So what are the steps for establishing a creditholder program?

If you are the administrator or board member in charge of setting up the creditholder program, you will need to establish a cash flow budget and a cash flow forecast using the best available estimates for the next three to five years. Obviously, the people setting up these forecasts will want to follow the instructions for cash flow budgets and cash flow forecasts in this book very carefully. These instructions call for specific footnotes for each item, since we believe it is vital to make your institution's budget crystal clear and easy to comprehend by prospective creditholders.

In some cases, a four-line summary—income, expense, running total, and cumulative total—is adequate for discussion purposes, but you want to have the budget, footnotes, and forecast available to answer more detailed questions.

Once you have completed these easy steps, approach your bank prior to meeting with your potential creditholders and discuss the creditholder program. In discussions with the banker, you should demonstrate that you understand how you arrived at the amount you wish to borrow. It also makes sense to show the banker how you plan to repay the line of credit. When you have agreed upon the amount for your line of credit, establish an umbrella account number for it that will be used by the bank to clearly designate the certificates of deposit or stocks and bonds coming in as collateral to be pledged to your organization.

The funds parked with your bank in a certificate of deposit or pledged as stocks and bonds will act as a secondary source of repayment for the bank. You fully intend to repay the line of credit from the operational funds in your budget as they arrive. These funds provide the primary source of repayment, and with the creditholders' funds you will have all the collateral that the bank requires. One bonus is that your collateral is in a highly liquid form—cash is as liquid as money can be—and this poses a tangible rationale for a reduced interest rate. Talk to your banker about lending to you at a couple of points above the interest being paid on the certificates of deposit.

This is also the moment to talk with the banker about any modification in the bank's standard hypothecation agreements. Each creditholder will be asked to sign a hypothecation (pledge) form. These are inevitably written in legalistic language in which the bank asserts its right to claim all your cattle and your firstborn child in the event of default. These forms, which tend to be fairly standard agreements, are normally designed to be used in commercial transactions, and they may be slightly different from what you or your creditholders expect. In a commercial transaction the collateral is typically promissory, and the bank wants to ensure that it has claims on whatever is out there. This may seem a trifle over the top for a creditholder program. After all, the collateral is in hand, the creditholder is a consenting adult who seeks no personal financial gain, and therefore the bank should expect each creditholder to shoulder no more liability than the amount that creditholder is pledging.

Because there is no risk for the bank, a clarifying statement from the bank officer or bank president may be in order. Just don't panic. Talk with your banker about this type of agreement. It represents a modest modification of terms and conditions, but still allows the bank to use an off-the-shelf agreement form. This saves the bank time and money, and it allows your creditholders to park funds with the bank without feeling that they will be dragged through town by wild horses if something goes wrong. We provide samples of this and other forms and letters in Chapters Eleven and Twelve.

Another approach that has been used by some of our clients is to pool the creditholder funds into one jumbo account, being mindful of the Federal Deposit Insurance Corporation (FDIC) limits on insuring accounts above $100,000. In this case, the bank is freed from having to set up and maintain each individual creditholder account with all the required forms and documents that bank regulators insist on. The nonprofit institution logs in each account as a deposit, places the entire sum in the hands of the bank, and then with some help from a bank officer, if necessary, sets up a spreadsheet that will automatically calculate the annual compound interest due to each of the creditholders who use certificates of deposit to participate. For creditholders placing stocks or bonds into the mix, the bank will have to provide a different arrangement, since the certificates need to be in the banker's vault to ensure coverage and no interest is paid on these accounts.

At this point you have marshaled your information in cash flow format, you have spoken with the bank to identify the size of your line of credit, and you have prepared the bank's staff for the torrent of creditholders who will be appearing at the bank to hypothecate funds. Now you need to meet with the potential creditholders, and the best place to start is with yourself.

Looking straight ahead into the mirror, ask yourself: *Am I ready to become a creditholder? At what level of commitment am I prepared to join?* If you have questions about your participation, this is a perfect time to resolve them with yourself before asking others. If you find yourself saying things like *I gave at the office with the sweat of my brow,* or *I really don't have the time or money to do this,* then it probably means that you will find it difficult to convince others why they should jump on board this train. On the other hand, if your mirror image smiles and says *I can do this* and *I know the reason why,* then set a dollar amount for yourself and walk or drive down to the bank. Present your funds or stocks and bonds to the friendly person who has been alerted to your creditholder program.

Although this exercise in self-understanding may seem trivial, social psychologists have presented some very compelling arguments for why it helps to explore actions on a conscious level, in an attempt to bring them into synch with unconscious concerns, particularly when dealing with stressful issues such as money.[1]

If your conscious and unconscious are in agreement, and you are ready to proceed, here's what will happen next. Okay, you are signed up to be a creditholder. Repeat this process with all your staff and your board members. Try to get as many people as close to the organization as possible to participate. Then with your bank account number and cash flow forecast in hand, you will want to sit down and discuss this matter face-to-face with a few key people in the community who are your supporters. Explain the circumstances that have brought you to the point where it makes sense to address the stabilization of your cash flow by creating a fully secured line of credit. Show them the budget and the forecasts. Tell them about all the others who have participated and ask them, and others in the community, to join you.

In describing the creditholder program, you should underscore that the creditholders still own their money. It is insured by the FDIC for up to $100,000 if they have purchased a certificate of deposit, or by the demigods of Wall Street if they are invested in stocks and bonds. This means that the creditholders will continue to collect all the interest or dividends these assets generate.

Certificates of deposit are time-based and may be purchased for a period from one month to a year or more. You should plan to oversubscribe the creditholders' pool, so people will know that in an emergency they will be able to withdraw their funds, although (as they are probably well aware) early withdrawal of certificate of deposit funds always involves a penalty from the bank. Some people may wish to withdraw their funds when the CD matures. In this case there is no bank penalty, but the organization must be prepared yearly to replace the withdrawn funds.

It is wise to think of the creditholder program as an ongoing opportunity for people to support your organization. It should be a regular feature of your institution forever, providing collateral for the organization's line of credit. The CDs are time-based, and it should be assumed that some current creditholders will withdraw their money when their CDs mature. Just as in personal life, for a whole host of reasons, your organization will do better the larger the number of friends and supporters who rally round it.

It is useful to note that some institutions, private schools being among the most obvious examples, make their creditholder program mandatory. In these cases, a deposit of a fixed amount is part of the annual contract entered into by the school and the student's parents. Some parents pledge stocks or bonds with a value equal to or exceeding the mandated amount. In the case of families on financial aid or where the enforced savings of a creditholder plan might be a hardship, one alternative is to request that some wealthier parents purchase additional certificates of deposit. The families on financial aid are then asked to pay a percentage point or two of an amount equal to the annual interest on the certificate of deposit. The families who participate in this arrangement are able to meet the mandate at an affordable cost, and the richer folks get a small bonus for their participation above and beyond the norm. For example, at a private school that will be featured as a case study later in this book, parents on financial aid can participate in the school's creditholder program at the required level of $3,000 per family for under $100 a year.

In any creditholder campaign, if you have been successful in answering the questions of your potential creditholders, the next step is to provide them with some options. They can simply go down to the bank and deposit funds that will be used to purchase a certificate of deposit. Banks normally offer certificates of deposit in preset amounts, such as $250, $500, $1,000, and up. Some creditholders will want to pledge stocks or bonds, and in that case, the bank will discount the value of the pledge and will usually ask that the certificates be placed in the vault before it will issue credit. Discounting stocks and bonds is a normal banking practice when these instruments are used as collateral. Don't be alarmed when this happens. Just accept the fact that bankers believe that stocks and bonds have values that go down as well as up over time, and the upside promise isn't enough to make them accept the downside risk.

Your potential creditholders will need some time to think about their participation, and if it is a particularly large sum, they may want to discuss this matter with their own financial advisers. Each creditholder needs to calculate what amount of money is acceptable to risk in this way. We have no experience of creditholder pools having failed, but that does not mean that they are completely safe. But then nothing in the world is completely safe. Prudence is always required even in seemingly safe situations.

Once they have decided to join, individual creditholders need to go to the designated bank to offer funds for certificates of deposit, or to pledge stocks or bonds. They must sign a pledge agreement that gives the bank access to the money they have pledged as collateral for the loan. Some institutions have designated a board member or a staff member as the creditholder coordinator, and this person can handle the funds and the paperwork for individuals who cannot make it down to the bank. When creditholders live a long distance from the organization's bank, the creditholder coordinator provides a valuable service, both to the creditholders and to the institution. When someone takes over the coordinating role in all transactions, it makes communication much more direct.

Banking at a distance may seem strange to some, but we have had clients that do precisely this when creating a creditholder group. A nationally prominent health care ministry has established an account with the bank that its management team deals with at home. For most creditholders, a trip to that bank is not in the cards; after all, who wants to travel a thousand miles to deposit a small check. Instead, the creditholders have wrapped their funds into a jumbo account and had their management deposit it for them.

Once the creditholders' funds or other assets are safely in the bankers' hands, the creditholders have one more responsibility to you: to inform you if they need to withdraw funds for an emergency, or if they do not plan to renew their certificate of deposit when it matures. In the latter case, they need to inform you well before the CD is actually mature. This information has real consequence, since you must sustain a specific level of collateral as a secondary source of repayment to the bank.

Once you have creditholders, we suggest that you issue a quarterly letter with a financial update, so that your creditholders hear from you at least four times a year. Communication with creditholders pays enormous dividends, and it helps to get into the habit of talking with them regularly, as triumphs in fundraising or disasters in ticket sales occur. These folks are on your side, but it is still their money, and they will want to hear the good news and the bad news. Share both kinds of news with them; they will really appreciate your candor. Make this contact part of your organization's yearly calendar, along with bringing in new creditholders each year.

Avoiding Pitfalls

As practitioners, we have seen some very strange things in the nonprofit world. Consequently, it comes as no surprise to us that the way institutions set up creditholder programs isn't always "by the book." Of course, we hope that people will follow our advice and that they will take our recommendations seriously and literally, but that is not always the case.

So long as human beings exist, any social endeavor will be subject to problems; creditholder programs established by nonprofit institutions are not immune. Here are some of the problems that we have observed over the past thirty years:

Not enough board and staff members were willing to commit to the creditholder program. So, despite a cost of participation at a level that meant that everyone could subscribe, only a few individuals signed up. These enrolled creditholders were in effect being asked to carry more than their fair share of the burden. Without adequate support, the creditholder program could hardly get off the ground.

The lesson here is that if your board decides to start a creditholder program, urge every member to participate, even if only at a minimum level. Plan to fully subscribe the program and don't stop recruiting creditholders until you have reached your goal.

Borrowing was not fully secured by creditholders. Acquiring debt as a new resource can be very exciting, but it is imperative that everyone on the board understand both its positive and negative consequences. Borrowing that is fully secured provides day-to-day funds as a resource in which the risk has been spread among many participants. By providing a dollar of collateral for every dollar borrowed, the board and staff can make sure that debt will be used responsibly.

A creditholder program is set up, then halted for some time. When this happens, new creditholders are not brought in to cushion the impact of other creditholders' leaving the program over time. The consequence is a fits-and-starts arrangement that leaves everyone wondering about the policy of the institution and leaves the bankers confused about their commitment of credit in relation to the institution's commitment of collateral. The lesson is simple. If you start a creditholder program, it makes sense to make it a regular part of your organization process and to regularly recruit new creditholders to make sure that your collateral is always sufficient to meet your expected and unexpected borrowing needs.

Resisting the Temptation to Go It Alone

Some of your stakeholders are bound to ask why you want to pay interest to the bank when the group could just handle the funding on its own. Saving interest is always on people's minds. Yet in this case, the marginal cost of interest provides the institution with an everyday resource and a highly dependable, emotionally detached banker who can be counted on to make careful decisions that reinforce the financial health of the organization.

For many people a convention in the nonprofit sector is that loans should come from special programs at foundations, such as program-related investment funds

(PRIs), or from financial organizations set up to address the special needs of non-profit institutions. We recommend that you think first of going to the bank. And why banks? Well, as the famous bank robber Willie Sutton put it so well, "Because that's where the money is."

Banks are a stable, predictable, efficient, and helpful resource. Bankers, unlike foundation program officers, may have only a passing interest in the mission of your agency. But with a liquid asset in the form of creditholders' cash, a sound plan, and a reasonable cash flow budget and forecast, your nonprofit can obtain working capital five or even six days a week. Unlike foundations, which change priorities and programs at the drop of a hat, bankers are in the business of renting money, and they are always open for business to qualified customers. What nonprofits need to qualify for commercial credit is the necessary cash flow sensibility and the highest possible grade of collateral, and both are within your reach.

For some people, only death, pestilence, and taxes inspire as much fear as visits to the bank to ask for money. So you will want to sit down with your financial committee chair or your board treasurer or even yourself and review the financial statements you will need for the banker. In an ideal world, you might take some time to quickly sketch out a strategic plan, a marketing plan for creditholders, and a brief description of how you will pay for expenses in the coming year. These need not be exhaustive planning efforts, but they do need to accurately reflect your best thinking at the time.

This preliminary work will pay a handsome dividend to you in the future, not only at the bank but in your fundraising efforts, in your day-to-day operations, and in your relationship with staff and trustees. Organizations using a consultant to assist them in preparing these materials have found that costs for the service are normally quite modest.

When all your homework is done, you will have an idea of how much you want to borrow, and you will have cash flow financial reports and plans to show how you expect to repay the loan. You have a plan for a creditholder group with enough funds to match the amount you wish to borrow, plus a little extra to allow individual creditholders to withdraw in an emergency.

You have prepared your annual cash flow budget, complete with footnotes, and you have generated a cash flow forecast. Furthermore, you and your trustees have agreed to institute a creditholder group. Board members have joined in to make their own funds available and to get others to participate. You are able to quickly determine the amount of money you will need to borrow by looking at your cash flow budget and noting the largest negative monthly totals. Or you may anticipate future borrowing needs by simply assuming that your line of credit should equal at least 10 percent to 20 percent of your annual operating budget.

When this is accomplished, you are ready to go shopping for a bank that will recognize your worth, offer you good terms, and work with you to meet your credit needs in the coming years. Start by calling the bank where you normally do business. Ask to set up an appointment with a loan officer and indicate that you are interested in establishing a line of credit. Don't be surprised if you encounter a tiny bit of resistance from the people at the bank. Some bankers have no idea that nonprofits qualify for, and can use, a line of credit. They may think that you are looking for a donation or an unsecured loan. Just be patient and remember that, while they are in the business of renting money, bankers are apt to be un-accustomed to dealing with nonprofit organizations.

What's going to happen at your first meeting? This depends on the banker, but don't count on too much. The first meeting with your banker should be viewed as a get-acquainted session, winding up with a specific request for a line of credit and some paperwork for the banker to review. Your banker will want to learn more about what you do, your mission, and your program, and will also be concerned with how the loan can be repaid. Make it easy for your banker to evaluate your current financial position, your prospects for the future, and the quality of your management. All these are perfectly normal questions for someone renting money.

When you head out to meet with your banker, the following items are help-ful to take along:

Financial statements:

- Current annual cash flow budget, with plenty of footnotes.
- A cash flow forecast that looks ahead a couple of years. The forecast will reveal your projected cash flow. The projected cash flow forecast is especially useful in identifying whether you will have sufficient cash to repay the loan.
- Three years of financial statements. (If you have been around that long; if not, your creditholders' cash will still ensure a warm welcome at the banker's door.)

Organizational plans:

- Strategic plan: A document demonstrating the fit between the organization and its environment. In plain English, demonstrate how you are pursuing your mis-sion and how your program or programs relate to the wider world in which you are operating. Placing this information in written form will assist bankers who need to get to know you better.
- Marketing plan: A plan for identifying and reaching your audience or clients. Your program for identifying and securing creditholders will impress the banker with your resolve to ensure the bank's safety in this transaction.
- Financing plans: A set of documents that might include a fundraising plan, a plan for generating earnings, and a sense of how you intend to use borrowed funds.

Diving In

Okay, so you have the paperwork, now what? Although you may anticipate questions, just remember this is not the Spanish Inquisition and your banker is not Torquemada, the Grand Inquisitor. Be prepared to answer questions, but remember that you have no need to be defensive. The bank is renting money, and it has a right to make sure that you understand your responsibility to repay it. However, since you are offering cash as a source of collateral—through your creditholders' account—the banker should be very accommodating and prepared to offer excellent terms on your line of credit, since the bank has no risk associated with your loan.

If you feel uncomfortable during this transaction, tell the banker. You are offering the bank an opportunity to earn income on your borrowing with virtually no risk, and you should be treated very well. If the experience or the terms do not suit you, consider going to another bank. Businesses shop around for banks all the time. While the products offered are pretty much the same, the treatment and service provided vary greatly.

When you decide on a bank or a banker you like and return to pursue your loan, there are certain details you will want to discuss. The following are some examples of the details that need to be ironed out:

A special account must be set up in the name of the organization. This account will be linked to the certificates of deposit and pledges from your creditholders. With some banks, this tiny deviation from standard operating procedure may require a little discussion on your part. The problem is that in some banks the communication between the people who handle certificates of deposit and those who make loans is less than perfect. By highlighting the need for a smooth link between the collateral and the credit, you are simply helping the bankers do their jobs better.

The creditholders' account will need to be established and administered by the bank in a manner that protects both sides. For your part, you need to be sure that the bank will inform its tellers or officers about the program so that your creditholders will not be treated poorly or turned off by bank employees who are unfamiliar with it. The bank, for its part, will be handling more accounts than usual to form your collateral, so they need to be sure that your level of collateral matches the loans in place.

You might encounter a banker who tries to tell you that larger certificates of deposit are necessary for this program. We suggest that you simply remind the banker that the bank's own brochures offer a wide range of choices and that the additional cost of a few keystrokes to link the certificate with the special account for your organization hardly outweighs the benefits the bank derives from having the credit fully secured with cash or cash equivalents. Or you might counter by setting up your creditholder account in-house using a variation of the agreements included in Chapters

Eleven, Twelve, and Fourteen, after they have been vetted by your attorney, and combining all your creditholder funds into one large account. You will be handling the paperwork and distributing the interest to the creditholders, and the bank will usually offer you a slightly higher interest rate for buying a larger certificate of deposit.

It is entirely appropriate for you to ask for a lower rate of interest on your borrowing. Again, the bank is not doing you a favor; you are offering the bank little or no risk. This normally would translate into borrowing at a rate slightly above the amount paid by the bank for the certificates of deposit.

The standard commercial security agreement that will be signed by your creditholders may need to be clarified—but not rewritten—by your banker. As the upcoming Northwest Folklife case study demonstrates, the bank's response can be clear and simple.

Although it should not be necessary, given the quality of your collateral, the bank may want to have receivables assigned to it for collection. For example, you might have a grant check sent directly to the bank from a government agency or foundation.

It is your responsibility to sustain the value of your creditholders' collateral. You may need to work out a communication plan between your organization and the bank that will allow mutual assessment of the appropriate level of collateral at any given point in the life of the loan.

Finally, if you encounter serious problems with the bank, try to figure out if the trouble is your problem or their problem. In the Northwest Folklife case study that follows in Chapter Twelve, the bank that had held the institution's accounts for years simply could not fathom the concept that adults in their community would consent to place cash and stocks and bonds in a collateral account for up to ten years, in support of the organization. Not believing that, the bank kept trying to defend itself with more and more exotic legal arguments. Just reading the reams of paper was exhausting. The answer was not to try to work it out with this bank. Instead, we marched down the street, placed our case before another banker, and within two working days had a signed agreement for a fully secured ten-year term loan.

Cash flow thinking and credit-based strategies can work on many different levels and for many different types of nonprofit institutions. In Chapter Eleven we demonstrate how these cash flow strategies can be put into action when you experience shortfalls.

USING CREDIT TO MANAGE FLUCTUATING CASH FLOW

In the course of day-to-day operations, any nonprofit may have moments when the funds available are not sufficient to pay for such essential items as payroll, or rent, or withholding taxes. When you're an administrator, your strategy for dealing with these moments says a lot about your leadership, particularly if you have known about this situation in advance. The most straightforward method for dealing with these temporary shortfalls is to have the foresight to set up a fully secured line of credit at your local bank before you need to use it. Once your line of credit is in place, all it takes is a telephone call and you can move on with the rest of your day.

In this chapter we introduce a case study that demonstrates how credit can be used to bridge the gap between income and expenses. It is one of three cases that reveal different aspects of our approach, and it's useful to start by summarizing some of their differences and commonalities. In the three case studies presented in this book, only the actual names associated with Northwest Folklife and West Sound Academy are used. The names of the other individuals and organizations have been altered, partly to protect their privacy and also because the other case study organization, Street Angels, is actually a composite of two different clients.

Each of these organizations called us in as consultants. With each, we started by asking the staff to prepare a cash flow budget. This information became the basis for solving the problem at hand. The board and staff members' understanding of the role that cash flow plays in their organization is what allowed them to develop a successful financial strategy.

In each case, certain themes will be apparent. We use cash flow budgets and forecasts extensively in our consulting work. Bankers played a major role by granting credit to the institutions and arranging for different types of loans. Similarly, creditholders were central actors in each situation, making sure that the institutions had the collateral needed to arrange for financing. You will also note that each institution's strategy with regard to its creditholders was different. This reflects the different risks and requirements that each type of borrowing places on creditholders.

For example, creditholders who are securing a line of credit have a very low level of risk. Funds have already been identified to repay the line of credit and, barring a major and unanticipated problem, the credit line should be periodically paid off as funds flow into the institution. These creditholders can sign up for a one- or two-year certificate of deposit, and if additional creditholders are recruited, their term of commitment may also be limited to a couple of years. Because a line of credit is meant to *revolve*, meaning—as we point out in Chapter Ten—it must be drawn down to zero for at least thirty days during the course of the year, it has a specific application: to smooth out cash flow, to bridge gaps between income and expense as they occur during the course of any one year's operations.

Creditholders who are helping an institution finance a shortfall or deficit are at higher risk. Their assets will be required for the term of the loan, or at least a certain percentage of that time, since repayment of principal and interest will diminish the level of risk each year. These individuals need to understand that they are participating in a long-term process and that their risk is correspondingly greater than it would be if they were just backing a line of credit. Of course, this risk can be mitigated to some extent by recruiting new creditholders on a regular basis to ensure that the pool of collateral is adequate to span the term of the borrowing. Some institutions oversubscribe their creditholder programs, which simply means that they recruit more creditholders than are necessary to collateralize their borrowing at 100 percent. We strongly urge all our clients to do this. In one of the upcoming case studies, West Sound Academy pegged its creditholder program at 120 percent of its borrowing level. This meant that some creditholders could withdraw their funds to deal with an emergency or a change in their situation without diminishing the overall collateral coverage provided by the program.

Finally, creditholders who are assisting an institution to use credit for a new venture are betting that it will succeed, often without a proven track record of performance. The level of risk for these creditholders is higher still, which is one good reason for the pool of participants to be as broad as possible, to spread the risk widely rather than concentrating it on a few individuals.

In the case of nonprofits using credit to start a new program or even an entire institution, one additional measure is needed to reduce risk. That is the ongoing recruitment of creditholders. In the case of a private school, each set of parents acting as creditholders would be replaced by new creditholders as their children graduate and move on.

Each of the three types of borrowing—a line of credit, a long-term loan for deficit reduction, or financing for a new venture—creates a different set of circumstances for the creditholders. It is important to acknowledge the risks and requirements of each up front.

The Street Angels Case Study: A Line of Credit for Stabilizing Cash Flow

Street Angels is a remarkable social service agency with a large and loyal following. Although financially successful and considered fiscally solid, the organization still experiences great fluctuations in cash flow during the year. It found that planning ahead to use credit can make a strong organization even stronger.

The folks served by Street Angels are among the poorest of the American poor. They include street people, abandoned and runaway children, the homeless, and the mentally ill. These people are often unable to work and in some cases can barely function at all. They are part of the penniless poor that are a familiar sight in cities across the nation. Street Angels was founded in 1978 by two couples, Joe and Jean Franklin and Tom and Tracy Topnagle, to assist people living on the street. Working with a board of prominent local people, they deal with more than 50,000 requests for service per year, or roughly 136 people a day.

Street Angels receives 60 percent of its annual operating budget of $450,000 in the form of fees for service under contract with the city. With foundation and donor support of $270,000, the organization operates a shelter and an evening meal program. Showers and spare clothes, along with counseling and day care, are part of the mix of services provided. Street Angels' approach of working with a local community college to provide classes for homeless people and of offering in-house vocational training programs has garnered additional support from donors and the community.

Each year the agency obtains grants from local foundations and corporations. It also raises close to $80,000 from its annual No-Show Ball, in which people are invited not to attend a social event during the hectic holiday season. Apart from the cost of invitations and return envelopes, the function is very low overhead, since people are more than willing to pay the $100 ticket price to not have to attend yet another fundraising event in town.

JJ and TT, as the founders are called, divide up the tasks of operating the agency, with the assistance of volunteers and counselors and a paid kitchen and laundry staff. Labor is the second-largest item on the budget, after food. The level of demand for the agency's services cannot be accurately predicted, since the staff is dedicated to taking in everyone who needs to be accommodated each night.

As chief financial officer of Street Angels, Tracy handles all the accounts, budgetary reporting, payroll, and taxes. We first met her when she called to ask about our consulting services after reading an article that had appeared in the newspapers about our work with another organization.

With precision Tracy outlined her problem. Big gaps occur each year at Street Angels, as she waits for the quarterly check from the city or the grant award from a foundation. Tracy must make payroll. The staff relies on her almost as much as the folks served by the agency do. She insists on paying the IRS payroll taxes religiously, and most of the vendors who supply food simply can't be put on hold. Over the years, she had maintained a small fund she called her "cookie jar account," and when she was short on cash, she would pull out a cookie or two. This year, the cookie jar was empty, depleted by a sudden surge in food prices, increases in the premiums for staff health insurance, the setup costs for a new educational program, and a strangely late payment from the normally predictable city. It was crunch time, and no more cookies were to be had.

Tracy told us they did not have a line of credit with their bank. The thought of borrowing had always made the founding couples squeamish, and after all, the money normally was there when it was needed. With our help Tracy reviewed her options. She needed funds now, payroll was due, vendors were stretched to the limit, her quarterly tax bill was pending, and calls to the city had resulted in nothing. We asked if the board was prepared to step in, since they are in effect the owners of the agency. Tracy told me that her request for funds at the last board meeting had met with confusion. The desire to help was there, but the members of the board couldn't figure out the right approach.

Board members struggled to imagine cutting programs or suddenly raising lots of funds. With no clear course to follow, Tracy had tried triage, the practice of dividing up creditors into categories according to the degree of damage they can do to the organization if not paid quickly. It just didn't help. There was not enough money to satisfy anyone, and she was very afraid of missing her payments to the IRS. Vendors were grumbling and the staff was getting uncomfortable. Tracy asked us to meet with the board the following Tuesday.

At the meeting, we explained that the function of credit is not to replace grants or earned revenue, and it cannot substitute for reasonable cuts in the budget. Credit is a resource that can provide funds when they are needed, funds that are paid back when they are not. Having access to credit, the social service agency could maximize its use of capital, saving money in some instances, and avoiding the consequences of nonpayment in others.

We talked about setting up a creditholder group. Surely, Street Angels had a mission that many people could support by making it possible for the organization to obtain credit. Street Angels provides an extraordinary service with its programs, and people in the city who knew about the agency were thankful that it was so successful.

We spoke of the reduced cost of going to their local bank and having instant access to below-market-rate loans with their fully secured line of credit, pointing out that this certainly beat taking annual losses from a mutual fund for a cash reserve. The board members agreed and asked the Executive Committee to draft a game plan for reaching out to creditholders.

Of the many ways in which a creditholder group can be structured, Street Angels chose an approach that was just right for them. Tracy, as the chief fiscal officer, met with their bank, got an agreement to establish a revolving line of credit that would be secured by certificates of deposit or stocks and bonds dedicated as collateral to the bank. She and Tom then went out and found individuals willing to participate. As the letters and forms that follow demonstrate, the agency was professional, thoughtful, careful, and correct when dealing with other people's money. And the Franklins and Topnagles still managed to maintain the warmth and enthusiasm that are the hallmark of the institution.

The board president of Street Angels sent a letter to supporters and friends explaining the concept and inviting participation. (See Exhibit 11.1.) The board president signed each letter, and on most he added a personal note.

They didn't want to overwhelm people with too many facts and figures, so they deliberately kept it general. Along with his letter, the board president included a short flyer that addressed the most commonly asked questions about creditholders. (See Exhibit 11.2.)

Once the individuals who received the letter inviting them to become creditholders had reviewed the questions and answers document, those who indicated an interest in participating were called by members of the board. Those who agreed to become creditholders were asked to sign the form shown in Exhibit 11.3.

How Street Angels Set Up the Creditholder Campaign

After the board president's letter went out, the board members divided the list of people to contact. The board members first reviewed the overall list, and all were asked to identify people whom they felt comfortable in calling to discuss the creditholders program. Each board member was given some talking points and a copy of the actual creditholder agreement.

EXHIBIT 11.1. STREET ANGELS CREDITHOLDER LETTER.

Street Angels
P.O. Box A
Seattle, WA 90543

Dear Friends:

On behalf of the entire Board of Directors I want to thank you for helping us have a remarkably successful year. Grants and donations are up. This year Street Angels has increased the ways we assist the people that we serve. We continue to provide a much-needed resource for the homeless and abandoned people of our city, opening pathways that might otherwise be closed to them. Your support in the past has been wonderful, and I am deeply appreciative. The lives of all who live in this fine city are indeed enriched.

Now I need your assistance to keep up our level of professionalism. Due to the unpredictable nature of our work, each year the agency experiences peaks and valleys in its cash flow. Most of our funding comes in big chunks from our contract with the city and from our popular No-Show Ball. This irregular pattern has made it difficult to maintain our operations without developing a way to smooth out our cash flow. I know I can count on you to help make the agency a more stable enterprise that is run with businesslike efficiency without sacrificing our goals to help others.

That is why I am pleased to tell you about a program we've jointly developed with First National Bank. First National Bank is offering certificates of deposit for twelve and eighteen months, at a rate that is competitive with other banks in our area. (See specific details on the enclosed flyer.) These certificates will act as our guarantee for a $100,000 line of credit. In this way, the agency will be provided with the cash flow stability necessary to continue our work, and you will receive the satisfaction of knowing that your funds are helping us manage our cash flow. Equally important, you are joining us in making it possible to continue the invaluable work of Street Angels.

Five members of the agency's Board of Directors have already signed up for this program. We now need other supporters to make our financial stability a reality. Won't you please consider it? I have asked a member of the Board to give you a call in the coming week to discuss this program and to answer your questions. I trust I can count on your support.

Sincerely,

John J. Jones
Chairman of the Board

P.S. I'm working to put my funds together. I sure hope you can too!

EXHIBIT 11.2. STREET ANGELS CREDITHOLDER GROUP QUESTIONS AND ANSWERS.

Street Angels is forming a Creditholder Group for the purpose of collateralizing a revolving secured line of credit to meet the working capital needs of the agency. The collateral will be certificates of deposit owned by individual Creditholders who have agreed to allow our bank, First National, to use the CD as security for the line of credit.

Why should I consider becoming a Creditholder for Street Angels?

With a secured line of credit, Street Angels will be able to meet its financial obligations in a more timely manner, thus reducing its annual interest and carrying costs.

What will the amount of the secured credit line be?

Street Angels has arranged to borrow $100,000 under this credit facility.

Aren't you just trading an interest charge from one vendor to another?

Yes, but we're trading a high-interest financing rate for a lower one. The interest rate on the secured line of credit will be 2 percent over the average interest rates being paid on the certificates of deposit. This will reduce our interest rate to approximately 5 percent from its current 7 percent.

Is there a minimum denomination of certificate of deposit I would have to purchase?

Yes. The minimum CD at First National Bank is $500. If this amount is more than you are willing or able to invest, the CD may be purchased jointly with other individuals.

What about the term length on the CD?

Your CD can be set up to mature each year or you may wish to set a longer term. Since better rates are available for terms longer than six months, you may want to consider a term of one year or beyond.

Who gets the interest on my CD?

You do. The CD and the interest it earns are yours. You will receive your interest in the same manner and at the same times as if the CD were not being used as collateral.

What risk is there to me as a Creditholder?

This program is not without risk. In the event that Street Angels does not meet its repayment obligation, the bank could move against the collateral to repay the debt.

EXHIBIT 11.2. STREET ANGELS CREDITHOLDER GROUP QUESTIONS AND ANSWERS, *continued.*

If the bank applied a portion of my CD to the repayment of the line, will I have lost that money?

Under the Creditholder Agreement between the Creditholder and Street Angels, the agency agrees to repay all or any portion of the funds applied by the bank at the same interest rate and term as provided for under your original CD. However, as a practical matter, circumstances leading to Street Angels' being unable to repay its line of credit would almost certainly have rendered the agency insolvent. If this were the case, Creditholders would be unsecured creditors of the agency pursuant to any insolvency or bankruptcy proceedings.

What if I need to get my money out earlier than the maturity date?

It's the goal of Street Angels to maintain a collateral base in excess of $120,000, or $20,000 more than our line of credit, to allow for early redemption. We ask that you advise us when you intend to terminate the CD so that we will know the level of our collateralization. Of course, as with any CD, you may be subject to a penalty for early withdrawal.

EXHIBIT 11.3. STREET ANGELS CREDITHOLDER AGREEMENT.

THIS CREDITHOLDER AGREEMENT is made as of _____, _____, by and between Street Angels, a Washington nonprofit corporation ("Street Angels"), and _____ ("Creditholder") for the purpose of setting forth the terms and conditions under which the Creditholder agrees to extend a security interest in certain collateral hereinafter described for the benefit of Street Angels.

Street Angels is a nonprofit corporation organized under the laws of the State of Washington and is exempt from Federal income taxes, except for income tax on unrelated business income, under Section 501(c)(3) of the Internal Revenue Code of 1986.

Street Angels desires to obtain and maintain a revolving secured line of credit with First National Bank (the "Bank"), for the purpose of meeting working capital requirements of Street Angels as such needs arise in the ordinary course of business. Street Angels has agreed with the Bank to secure the line of credit with a first security interest in Certificates of Deposit provided by the Creditholders and others (together referred to as the "Creditholder Group") pursuant to the terms as set forth in the "Security Agreement for Savings Accounts, Share Accounts, Time Certificates of Deposit and Time Deposits," attached hereto as Exhibit A and hereinafter referred to as the "Security Agreement."

The Creditholder, in support of the mission of Street Angels, is willing to provide such a security interest in a Certificate of Deposit owned or to be purchased by the Creditholder in order to assist Street Angels in meeting its working capital requirements at a minimal cost to Street Angels.

THEREFORE, in consideration of the mutual benefits to be received by Street Angels and the Creditholder, the receipt and sufficiency of which are hereby acknowledged, Street Angels and the Creditholder agree as follows:

1. Collateral: The Creditholder has or will purchase a Certificate of Deposit from the bank in the amount of $ _____ , identified as CD# _____ , maturing on _____ , (the "Collateral").

2. Certificate of Deposit: The Certificate of Deposit and all earnings thereon are and at all times shall be the property of the Creditholder, subject to the terms of the Certificate of Deposit and to the Security Agreement. The Creditholder will look solely to the Bank for payment of interest on the Certificate of Deposit, so long as the Bank has not applied all or any portion of the Collateral to the obligation of Street Angels.

3. Protection of Collateral: Street Angels acknowledges the trust the Creditholder is placing in Street Angels to provide the Certificate of Deposit as Collateral. Street Angels therefore agrees:

(a) Street Angels will at all times abide by the terms and conditions of the promissory note and any other documents required by the Bank to obtain and maintain the secured line of credit, including the obligations for payment of interest and principal in a timely manner and the provision of information;

(b) Street Angels will strive to always maintain no less than 120 percent of the lesser of (i) the maximum loan balance outstanding or (ii) the approved line of credit amount, in collateralized Certificates of Deposit with the Bank;

(c) Street Angels will provide the Creditholder with regular and ongoing information as to the status of the secured line of credit and Street Angels's financial position. This information, as described below, will be provided semiannually to the Creditholder:

(1) Secured Line of Credit Information, including loan balance outstanding under the secured line of credit, total collateral securing the loan balance, and anticipated repayment date of outstanding loan balance.

(2) Street Angels's Financial Information, including interim financial statements and audited financial statements.

(d) In the event that the secured line of credit goes into default for any reason, Street Angels will notify the Creditholder within five business days of receiving such notification of default.

4. Withdrawal of Collateral: The Creditholder agrees that it will notify Street Angels on or before the Creditholder terminates the Security Agreement with the Bank.

5. Collateral Applied: If the bank applies all or any portion of the Collateral to payment of Street Angels's obligations under the secured line of credit, Street Angels agrees:

(a) It will immediately notify the Creditholder as to the amount of the Collateral provided by the Creditholder that has been applied to Street Angels's obligations;

(b) It will pay periodic interest to the Creditholder on that amount of the collateral applied to Street Angels's obligations at the same rate and at the same times as provided for under the Certificate of Deposit;

(c) It will repay to the Creditholder the sums applied by the Bank on the maturity date of the Certificate of Deposit.

EXHIBIT 11.3. STREET ANGELS CREDITHOLDER AGREEMENT, *continued.*

6. <u>Notices:</u> Any notice or other communication required by or under the terms of the Creditholder Agreement will be in writing, addressed to the appropriate party, and delivered personally or sent by U.S. mail as follows:

> Street Angels
> Creditholder Coordinator
> Attention: Finance Manager
> P.O. Box A
> Seattle, WA 90543

Creditholder's Address

_____

_____

7. <u>Binding Effect:</u> The rights and obligations of the Creditholder under this Agreement shall inure to and bind the heirs, executors, administrators, successors, and assigns of the Creditholder. The signature of the Creditholder represents that the Creditholder has had the Creditholder's attorney review this Agreement and the Security Agreement or has chosen to waive such opportunity.

When executed by Street Angels and the Creditholder, this Agreement is effective as of the date first above written.

Street Angels　　　　　　　　　　　　　　　　CREDITHOLDER
a Washington nonprofit corporation　　　　　_____
　　　　　　　　　　　　　　　　　　　　　　　　　　Name

By: _____

_____

The financial officer of Street Angels acted as a technical backup, in case a board member needed more information or support. She also placed follow-up calls to track which board members needed assistance. The board president kept track of each board member's status and talked to the financial officer several times a week to find out who had signed up and for how much. In a nice surprise, a couple of people who had agreed to be creditholders without specifying the amount of their participation signed up for $10,000.

In thirty days Street Angels had $120,000, which was enough to oversubscribe the $100,000 line of credit. Having access to credit immediately provided Street Angels with a means to stabilize its cash flow.

In the year following the creation of the creditholder program, Street Angels saw a dramatic increase in donations. Our sense is that as more people in the community saw the organization through the eyes of creditholders, more were encouraged to provide support. The action of the board and staff in setting up the creditholder program was seen as a positive step in the development of a more self-sufficient institution, and this also encouraged higher levels of giving.

Street Angels exemplifies the key lessons to be learned from setting up a creditholder program:

- The board of directors needs to understand the importance of stable cash flow to an organization. It needs to grasp the creditholder concept, and members need to personally participate and recruit others.
- The arrangements with the bank need to be set up before anyone approaches potential creditholders, so that individuals who decide to join can do so at once.
- The communication from the board president to the potential creditholders needs to be clear, reasoned, and straightforward. It also needs to be backed up with some answers to commonly raised questions.
- Finally, the agreement between the creditholder and the organization needs to be formal; it must be articulated in correct legal terminology, including the occasional obscure phrase of the type that so often blights the linguistic landscape when lawyers draft contracts.

In the Street Angels case study, we have not included the hypothecation agreement between the bank and the creditholders, even though each Street Angels creditholder was asked to sign one. Hypothecation and more is coming up in the next case study, in Chapter Twelve, which looks at a slightly more challenging form of borrowing.

CHAPTER TWELVE

USING CREDIT FOR DEALING WITH DEFICITS

Few things inspire terror in the hearts of administrators and board members as much as an unanticipated shortfall near the end of the fiscal year. Yet deficits happen—and often to groups that do not deserve them. Circumstances beyond the immediate control of the board and staff can sometimes result in negative numbers even at the end of an otherwise rosy year.

So deficits happen. For the literal-minded, we are using the terms deficit and shortfall interchangeably. We are not referring to the national budget. Instead deficits or shortfalls are the financial position an institution finds itself in at the end of a year when it lacks the cash to pay for all of its current expenses. When this happens unexpectedly and the rent or staff do not get paid, everyone, from the board president to the janitor, is annoyed, if not actually enraged.

In this chapter we offer you some effective strategies for understanding why deficits occur and for dealing with them when they do. These include finding out why the problem occurred in the first place, weighing your options, and then, in certain circumstances, putting into place a term loan, one that extends for more than a year, to give you time to solve the problem. This use of long-term credit, in contrast to the short term associated with a line of credit, is often the answer, as the Northwest Folklife Festival case study demonstrates. We also critically explore some alternative measures, such as emergency fundraising campaigns and cost-cutting tactics. And we talk briefly about the psychological challenge of acknowledging shortfalls in the public arena.

What to Do When an Unexpected Deficit Appears

We are frequently called upon to talk about unexpected deficits, usually at 11 P.M. on the Friday before a crucial board meeting. When the telephone rings at this hour, we know that someone desperately needs to talk about fiscal things that are not going well down at their shop. Here are some of the questions and answers that usually flow from these late-night telephone meetings:

We have suddenly discovered a huge deficit. Before we burn the chief financial officer at the stake and explore Chapter 11 proceedings, is there anything we can do?

Before running for the firewood and matches, you need to correct or take care of the problem created by the deficit, and you need to do it in a way that is least harmful to the organization. Shakespeare was wrong: Hell hath no fury like an administrator or a board member who feels betrayed by suddenly learning of a deficit. Be gentle; find the least painful way to solve the immediate financial problem, and at the same time begin to put into place or refine systems designed to prevent a similar situation in the future.

While assigning blame has its own satisfactions, it is usually necessary to dig a little deeper to find out what went wrong in the fiscal area. Assuming that you and everyone on the board understood the financial reports, and that the CFO was straightforward in sharing information, the problem may be wrapped up in the policies and practices of the organization, or it may be caused by external factors beyond anyone's control.

If it appears that the institution is bleeding to death in front of your eyes, it may seem too difficult to pause for a moment's reflection before acting to cure a deficit. Yet it really does make sense to stop for a moment and try to explore the reasons that the deficit occurred. Has it been growing for some time? Given the vagaries of fiscal reporting in many nonprofit organizations, things could have been cooking for a while before anyone smelled the smoke. Look first to the financial reports. Do they reveal a problem? Often a trend has been in the making, but it was not candidly disclosed to the board, or it was ignored in an act of massive denial by members and staff.

To face up to the circumstances that contributed to the shortfall, you have to be willing to ascertain whether the problem is chronic or acute. If it is chronic, then the shortfall is a signal that the fundamental viability of the institution is threatened and major change is necessary for survival. If, on the other hand, the problem is acute, corrective actions stand a good chance of success if you manage to buy time to allow them to work. In either case, it makes sense to attempt to "fix the money," either as the first step in rebuilding or as the last step in managing the liability of eventual dissolution.

Does the deficit follow Linzer's Law of Littles? To wit, did lots of little items, such as small losses of income or small extra expenditures, come together to form a sizable deficit? For instance, those small increases in printing costs, coupled with a higher bill for electricity, and the slightly above-expected expenses for the board retreat may all seem inconsequential, but they can add up. If things are subtle, and there's a lot of room for subtlety with two bottom lines to address—fiscal solvency and mission, small items can gradually create big deficits. One answer is to refocus in just the opposite way, to look carefully at the big picture. See if you can spot any patterns or trends that reveal problems. Then return to an examination of actual cash flow on a monthly basis, looking at total income, total expense, and the running or cumulative total. These numbers can often help to point out when things started going south.

Before you do anything rash, you might want to check on the following items:

First, make sure that no one made off with the funds. Is there an address in Bora Bora where you could send a note inquiring about the loss? This sounds funny, but it isn't. People who work for nonprofit organizations may be devoting themselves to the public good and social purpose, but some still harbor felonious tendencies. The commercial world is not the only place where people embezzle funds. Good controls and commonsense ideas, such as separating the function of opening the mail from the task of posting checks to the account, can help. Trust us; even though the accountants are still one step behind the crooks, they still have excellent advice to give in this department. The accountants, that is.

Second, you might consider whether the problem has emerged while you were engaged in a capital campaign or just past the finish time. Does the deficit result from the postpartum letdown that follows an ambitious capital campaign? We can't tell you how many times we've heard executive directors moan about the deficit in operating income that hit just after a capital campaign. You are trying to feed two mouths when you raise capital, and without a tremendous effort, the operational budget—the daily grind that no one loves to contribute to—will come back to haunt you. Beware the capital campaign: it can be a real deficit maker!

Third, it makes sense to quickly review your balance sheet to see if restricted funds are clouding your vision of your fiscal health. We have touched on the distorting effect that restricted funds can have on the institutional bottom line, but it is worth mentioning that many administrators and board members fail to spot a cash flow problem because the only financials they are looking at reflect the institution's assets and its liabilities. When this happens, individuals frequently cannot accept the fact that they glossed over the bad news when it was reported to them. Did we mention before that denial is sometimes more than a river in Egypt?

Is there a long-term solution to shortfalls?

For organizations that assess their financial shortfall as being acute and therefore highly situational, a conventional credit instrument that may be useful is a term loan. Shortfalls happen, often for reasons beyond an organization's immediate control. The weather was terrible and no one came to the major fundraising event; the political party in power got booted and the new guys closed the state agency that provided core funding; the auditor missed an innocent mistake by the bookkeeper, and you have less money in the bank than anyone thought. In cases like these, it is important for everyone to slow down and try to look calmly at the deficit. If that is not possible, bring in an outsider, a professional with no stake in the outcome. That person can examine the situation objectively and perhaps unlock the mystery of whether this deficit is an anomaly or a long-standing problem that has just surfaced this year.

It is important to honestly gauge the magnitude of the deficit. How big is it? Could it be brought under control if converted to term debt and paid off, just like a mortgage, over five or more years with reasonable interest payments?

Term debt is borrowing that is stretched out over a fixed period, say sixty months (five years), with regular payments that are divided up into interest and principal. It is different from a line of credit, which needs to be completely paid back at least once during the year. This requirement for a line of credit ensures that it will be used only for timing and not for debt or new ventures.

The advantage of term debt when you have a deficit is that it allows you to slowly and deliberately pay off your obligation. The obvious disadvantage is that your deficit may be an indication of underlying operational problems that need to be resolved before you can make money in the future. You and the board need to make this determination. You also need to put together enough collateral to persuade the bank that it will be protected if it rents you money over a longer period of time.

As a first step, board members may want to establish an internal creditholder group before reaching out to the community. The board members are liable for the financial well-being of the organization. It makes good sense that they would step in first to provide collateral. By offering the banker a liquid asset to collateralize the term loan, they are shouldering the responsibility for curing the problems that caused the deficit. However, once the board has committed some assets to the long-term effort, it is entirely appropriate to reach out to the community for additional creditholders.

After analyzing their situation, many of our clients have repositioned their deficit with their banks. Having a fully secured line of credit already in place means that they have some borrowing history with the bank. This foresighted use of credit saves time and energy when attempting to obtain a long-term loan.

What are the standard operating procedures people typically use to deal with shortfalls?

In our experience, the approach usually taken by board and staff members when confronting a fiscal crisis is either to call for more funds to be raised or to insist that expenses be cut, or some combination of these two tactics. When we suggest the counterintuitive idea of going further into debt to solve the problem, it is generally viewed as a lousy idea. Instead, people ask us earnestly, "Shouldn't we embark on a massive fundraising effort to cure the accumulated deficit that has recently come to light?" To which we always reply: "Doesn't it make sense to first ask why you waited until you'd accumulated a deficit to embark on a massive fundraising campaign?"

If your fiscal reporting did not warn you that a problem was coming, that should be a real concern and needs to be addressed. Then, after examining the problem, it may make much more sense to translate the deficit into term debt and develop a strategy to pay it off over time. Some organizations have found that crisis-driven fundraising—the kamikaze approach to development efforts—will work in the short run, but that it is hard to sustain momentum over the long haul. Fundraising needs to be viewed as a disciplined, ongoing activity, not the end product of poor financial monitoring and inadequate planning for the credit needs of the organization.

The problem is that raising money on an emergency basis will probably take more time than anticipated, and may completely interfere with the operations of the institution. Fundraising typically takes time, if the sums are large, and that means a slow response to an immediate situation.

By contrast, the short-term solution of slashing expenses may solve the immediate shortfall problem but have serious consequences as program capacity is diminished. The long-term effect of a slash-and-burn policy may be difficulty in obtaining institutional support or donor contributions as the programming levels are reduced through austerity.

Attempting to combine cuts in expenses and increasing revenues through fundraising efforts has problems of its own. While it is true that some trimming may be useful, it should be done thoughtfully. Similarly, raising additional funds is always a good idea, although you must be careful to avoid stepping on your own ongoing fundraising requirements.

What it all comes down to is a policy that weighs short-term action against long-term results. The one common denominator is that all three tactics are inherently time-based. You need to examine the relationship between time and money, since lack of time, not lack of money, is often the problem that nonprofit organizations face.

Our suggestion to institutions confronting a shortfall is to think about going to the bank to talk about the situation. Comfortably seated in your banker's cozy office, display your cash flow position and your forecasts. Ask your banker to assist you in obtaining a term loan to buy time, thus enabling you to implement the graceful reduction of expenses, or to allow for a more relaxed, although still earnest, approach to fundraising.

In times of fiscal crisis there are always folks who lobby for jumping ship and taking their chances in the courts. We have lost count of the number of times that we have been confronted by upset board members who want to discuss bankruptcy. Yet this is rarely a viable option in the nonprofit world.

Compared to businesses, which have a high decimation rate, relatively few established nonprofit organizations actually go out of business. Instead, they may contract into smaller and smaller versions of themselves, or they may translate their mission into another social purpose. So, for example, an agency that was set up specifically to assist immigrants from a particular religious, racial, or ethnic group may simply move on to assist members of another group as the original immigrants become settled and no longer need assistance.

This cheery note notwithstanding, some organizations do go out of business. The question that you and members of the board must ask when contemplating this possibility is whether you will be better served by dealing with an institutional lender in working out the obligations of the organization, or with an assortment of creditors who, in their genuine anxiety about competing with each other for what is left of the funds, may rush to litigate.

Another response to financial trouble is for some board members to reach into their pockets. Whatever the reason for the deficit, well-intentioned board members will often step forth and offer to lend the institution money to get it over the hump created by the deficit. We suggest that you decline this offer, even though it is a wonderful gesture and probably a heartfelt one to boot. The reason for saying no is actually heartfelt too. We suggest that board members not lend funds to their organization. Their relationship with the institution is much too important to be cluttered up with personal issues regarding its financial situation.

In our experience, board members who lend money often propose the most draconian austerity measures when times are tough for the institution, sometimes to their own and the organization's detriment. Board members can donate money, help with fundraising, pledge funds as collateral, and get others to join them in these activities. All these are positive acts. Let the bankers lend. The board should stop worrying about the marginal cost of interest and get on with the business of the organization with a clear conscience.

In every financial dust-up there is at least one board member who notes, "My business could not survive if it ran out of money each year, so how can our nonprofit endure these losses?" To which we respond that deficits are not losses, at least not in the sense of losses in the commercial world. In business, at the end of the year, a company tots up its disbursements and its receipts, and if it's had greater expense than income, declares a loss. This declaration has enormous implications for dividends paid out, for the reputation of the company, for stockholder satisfaction, and for the public assessment of the value of the company, and it has real tax consequences. This is so because distribution is an essential component of any commercial entity.

But for nonprofits, a deficit is often just a shortfall of funds at a moment in time. It may have absolutely no adverse meaning for the long-term health of the organization. For example, an organization with cash-based accounts ends its fiscal year with a check from a major funder in the mail, but not in hand. The deficit is recorded, but two days later the check arrives and no financial crisis occurs.

As purely cash-flow entities, nonprofit organizations send confusing signals to commercially oriented participants when they have a shortfall, even if it may actually pose no great threat to the organization. That is, it poses no great threat *if* a method can be embraced that will deal with the deficit, a method that will buy time and allow for analysis of the shortfall and the adoption of measures to address the deficit. Our approach is to recommend that you create a multiple-year cash flow forecast, set up a creditholder fund as a source of collateral to establish term debt, go the bank with your collateral and your plan, and then get on with your mission.

Moving Forward by Looking at Cash Flow

After we have answered the most commonly asked questions about shortfalls, and if the resistance to the idea of borrowing to get out of debt has diminished, we address the mechanics of moving the institution forward. This step requires that we take a hard and objective look at both the past (to spot the reasons why the shortfall occurred) and the future (to chart out a possible course of action). As part of any assessment of an organization's shortfall, it is productive to establish a multiple-year cash flow forecast. Looking back through three years of cash flow reports based on actual figures will provide a sense of history. The cash flow budget analysis often reveals when the financial woes started. By exploring the historical events surrounding a decline, insight may be gained into the problem—or, more likely, the constellation of problems—that contributed to the gradual development of financial concerns.

Looking ahead helps you see any trends or patterns that are slowly unfolding. This is where the Cash Flow Forecaster comes in so handy. It makes good sense to drop the prior year actuals for monthly income and expense into the program. Assumptions about future activities can then be analyzed rapidly.

By projecting cash flow into the future, an organization can forecast its intent in a concrete manner. This forecast creates automatic benchmarks that can be used to evaluate progress on an incremental basis. It also helps the banker see how the funds will be repaid. The forecast budget is an organizational strategy expressed in numbers. It gives heft to the goals and objectives the organization adopts and creates measures that can be independently weighed by funders, the banker, or by creditholders.

Multiple-year cash-flow forecasting has links to term debt. Forecasts, in a complex world, are usually pretty fuzzy. But that does not mean they are not useful for helping envision the future—or that they can't provide measures to enable your institution to work toward a desired outcome.

The multiple-year cash flow forecast will not be perfect, nor should it be. The object is to create an ordinary, good-enough sense of the direction the organization is heading. The multiple-year cash flow forecast allows for all sorts of corrective actions to be taken in the moment. It is the cumulative effect of these small but significant corrective actions that often contributes to organizational success.

With all those numbers, multiple-year forecasts may seem difficult to construct, yet what would have been a real chore—back when Bob Cratchit was clerking for Old Man Scrooge—can be accomplished with far less huffing and puffing today. The Cash Flow Forecaster provides an easy way to establish multiple-year forecasts with entry screens like the one shown in Exhibit 12.1. Simply start with the actual income and expense figures from the first year in your sequence. Then, using the actuals for that first year, adjust the increased or decreased percentage of income and expense to conform to what you believe will happen in the future. The percentage increase or decrease can then be plugged into the three-year or five-year forecast. In some cases, you may wish to go further out—which isn't a problem, as the Cash Flow Forecaster allows you to make projections out to twenty years.

The Forecaster will configure these numbers into a cash flow curve, and when you add your estimates for the coming years, it will automatically adjust the amplitude of the curve to reflect your thinking. The numbers in the monthly cash flow segment of the Forecaster will serve as a guide for analysis, and you will often spot trends or patterns in the upward or downward movement of the curves when the numbers are represented graphically.

All this is more than an abstract exercise. A multiple-year cash flow budget is your ticket to a meeting with your banker. Before you schedule that meeting, here are some thoughts to consider. Bankers rent money. To do this, they offer a variety of products designed to balance their risk with their financial rewards. At best, money renting is a subjective business, and it is made more so in the nonprofit sector because of the lack of systemwide comparable figures. A multiple-year cash flow forecast that is simple and consistent with your annual budget will be a considerable help to the banker and to you. The cost of borrowing is clearly enumerated, so that the banker and board members can all see the impact of borrowed funds on the organization, the requirements for repaying debt service, and the time frame within which all this activity is taking place.

In one case we worked on, a foundation-appointed management consultant issued a private report to the board of a prominent social service agency. The report strongly discredited the fiscal skills of the agency's executive director. Shortly thereafter, a mistake on an audit suggested more funds in hand than were actually available. Because the executive director's financial reputation had been tarnished, the board members ignored her warnings about the lack of funds, following instead the erroneous figures on the audit. The board moved in and went on a spending spree. We were called in when a large but mysterious deficit emerged that threatened the future of the institution.

Going though two years of cash flow records with the bookkeeper, we reconstructed the cash flow accounts and found the problem. Funds were being held for other organizations from a series of small one-time grants. This organization was acting as fiscal agent for a group of smaller service organizations, and payment to them had spanned two fiscal years. Instead of showing these funds as belonging to someone else, the annual audit had treated them as revenue to the agency. When we developed a monthly statement of cash flows, the problem was immediately clear. A careful assessment of cash flow would have spotted this problem and alerted the organization to its existence. Instead, the board spent money that it did not have, and the executive director became depressed over having been mistrusted after twenty years of successful administration. The net effect of this chain of events was a shortfall that the organization chose to use as the basis for making an impassioned plea for emergency funds from local foundations.

Did it work? Far from perfectly. The city's foundation community responded with a short-term bail-out, but then punished the organization harshly by denying funding for a major initiative that had been slated to carry the organization through the next five years.

Protecting Your Reputation

"Won't our name be mud as soon as anyone learns we've run out of money?" Board members or staff often ask us if their institution's golden reputation will be ruined by any

EXHIBIT 12.1. CASH FLOW FORECASTER:
THREE-YEAR SCREEN.

1. Month to begin analysis (use 1–12, e.g., March = 3)   Start Month: | 1 |

2. Year to begin analysis (e.g., 2002)   Start Year: | 2006 |

3. Cash on hand at beginning of analysis   Beginning Cash: | $50,000 |
   (If debt, enter as a negative amount)

4. Enter first-year monthly Income and
   Expenses in the table:

	Income	Expenses
January-06	$ 30,000	$ 41,000
February-06	$ 32,000	$ 40,000
March-06	$ 38,000	$ 35,000
April-06	$ 45,000	$ 32,000
May-06	$ 50,000	$ 30,000
June-06	$ 40,000	$ 35,000
July-06	$ 30,000	$ 40,000
August-06	$ 25,000	$ 45,000
September-06	$ 20,000	$ 42,000
October-06	$ 35,000	$ 35,000
November-06	$ 40,000	$ 30,000
December-06	$ 45,000	$ 25,000

5. Enter projected year-to-year percent changes in income and expenses: For increasing percent changes, enter positive numbers. For decreasing percent changes, enter negative numbers.

	Percent Change in Yearly Income:	Percent Change in Yearly Expenses:
Projected percent increase (decrease) from year 1 to year 2:	12.000%	9.000%
Projected percent increase (decrease) from year 2 to year 3:	7.000%	11.000%

public discussion of their shortfall. Even though shortfalls happen from time to time, even in the best-managed organizations, administrators and board members affiliated with an institution that has incurred a shortfall often genuinely believe that they must fix the problem before they tell anyone about it. They apparently believe the problem will stain their reputation in the community or among funders, and therefore must be kept secret or disguised in some other fashion for as long as possible.

Financial difficulties spark powerful emotional reactions—blame and shame, to say nothing of guilt and anger. Some directors react by hectoring the board to get out there and raise more money. Others combine this tactic with draconian measures to create austerity. Others weep and offer themselves up to the community as victims of circumstance, and everyone assumes the worst possible consequences.

Perhaps the worst thing that you can do is to feel ashamed of the shortfall. The best thing that you can do is to assess the damage, develop some plausible multiple-year forecasts and plans for resolving the problem, and, if you haven't already done so, schedule an appointment with your banker.

For many administrators and board members, going to the bank in the midst of a financial crisis seems like exactly the wrong thing to do. People seem to believe that the banker will ask lots of probing questions and embarrass everyone, record your sorrow-laden information, turn you down flat, and then write a note to the bank's contributions committee suggesting that your organization be permanently removed as a candidate for community service grants. It's a pretty grim picture, all in all.

Happily, it's not true, as our next case study clearly shows. Remember, your organization is going to provide the banker with a dollar of collateral for every dollar that you borrow, over the life of the loan. You have completely removed the downside risk for the banker. As long as your collateral is liquid and the bank is assured of repayment, the banker is going to be your professional friend—and will also work with you to assess your situation, weigh your assumptions constructively, and in many cases offer a host of nonfinancial forms of assistance.

After all, you do not have to sell the banker on the idea of lending you fully secured funds. All those multiple-year cash flow forecasts and plans are designed to convince you, your staff, your board, your creditholders, and your donors that you are viable and going to be all right in the end. It is you, not the banker, who needs to be comfortable and sure that your plans will work.

In the Northwest Folklife case study, all the elements of the human drama as they relate to deficits are played out. The robust nature of the problem and the steps taken to resolve it make for great theater.

The Northwest Folklife Case Study: Addressing a Major Financial Shortfall

Northwest Folklife produces an annual festival that is one of the most popular public events in the Pacific Northwest. For the past three decades, people from all over the region have flocked to the festival on Memorial Day weekend.

A free event, the Northwest Folklife Festival is operated by a small nonprofit that has managed, through volunteer effort and remarkable community participation, to sustain itself on income from concessions, a small number of corporate sponsors, and a handful of grants from local arts councils and foundations. People attending the event also contribute by buying buttons and making small donations on the festival grounds.

In 1997 the organization received a major multiyear grant from a large national foundation. The original proposal had been written by the founding director to enable the Northwest Folklife Festival to expand into a year-round program with an entrepreneurial twist. Educational programs, bazaars, publications, record releases, and product sales were seen as the answer to providing the money the festival needed to survive.

Board members were pleased with the multiyear grant. Although all were enthusiastic supporters of the festival and eager volunteers at the event, they had no history of raising money. In the capable hands of the director, the staff was increased to develop the new moneymaking ventures.

As expenses climbed, board members talked about how investment was part of any businesslike operation, and the festival was simply ramping up its human capital to take advantage of the multiple markets its new divisions were designed to tap. The foundation grant paid for the salaries and most of the new expenses, and the foundation officials were encouraging even more aggressive market-oriented activities.

The foundation's grant also obscured some of the financial problems that were occurring with Folklife. The lack of successful fundraising by the board members seemed less important now that funds were arriving from another source. The surge in funding also reduced the priority that should have been paid to some unproductive aspects of the festival, such as carefully monitoring vendors who were not fulfilling their obligation to pay a percentage of their gross sales to the organization. Money was changing hands too quickly and in too great a volume for the organization's volunteers and staff to ensure that all collections were correct and complete during the busy event. The balance sheet was looking good, everyone was optimistic, and the slightly murky financials seemed less important as the funds rolled in for new staff and new programs.

Then, as so often happens, disaster struck. At first, it seemed minor. Bad weather over Memorial Day weekend kept the crowds home, and revenues from the festival were sharply cut. Then slowly, very slowly, the individual money-making enterprises failed to perform as predicted. The entrepreneurial concept still seemed correct, and the foundation continued to support the effort, but the returns were just not there, which was particularly disappointing in light of all the effort by the staff.

The financials were cloudy, and young and earnest business managers came and went. The board asked good questions, the director provided good answers, and still the overall fiscal picture was opaque. A five-year-old unsecured line of credit with a large branch of a national bank was now fully extended. The bank's president was a big supporter of the festival and a friend of the director, and he had been the one to urge the local branch to extend credit without collateral.

Then vendors began to call, and the business manager and the director spent more and more time fending off their concerns. The Finance Committee met and met again. There was serious talk about doing something, anything. Finally the Finance Committee recommended that the board raise more money to under-write the festival. Yet, even with urgently needed capital as a goal, the board still found itself unable, unwilling, or just plain uncertain about how to raise funds. Grumbling about the director began to surface, and as the next Memorial Day rolled around, everyone's hopes were pinned on good weather—glorious, sunny, good weather.

Memorial Day 1998 went down on record as one of the wettest and coldest weekends in the history of Seattle. The festival took a huge hit. Its limited weather insurance did not help one bit; the policy, prepared by clever underwriters, re-quired a fraction of an inch more rain than had fallen.

The board met, the staff groused, and the director tried to find a way to work everything out. The financial picture was still cloudy, so the board met with the director and hired an expert with serious corporate experience to come in and "clean up the books." No one liked what she found. The festival had maxed out its line of credit at $160,000. Vendors needed to be paid and were getting angry. The deficit, when all was totaled, exceeded $450,000, which on a budget of less than $1.3 million was frankly unacceptable.

The bank was alarmed and threatened to call in its line of credit. Vendors threatened suit. The board asked for and received the resignation of the direc-tor. The local funding community had already turned its back on Folklife, and headlines appeared in the local papers heralding the festival's demise.

The chairman of the Folklife board, Irene Namkung, acted quickly. She so-licited ideas for a possible replacement for the director, and with board approval she initiated a process for hiring a new executive director. Michael Herschensohn was hired by Folklife at a moment when the situation looked very grim indeed. A skilled fundraiser and experienced nonprofit professional, he had formerly been the director of Seattle's Museum of History and Industry.

With leadership from Irene Namkung and her husband, John Ullman, the board rallied and refused to give up on Folklife. We were called to meet with the board. We suggested that they consolidate their debt and ask their bank to grant them a long-term loan. They would provide collateral and the bank would lend them money, to be paid back in monthly payments over a ten-year period. We recommended forming a creditholder group to provide collateral for the loan. It took a while for people to understand this concept, but within weeks the board had secured creditholder deposits for over $500,000 on a long-term basis.

Normally, this would have been enough for the bank to offer a term loan for the $450,000. But in the real world, things are not so simple. Because the overdue line of credit had been unsecured, and because it had fallen into the hands of the collection division of the bank, things got complicated in a hurry. The bank's lawyers stalled and then began to create more and more conditions, until finally the credit agreement became a massive document, full of fine print and enough clauses to make your teeth itch.

Although the bankers understood that they would have first-rate collateral to cover every dollar that they loaned, the idea that a nonprofit organization could garner enough community support to secure a long-term loan seemed hard for them to accept.

At this point, Michael and Irene talked to the board and the staff, and together they decided it was time to approach another bank. We suggested one that was local and smaller. The deal was put together with Redmond National Bank (now Venture Bank) within two business days after the first meeting with the loan officer. Using a slightly modified standard collateral agreement helped to speed things up.

Once the credit was in place, Folklife was able to pay off its debts to its creditors and was solvent once again. The self-sufficiency of this action prompted favorable publicity, and this in turn made Folklife more attractive to donors. A major creditholder came forth with a significant challenge grant of $200,000, to be matched two-to-one. Suddenly the pendulum was swinging the other way.

Folklife was soon in excellent shape thanks to solid fundraising efforts, improved weather—at least by Seattle standards—at following festivals, and an outpouring of support. It built up a sizable surplus and began to carefully pay down its loan, making sure that it sustained its operational needs while meeting its obligations to the bank.

Executive Director Michael Herschensohn enjoyed pointing out that, by using credit and incurring term debt, the stability and vitality of Folklife was restored.

Having collateral when he needed it enabled him to obtain the credit necessary to deal with the Festival's deficits and to move toward a brighter future.

After five years, the brighter future was realized when the organization mobilized enough funds to pay off its term loan, five years ahead of schedule.

Exhibit 12.2 shows you what the press release announcing this ray of sunshine looked like.

EXHIBIT 12.2. FOLKLIFE PRESS RELEASE.

Just in time for its 33rd Festival coming up May 28 to May 31, Northwest Folklife announces the elimination of its long-term debt five years ahead of schedule. Generous donors, a responsive board and the careful management of limited resources made it possible for the grassroots folk art organization that is known nationwide for its incomparable Festival to achieve this impressive goal in hard economic times. "Few local arts organizations have the community behind it the way Folklife does," says Executive Director Michael Herschensohn.

In the summer of 1998, the board of directors of Northwest Folklife learned to its dismay of vendor and performer debts of $450,000. The board hired a new management team and sought the advice of consultants Richard and Anna Linzer of Indianola, Washington. With their help, Folklife created a creditholder fund underwritten by cash and stock from over 35 loyal Folklife supporters. Their money backed Folklife's loan from the Redmond National Bank and signaled their faith in the new management, the board and the community's commitment to sustaining the organization.

Major gifts from an anonymous donor and Ed Littlefield Jr. expedited debt reduction, as did restricting the board's contributions between 2000 and 2003 to paying down the debt. The participation of the Board of Directors led by presidents Irene Namkung, Scott Scher and Ed D'Alessandro was a critical factor in reaching this impressive goal. The generosity of donors at the Festival also played a major role with individual contributions rising from $80,000 in 1999 to $240,000 in 2003. These gifts made a huge difference.

"Offering a free festival is a big challenge," made easier, Herschensohn notes, "by gifts of time from performers and other volunteers, by support from the Mayor, the City Council and our Friends at Seattle Center and by creative fundraising."

With the debt gone, Folklife can now dedicate itself to building a stronger staff infrastructure. Staff and board agree that the work is only beginning and that success requires everyone continuing to be as generous as they have been over the last few years.

On Wednesday, May 5 at 10:30 A.M., there was a ceremonial burning of the loan papers at Center House in Seattle Center, accompanied by a song composed for the occasion by celebrated Seattle folk artists Jere and Greg Canote.

Now that you know the happy ending, here are some of the documents that were used to follow up on the successful management of the Northwest Folklife financial shortfall. It is important to understand that the board and staff of Northwest Folklife responded to their financial crisis by immediately turning to their closest friends and supporters to become creditholders. The calls from board and staff members elicited a strong response, and very quickly thirty-five supporters were recruited to participate as creditholders.

From this core group the funds needed to secure the long-term loan that relieved the organization of its immediate fiscal crisis were obtained. But the folks at Folklife did not stop once the immediate problem was addressed. They used the forms and agreements that they drafted for the first round of creditholders as the basis for contracting with other individuals who were recruited to continue the creditholder program. The focus of this round of creditholder recruitment was to obtain $150,000 to collateralize the Northwest Folklife line of credit.

Exhibit 12.3 is an example of the letter that was sent to second-round creditholders by a local political leader, James Compton, to encourage others to become creditholders.

The letter from James Compton was accompanied by a letter from the executive director of Northwest Folklife, Michael Herschensohn. This letter, shown in Exhibit 12.4, provided greater detail and included a fuller description of the creditholder program.

The letter from the executive director was accompanied by a document that provided a description of the purpose of the creditholder program, additional information. It invited the participation of recipients of the letter to fill out the enclosed form and to become creditholders. For creditholders who pledged stocks and bonds, the separate letter shown in Exhibit 12.5 provided the information necessary to communicate the information that the bank required from these creditholders.

Once individuals agreed to become creditholders, Northwest Folklife sent the simple note shown in Exhibit 12.6 instructing the new creditholder on the signatures and documents needed to enroll in the program at the bank.

Exhibit 12.7 is a sample of a letter of agreement with the bank to modify the terms of the standard security agreement entered into with creditholders. Northwest Folklife gave this draft to the Redmond National Bank. The Bank chose not to copy this letter in its original form, and instead responded with the Redmond National Bank letter that follows later in the chapter, in Exhibit 12.8. Please note that the suggested modifications include a provision whereby Northwest Folklife gives written instructions to the bank regarding the withdrawal of collateral being returned to a creditholder. Northwest Folklife developed a plan for withdrawing excess collateral and returning it to the creditholders in a way deemed equitable to all creditholders.

EXHIBIT 12.3. COVER LETTER TO PROSPECTIVE CREDITHOLDERS.

Folklife Festival
Education Programs
Folklore Research
Cultural Programs
Publications
Recordings

Northwest Folklife

*Imagine Memorial Day weekend without
Folklife, the largest free festival in the world.
We simply can't let that happen!*

—Irene Namkung, Board President

April 12, 1999

Dear Friend:

When Folklife trustees discovered a debt of nearly $450,000 last August, the organization came incredibly close to shutting its doors. Luckily, there were many, many people who refused to see Folklife disappear. The board of directors instituted a system of financial controls and reorganized the management team. And, they created a Creditholder Program which allowed caring community members to place cash or stock with our bank to secure a loan to pay creditors and provide the cash flow to ensure a festival in May.

As happy as we are that Folklife is saved for 1999, we must make sure it is safe for years to come.

Jim Compton, Folklife Supporter

The world of banking includes lots of forms and lots of paperwork. It may seem cumbersome to people who are not bankers, but it all has an important function to serve within the regulated world of banking. Or, at least within the legal staff's view of the world of banking. Having vented, it is now possible to see that the letter in this case is trying to address an important distinction between creditholders and those individuals who pledge funds in commercial transactions. In many cases, commercial loans require that the investors or owners of a business make their assets available to the bank as collateral. In these instances, the bank is serious about extending its potential recovery pool as broadly as possible. After all, the people pledging their assets are expected to be anticipating profit from the transaction.

Creditholders are different from investors in a commercial activity. Creditholders do not stand to gain anything other than the interest on their certificate of deposit or the normal returns from stocks and bonds. They are parking money

EXHIBIT 12.4. LETTER EXPLAINING
THE FOLKLIFE CREDITHOLDER PROGRAM.

Folklife Festival
Education Programs
Folklore Research
Cultural Programs
Publications
Recordings

Northwest Folklife

Dear Folklife Supporter,

The Creditholder Program has been incredibly successful! We are close to finishing the program's first phase and with your help, we'll complete the next one very soon. To secure Folklife's future and to keep the Creditholder Program going for the next several years, we estimate requiring about $150,000 in new cash or stock before the Festival in May.

Here's how the Creditholder Program works. You place cash or stock with our bank:

• The funds act as backing for our long-term loan and partially secure our line of credit.

• When you put cash in the program, the bank issues you an interest-bearing certificate of deposit, which secures an amount equal to your cash.

• When you put stock in the program, the bank generally accepts a percentage of its market value as security while you continue to earn money on your investment.

• You commit your collateral for the ten-year life of the loan. If special circumstances require you to withdraw your funds, Folklife agrees to make every effort to find replacement funds.

Without a doubt, Folklife's power comes from the ownership every participant has in it. If you and 100 other loyal "owners" put up as much as you possibly can, we can keep Folklife stable. Naturally, as with all loans, there is some risk. If Folklife defaults, the bank can use creditholder funds. If we are not able to find replacement funds, your money could be tied up for the life of the loan. I've enclosed a description of the program, a form you'll need to fill out, and an envelope for sending it back with your check or information about your stock. Most creditholders have placed between $2,500 and $100,000 with the program.

It is a focus of the board and management to make Northwest Folklife self-funding from ongoing programs, including event revenue and fundraising. It is our intention to pay off the loan in five years or less.

With your help, we can build the infrastructure for the future with the confidence that Seattle Center will come alive with music and magic every Memorial Day weekend for years to come.

Sincerely,

Michael J. Herschensohn, Ph.D.
Executive Director

P.S. I am delighted that Folklife is well on its way to a stable and secure future—and you can help make sure it happens.

EXHIBIT 12.4. LETTER EXPLAINING
THE FOLKLIFE CREDITHOLDER PROGRAM, *continued.*

Folklife Festival
Education Programs
Folklore Research
Cultural Programs
Publications
Recordings

Northwest Folklife

The Northwest Folklife Creditholder Program

Make an Investment in Your Community
We're asking caring community members to invest in Northwest Folklife by becoming a Creditholder. The term *Creditholder* has been coined to refer to friends, associates, and constituents who agree to provide cash or stocks as collateral for Folklife's loans with Redmond National Bank. As a Creditholder, you're banking that Northwest Folklife supporters and Northwest art funders won't let Folklife down.

The Short-Term Strategy
The bank is providing a line of credit to Folklife, which must be paid back annually. The line of credit helps Folklife, clearly a seasonal operation, get through those times of the year when expenses exceed revenue. The line of credit limit is $150,000 and requires $50,000 as collateral for this loan.

The Long-Term Strategy
This strategy consolidates Folklife's $450,000 debt into a ten-year loan. The loan is set at the current prime interest rate for five years, and will be adjusted at that time to the then current prime rate for the remaining life of the loan.

How a Cash Pledge Works
The bank purchases an FDIC-insured Certificate of Deposit in your name at the prevailing interest rate. The CD is invested for a minimum of twelve months and automatically rolls over at the end of the term.

• Interest from the CD belongs to you.

• Through an assignment, Creditholders place the CD as security for Folklife's loan and line of credit. All paperwork can be handled through the mail, by overnight courier, or in person with Redmond National Bank.

• At CD maturity, you may request that Folklife replace your CD with collateral from another Creditholder. Folklife commits to finding a replacement as quickly as possible, however, your CD will not be released until replacement funds are in hand.

How a Stock Pledge Works
Creditholder stock certificates are pledged to the bank for a period of twelve months or more. The bank issues a receipt for the stock, which remains in your name.

• Dividends and any growth in stock value belong to you for as long as Folklife's loan is in good standing.

• Through an assignment, a Creditholder places the stock as security for Folklife's long-term loan and line of credit. Paperwork can be handled through the mail, by overnight courier, or in person. Stock certificates should be sent via overnight courier or brought to Redmond National Bank.

• The bank reviews the market value of the stock quarterly. Should there be a loss in stock value and for as long as the loan is in good standing, Folklife is responsible for making up any difference in value.

• If, as a Creditholder, you decide to discontinue participating in the program prior to the repayment of debt, Folklife will make every effort to replace your stock with collateral from another Creditholder. Folklife commits to finding a replacement as quickly as possible; however, stock will not be released until repayment funds are in hand.

Risk
Stock and CDs belong to Creditholders unless Folklife defaults on its debt. In which case,

• Folklife will offer Creditholders the opportunity to replace security with funds to cover the amount of the original assignment.

• Redmond National Bank will have the right to keep collateral as payment for the defaulted debt as well as any dividends or increase in stock value it might hold at the time of default.

• Folklife strongly advises all potential Creditholders to consult with their financial and legal advisers prior to making this commitment.

Reporting
Folklife will keep you informed of our progress and success quarterly.

How to Become a Creditholder
Complete the form on the back of this page and send it to:
Northwest Folklife, 305 Harrison Street, Seattle, WA 98109-4623, or give us a call at (206) 684-7300 and ask for Valerie or Michael.

EXHIBIT 12.4, *continued.*

The Northwest Folklife Creditholder Program

Please fill out the appropriate sections below and return to Northwest Folklife.

Upon receipt of your check or stock certificate, the bank will send you a deposit receipt and documents that assign your stock or CD to Northwest Folklife's bank debts. All processing can be handled through the mail, overnight courier, or in person.

Name: _____

SS#: _____

Address: _____

_____

Telephone: Home ( ) _____

Work ( ) _____

E-mail Address: _____

Referred By: _____

Cash (which will purchase a Certificate of Deposit in your name):

Amount: $ _____ ,

Number of years: _____ , minimum 1 year

Please attach your check and a copy of your driver's license or other picture ID to this form.

Stock:

1. Complete the information below and return this form to Northwest Folklife.

2. If necessary, contact your broker to request a stock certificate in your name.

3. Once you have the certificate in hand, call Northwest Folklife to arrange for taking it to the bank.

Name of Stock: _____ Number of Shares: _____

Date Stock Certificate Requested from Broker: _____

Date Stock Certificate will be available: _____

Other Potential Creditholders

Please send Creditholder information to the following people I know who would be interested in participating:

1) _____

2) _____

Please Return to:

Northwest Folklife, 305 Harrison Street, Seattle, WA 98109-4623
For more information call Northwest Folklife at (206) 684-7300

EXHIBIT 12.5. LETTER FOR CREDITHOLDERS PLEDGING STOCK.

Folklife Festival
Education Programs
Folklore Research
Cultural Programs
Publications
Recordings

Northwest Folklife

John and Jane Doe
Seattle, WA

Dear John and Jane:

We have been successful in negotiating a ten-year term note with Redmond National Bank. [Now Venture Bank.] The debt is partially secured by your stock. Enclosed are the documents required by the bank in order to complete this transaction.

Since you agreed to have your stocks serve as collateral for a term that is less than ten years, it is our goal to continue adding new Creditholders to our program and thereby having security over and above the requirement. In the event that you desire a release from your assignment, we may need to replace it with that of a new Creditholder. Please read the documents carefully and obtain advice from financial and legal counsel prior to signing.

By signing below, you acknowledge that: a) neither Northwest Folklife, its board, staff, or affiliates have provided you with any legal or financial advice with regard to the Creditholder Program or in connection with the enclosed documents; b) Northwest Folklife has advised you to consult with financial and legal counsel with respect to the terms, legal effect, or obligations contained in these legal documents, prior to signing; c) the assignment you are providing secures a ten-year term note; d) in the event you wish a release of your assignment, you will provide Northwest Folklife with a minimum of 60 days' notice so that Northwest Folklife can attempt to find a replacement for the assignment, and e) Northwest Folklife cannot guarantee that a replacement for the assignment will be found or that Redmond National Bank will accept such replacement.

Please sign and return one copy of this letter with the executed documents and retain the other copy for your files. On behalf of the board and staff of Northwest Folklife, I thank you for your generous support.

Yours truly,

Michael Herschensohn, Ph.D.
Executive Director

I hereby acknowledge that I have read, understand, and agree with the statements above:

Creditholder(s): _____

_____

Date: _____

EXHIBIT 12.6. BANK SIGNATURE AND DOCUMENT INSTRUCTIONS.

Folklife Festival
Education Programs
Folklore Research
Cultural Programs
Publications
Recordings

Northwest Folklife

Dear Creditholder,

Thanks for participating in our Creditholder Program.

In order to complete this agreement, please:

1. Sign Assignment of Deposit Account.
2. Sign Signature Card.
3. Provide Social Security Number.
4. Please provide a photocopy of your driver's license or other ID.

Mail the complete package to:

Northwest Folklife
305 Harrison Street
Seattle, WA 98109-4623

If you have any questions, please call our office at (206) 684-7320.

with the bank to assist a nonprofit that they support, and they may wish to restrict or limit the level of liability they have for the organization's destiny. This is very understandable. Creditholders have made a judgment to risk their funds, however modestly—that is, to hypothecate them and to sit back and hope that all turns out well for the nonprofit they are supporting. They are not shouldering the entire burden of the nonprofit enterprise, and it is appropriate that their liability be limited only to the amount they have pledged.

In an attempt to limit creditholder liability, the executive director of Northwest Folklife asked the bank to clarify a provision in the off-the-shelf Commercial Pledge and Security Agreement, which grants the bank wider authority to seize an investor's assets or property. The bank's letter in response is a careful delineation of the limits that are being self-imposed by the financial institution on the creditholder program.

Even with two cooperative parties involved, some questions remained to be answered in this transaction. Exhibit 12.8 is a follow-up letter, again from the bank

EXHIBIT 12.7. FOLKLIFE'S DRAFT BANK MODIFICATION LETTER.

Michael J. Herschensohn
Executive Director
Northwest Folklife
305 Harrison Street
Seattle, WA 98109-4623   Re: Loan No. xxxx

Dear Mr. Herschensohn,

It is recognized by the Bank ("Lender") and Northwest Folklife ("Borrower") that the form of Commercial Pledge and Security Agreement, used by the Bank for the pledge of collateral by Northwest Folklife Creditholders ("Grantor") to secure the Loan (the "Security Agreement") should be modified to express the intent of the Northwest Folklife Creditholder Program. Accordingly, each Security Agreement hereby is modified and amended as follows:

1. The Collateral pledged under the Security Agreement does not include any property or accounts of a Grantor in the possession or subject to the control of the Lender not specifically listed in the Security Agreement, and the section on Page 1 of the Security Agreement headed "Collateral" is hereby amended to delete the second paragraph of same, which starts with the words "In addition" and ends with the word "media."

2. The paragraph on page 1 of the Security Agreement headed: "Income and Proceeds" hereby is deleted in its entirety and of no effect. Income and Proceeds from the Collateral shall be the property of and go to the Grantor.

3. Collateral pledged under the Security Agreement may be released back to the Grantor at the request of the Borrower, provided that there remains after such release sufficient Collateral to satisfy the condition of the Loan. Lender agrees promptly to release such Collateral to Grantor(s) pursuant to written instructions from Northwest Folklife. In the event the Lender deems that there would be insufficient Collateral remaining after such a release to satisfy the Loan conditions, Lender promptly shall give written notice of same to Northwest Folklife.

4. The term "Grantor" is deleted from the section headed "Events of Default" on Page 3 of the Security Agreement. The Events of Default stated therein shall apply only to such an event occurring only in respect of the Borrower.

Sincerely,

Redmond National Bank

By:
Accepted this _____ day of _____ , 1999
Northwest Folklife
By:

EXHIBIT 12.8. COMMERCIAL AGREEMENT MODIFICATION LETTER.

REDMOND	PO Box 2079	tel: 425/881-8111
NATIONAL BANK	Redwood, WA 98073-2079	Fax: 425/883-1767

Michael Herschensohn
Executive Director
Northwest Folklife
305 Harrison Street
Seattle, WA 98109-4623

Re: Commercial Pledge and Security Agreement

Dear Michael:

You have indicated that some of your Creditholders have questions or concerns about the wording of a couple of paragraphs in the above-referenced document. In an effort to address those concerns, I would like to take this opportunity to share with you our views on the issues included.

Regarding the section on Page One, headed "Collateral," the second paragraph specifically refers to property "in the possession of the Lender." We claim **no rights** to collateral or property not in our possession, and not consciously pledged by a Grantor.

Regarding the section on Page One, headed "Income and Proceeds," we **cannot** waive our rights to stock dividends and stock splits, because they directly affect the value of the collateral we hold; but we have no interest in collecting cash dividends. Those belong to the Grantor.

Regarding the section on Page Three, headed "Events of Default," the various circumstances that could arise with respect to a Grantor **may** cause the Bank to take some action. It is our view that unless a listed event becomes a reality with respect to a Grantor, **and** that event jeopardizes either the financial condition of the Borrower or the value of the collateral pledge to the Bank by the Grantor, the Bank will **not** take any remedial action.

I hope that this letter has addressed your concerns as well as the Creditholders' concerns. We very much appreciate our banking relationship with Northwest Folklife and look forward to a long and mutually beneficial relationship.

Sincerely,
Senior Vice President and Credit Administrator

---

in response to the executive director's request for clarification on the meaning of the Commercial Pledge and Security Agreement. The Redmond National Bank letter satisfied the questions that were being asked, while still protecting the rights of the bank.

These documents provide a helpful illustration of the limits of standard banking forms when used in a creditholder program. The standard forms make it easier for the bank and should be used whenever feasible, but a nonprofit organization establishing a creditholder program needs to ensure that the form's wording and its interpretation do not treat creditholders unfairly. This is yet another reason why it is helpful to enlist an attorney to assist your organization as you put the written infrastructure of the creditholder program together. The expense of counsel has proven to be well worthwhile.

Consistent with the idea that creditholders want to be well informed, the letter shown in Exhibit 12.9 was drafted and sent by the Northwest Folklife Board President Irene Namkung to existing creditholders, updating them on changes

EXHIBIT 12.9. INFORMATION UPDATE FOR CREDITHOLDERS.

Folklife Festival
Education Programs
Folklore Research
Cultural Programs
Publications
Recordings

Northwest Folklife

Dear Folklife Supporter,

Northwest Folklife's road to recovery has required many changes—changes that are making Folklife stronger, more innovative, and more efficient. Changes that make supporting Folklife a sound decision.

With Michael Herschensohn on board as executive director, Folklife now has the fundraising expertise it needs in house. His work in the field of fundraising goes back some 20 years. As the director of Seattle's Children's Museum, Michael directed a capital campaign that raised more than $4.5 million. At the Museum of History and Industry, he increased contributed income by 200% and balanced the budget.

A new staff of professionals trained in the fields of fundraising, financial management, and marketing are in place as is a strategy designed to take full advantage of the widespread community support for Folklife. Folklife's fundraising plans call for reaching out to every corner of the community—corporations, foundations, government agencies, and individuals. Plans for raising funds at the Festival itself are in place. Northwest Folklife is now an organization operating at high professional and fiscally responsible levels.

Your participation in the Creditholder Program ensures our success. Thanks for playing your part to keep the traditional arts alive.

Sincerely,

Irene Namkung
President, Northwest Folklife

at Northwest Folklife, and emphasizing the fundraising, financial management, and marketing skills of new staff members.

How Northwest Folklife Approached the Press

In a speech delivered at a conference on nonprofit financial management held in Seattle, Irene Namkung, the board president of Northwest Folklife, discussed how the organization managed its relations with the press during the fiscal crisis. These are her remarks:

> We went into the 1998 festival thinking that we were $200,000 in debt, and hoped we could make this amount up with more active solicitation and good weather. We had the worst weather in the twenty-seven-year history of the festival. By the end of July we knew that the debt was in the $400,000 range.
>
> As staff was being bombarded by calls from distraught creditors, news of the organization's plight broke in the *Seattle Times*. The focus of the early stories was Folklife's inability to pay artists for their Festival compact disc sales. The inability to pay the artists, who perform at the Festival for free, was intensely painful for the board members, several of whom were creditors themselves.
>
> Although the creditors could have forced Folklife into bankruptcy, no one on the board suggested that they should walk away from the Festival or the debt. Although the media asked hard questions about Folklife's management, reporters from the *Seattle Times* and the *Seattle Post-Intelligencer* also reported Folklife's need for help and the steps they were taking to rectify their situation. A turning point came in the form of Jim Compton's very sympathetic op-ed piece in the *Seattle Post-Intelligencer.*
>
> After local foundations and corporations that had bailed out other cultural institutions were not responsive, the board faced up to the fact that Folklife was $450,000 in debt and needed a different way to solve its problem.
>
> As creditholders were being recruited, the organization released information on the program, timed to coincide with the sending of reimbursement checks to more than 300 Festival performers. The newspapers picked up on this. In the months that followed, more articles on Folklife appeared, and in each the self-sufficiency and determination of the organization were underscored. Clear signals from the board president and the executive director in separate interviews helped to reinforce the idea that Folklife was moving ahead, did have a viable plan, and could use still more support from the community.
>
> It was just the right combination of messages to inspire people to step forward, to contribute, and to boost the fundraising efforts of the Festival. In addition to allowing us to pay our debt and continue to stay in business, the

Creditholder Program has brought us favorable publicity. This in turn made us more attractive to donors than we would have been had we simply been floundering in our debt.

Lessons from the Folklife Case Study

The Northwest Folklife case study represents a shining example of how an institution can respond creatively to a dire financial situation.

As the case study illustrates, the first bank that Folklife dealt with had difficulty with the creditholder concept, which prompted the board president and the executive director to sit down with another banker to work out the plan that saved the institution.

We do not want to leave you with the impression that it is only the occasional banker who may have difficulty with the creditholder concept. So, in the spirit of full disclosure we will share with you another obstacle on the road to curing a serious shortfall.

Perhaps the most difficult lesson that we have learned over the years is that the creditholder concept does not always fit neatly into the system of accounting used by nonprofit institutions. We have seen organizations that created creditholder groups to confront a serious deficit arguing with their accountants about how to handle this important issue in composing their audit.

Before showing you how to deal with this paradox, let's examine what is happening when the accountant is unwilling to count creditholders' participation as an asset. To start off on the right foot, let's make the case for the accountants. Your creditholders' participation may pose a problem for your accountant because the funds placed in the bank's hands or pledged as stocks and bonds do not actually belong to you. The funds belong to the creditholder, and the creditholder has hypothecated or pledged them to assist you in securing credit. Remember, the creditholder accounts do constitute an asset that the banker is using to lend you money. And because of the willingness of creditholders to assume responsibility if you default, these assets can have a powerful impact on your financial future.

Semantics aside, you might well ask why cash sitting in the banker's vault would not be considered as having value to your organization in the accountant's scheme of things—particularly when the same accountant who is forcefully expressing an opinion about the asset value of creditholders will gladly assign a full asset value to an endowment. Many endowments are created as irrevocable trusts, the principal of which you will never be able to touch. This is potentially very confusing to anyone who looks just at the assets and liabilities of your accounts, since liabilities can be reduced by the value of assets, even if the assets can't actually be spent. In a literal sense, the accountant is taking a permanently restricted account that itself cannot be converted into cash and showing it as an asset of the institution, along with all sorts of other assets.

Yet, all that said, the dollars belonging to your creditholders do not in fact belong to you. They are being parked at your bank and they can assist you, but they are not on your balance sheet.

Our solution to this paradox is to suggest that the accountant who is your auditor needs to be informed that you have created a creditholder group. The concept of a creditholder group may need to be explained, and the auditor needs to acknowledge that the assets pledged by the creditholders, even though they do not technically belong to your organization, are a quantifiable form of goodwill and they must enter into any calculation of the audited accounts. Otherwise, the auditor will count any fully secured debt that you have, since your organization is responsible for that, but will discount the creditholders' participation, since these assets do not technically belong to your organization. However, after booking the cash in the bank as a debit, and the secured loan as a credit, the accountant can add a very prominent footnote regarding the creditholders' participation:

> Footnote 1: This is a contingent liability and is fully secured with assets not the property of the organization. If not repaid as expected from future earnings, it will be treated as offset by an in-kind donation of securities owned by the creditholders.

In simple English, you have access to a real asset, but not one that you or your accountant can claim that you own. As the Northwest Folklife case study illustrates, creditholders' assets triggered the lending that saved Folklife. In the real world, financial strategies that work must be given their due, even if they are only credited in an explanatory footnote in the institution's audit.

Northwest Folklife shows that you can endure the announcement of a deficit. You need to shift your thinking to cash flow and assess your situation carefully. A multiple-year cash flow budget is a good start. Then, if your problem can be solved by changes that you can introduce over time, you can start by forming a creditholder group. Your organization can weather the storm by doing something similar to this:

- Develop a multiple-year forecast that lays out your game plan for dealing with this financial crisis.
- Form a solid and supportive group of creditholders who are backing you with cash.
- Approach the banker—and if you don't get a cooperative response, remember that you can find a banker next door who will be more responsive to your request to obtain long-term financing.

- Feel confident that over time, with some delicate cuts in expenses and some modest increases in fundraising, you will be in the clear.

All is not doom and gloom in the nonprofit world. Yes, shortfalls do happen, but they can be sensibly addressed—and windfalls happen as well. As discussed in Chapter Thirteen, they too need to be addressed sensibly.

CHAPTER THIRTEEN

WINDFALLS AND OTHER SURPLUSES

An attorney's letter arrived at the nonprofit institution in the morning mail announcing that a long-time supporter of the organization had passed away and left it a big chunk of her estate. Suddenly all those years of careful cultivation, of long luncheons and small quiet dinners, had paid off. The prize was in hand and the delightful prospect of dealing with newfound riches was a cause for celebration. At the next board meeting, trustees were positively giddy with all the ideas for using the unrestricted bequest as a springboard to financial security. After an impassioned debate, they decided to use the funds to create an endowment, and not only that, but an irrevocable trust to be named after the benefactress.

Key Issues and Questions

Had the board members applied a cash flow perspective to this gift, their decision might have been different. In this chapter we demonstrate that turning gold into dross, metaphorically speaking, may not be a wise strategy for most nonprofit institutions. We take a careful look at the financial implications of building and sustaining an endowment. Along the way, we do a little math and then explore some of the financial thinking that underpins large reserves, suggesting that capital accumulation is not helping the institutions who hoard, their constituents, or their communities. Instead, we describe a safe and sane way to face an uncertain future and still get more mission with less money in your coffers.

What's the other side of the coin with regard to endowments?

Endowments are very popular. Almost everyone in the nonprofit sector wants an endowment, a cash reserve, or a capital campaign to construct a new building or to renovate existing space. In other words, board and staff members are pursuing strategies to accumulate capital for their institutions. Yet endowments are rarely an efficient way to address issues of fiscal solvency.

An endowment, as we define it, is an irrevocable trust, a legally binding agreement in which funds are given to an institution with the understanding that the principal is to be maintained in perpetuity. (This definition has some exceptions, for instance, if a specific sunset clause is included in the original trust agreement.) Only a portion of the income earned can be spent. Quasi-endowments are different insofar as their funds are more like a cash reserve that has been restricted by the board of directors of the institution.

When an organization decides to accumulate capital, it is choosing to trade current pursuit of its mission for future financial security—which turns out to be an illusion. To accumulate capital for an endowment or other reserve fund, established nonprofit organizations spend money to raise contributions. The money raised generally is then invested conservatively. Inflation and endowment terms dictate that a certain amount be put back into the principal for the endowment to maintain its purchasing power. Taking these factors together, it is clear why the future yields are actually very low.

Henry Hansmann, a Yale law professor who is an expert on the law and economics of nonprofit institutions, has a blunt assessment of endowments. He contends that hoarding diverts universities from their core mission of educating students and making breakthroughs in science and other fields. "They can contribute more to society by building a great university than they can by building a great endowment," he says. "A stranger from Mars who looks at private universities would probably say they are institutions whose business is to manage large pools of investments and that they run educational institutions on the side . . . to act as buffers for the investment pools."[1]

In an article examining New York University's decision to spend current funds rather than build its endowment, Hansmann and his allies agree that administrators in other universities are wrongly making a fetish of the size of their universities' endowments. "Saving is worthwhile only if you have a better use for the money in the future than you do now. With universities, there is no particular reason to believe that there will be a better use in the future and every reason to believe the reverse is true."[2]

Hansmann's way of thinking has won some converts. "There is a bit of push-back," says Trish Jackson, a vice president of the Council for Advancement and Support of Education. She notes, "How can we justify endowments over $1 billion? Are we shortchanging today's students for tomorrow's students?"

As we mentioned earlier, nonprofits have two bottom lines: the immediate pursuit of their social purpose and long-term fiscal solvency. An endowment is a financial device that defers the immediate gratification of current operational needs for the imagined long-term benefits of fiscal solvency. The financial strategies that organizations adopt, including endowments or lines of credit, are simply ways to confront the need to deal with financial solvency over time.

According to an article in the *Chronicle of Philanthropy*, many privately held endowments in this nation spend less than 5 percent each year to fulfill the mission of their organization.[3] In this day of 3.5 percent inflation, plus the extra point or two that inflation in the nonprofit world is often assumed to have, you can see that even at 5 percent, endowment earnings barely contribute enough to match current inflation, to say nothing of operational needs.

Inflation will increase again, despite all the efforts of the Federal Reserve Bank. It may already be higher than what we're talking about here. Many economists believe that the government significantly understates inflation in its official calculations. Yet, despite the low-ball inflation figures, we are already seeing an increase in inflation in the housing, energy, durable goods, and general living expense markets despite the Fed's policies. None of this is good news for institutions that are hoarding.

Michael Porter and Mark Kramer have addressed the question of the inefficiency of endowments in another way. They calculate that a dollar donated to a nonprofit organization and spent within a year will generate a dollar's worth of mission. The same dollar contributed to an endowment, a foundation, or a donor-directed fund will take somewhere between forty and a hundred years to equal the value of the original dollar. That's a long time to wait, particularly if you are trying to feed starving children.[4]

Endowments will not save you in times of need.

An irrevocable trust (an endowment) is useless in the face of fiscal crisis. You can't touch the principal—and neither can your banker, so you can't borrow by using it for collateral. For this reason, it is technically possible for a nonprofit organization to be, at the same moment, both fiscally solvent (at least on paper) and bankrupt. Since you can spend only a portion of the interest, you may have an impressive endowment, but you won't be able to mobilize the money to pay your bills. In this case, interestingly enough, the courts will not liquidate the endowment. Instead, they will transfer the principal to another nonprofit institution, leaving trustees still on the hook to creditors.

Recently a number of high-profile institutions have raided their endowments. While it is painful to watch the machinations trotted out to justify these actions, it is still true that in cases where the endowment is part of a restricted trust, the funds used for these purposes provide the basis for potentially messy court battles.

Competition in the nonprofit world tends to be quietly understated. So if the pool of resources is constant, this certainly might seem to provide a justification for gathering as many rosebuds as you may, while the getting is good. Endowment building has become something of a blood sport for many large institutions. The competition for donor dollars is quite overt.

The problem is that inefficient use of funds harms everyone: the institution, the community, and the clients and constituents of nonprofit organizations. When excess funds are devoted to endowments, less money is available to meet the organization's operational needs. This means that clients and constituents receive less service or have to pay a higher price.

In addition to permanently restricted funds such as endowments and temporarily restricted funds such as cash reserves, capital can also be accumulated in the form of buildings and equipment. The ownership of property and tangible goods is very much part of the tradition of the nonprofit sector. This use of capital is also inefficient.

When an organization decides to accumulate capital in an endowment, it is choosing to trade current pursuit of its mission for the illusion of future financial security. To accumulate capital for an endowment or other reserve fund, established nonprofit organizations will spend a median of twenty-six cents to raise a dollar in contributions. A *median* is simply a statistical measure that indicates that half of a population is above the number and half is below. So in this case, half of the group is spending more than twenty-six cents to raise a dollar and half is spending less.

How do we figure the cost of an endowment versus the benefits to us?

"Nonprofit organizations are not required by law to disclose information about their endowments—and many prefer not to tell the public much about the size or operations of the funds," says Harvy Lipman, writing in the *Chronicle of Philanthropy*.[5] For this reason, it is not surprising that exact figures for returns on investment or spending policies of endowments cannot be definitively stated.

As an example of the fiscal efficiency of endowments, the following quick formula helps to assess the amount of funds available each year to fulfill the mission of the institution. This formula attempts to pull together some of the information that is known about endowment investment and spending policies and to make some guesses that help to demonstrate the relationship between the costs and the benefits of these investments.

Using $100,000 as a basis, apply the following assumptions:

Goal of the endowment campaign	$100,000
Estimated cost of campaign (28 cents per dollar)	$28,000
Annual yield after management fees (6 percent)	$6,000
Annual amount returned to principal (3.5 percent)	($3,500)
Deduction for inflation in the nonprofit sector (1 percent)	($1,000)
Balance of annual spendable income from the fund	$1,500

To recapture the sum spent to raise the endowment, in this case $28,000, the institution will not receive a penny of real appreciation for close to nineteen years. That is unless there is a significant change in the level of yields, the average rate of inflation, or the higher level of inflation experienced within the nonprofit sector. In some cases, endowments are reported as having much higher annual returns and in others lower returns. If you are thinking about an endowment, plug in your own numbers and take this formula out for a test drive.

Regarding the costs, the Association for Health Care Philanthropy has studied the cost of fundraising campaigns for years. Its figures indicate that member organizations spend a median of 28 cents to raise a dollar.[6] As discussed in Chapter Six, the association's figures indicate that actual spending, especially for organizations less than five years old, can approach three times that level.

Retained funds invested 60 percent in stocks, 30 percent in government securities, and 10 percent in cash equivalents are considered prudent. For our purposes here we use a 6 percent return. Management fees and investment charges can total half a percent annually.

To sustain the buying power of the fund, an amount equal to an estimated five-year rolling average of inflation needs to be returned to the fund. The current estimate for inflation is 3.5 percent.

Inflation in the nonprofit world is generally considered to be slightly higher than inflation in the rest of the economy. As Baumol and Bowen note in their classic study of the economics of the performing arts, inflation in the nonprofit sector tends to outpace that of the commercial economy for three reasons: the nonprofit sector is more labor intensive, the smaller economy of scale for nonprofits produces higher costs for these organizations, and since there is no incentive to invest in advanced technologies in the tax-exempt environment, nonprofits have lower levels of technology with which to compete.[7]

Clearly, one of the key assumptions included in this formula is the cost of raising a dollar, which can vary a great deal. It is often difficult to make a judgment about this because of the intense pressure in the philanthropic community to report low costs for development efforts. Institutions tend to underreport their costs, bury them in other accounting categories, or face losing support from donors.

If you pencil in the actual costs of raising money, you will see one reason that endowments are an inefficient fiscal device. If the total cost of raising endowments or cash reserves is included, it may well take years before institutions realize a penny of positive appreciation.

In other words, we believe that the history of endowments in this nation shows a poor track record of meeting the needs they are supposed to address. The spending policy of most trusts simply maintains the status quo for their institutions.

To glimpse just how much capital needs to be accumulated to generate even small amounts of interest, J. Gregory Dees states that it takes about $20 in money raised to generate $1 in annual income from an endowment. And as he notes, not many institutions can afford to raise twenty times the cash needed for annual core operating expenses.[8]

Of course any discussion of capital obtained from the stock market inevitably leads to defenses of investment along these lines: "Didn't the stock market produce an average of 10.4 percent, before inflation, from 1926 through 2003?" How many times have you heard a statement like this? Well, some research strongly indicates that it is not true. Once you factor in the effects of inflation, brokerage charges, investor tendency to buy high and sell low, and taxes for commercial transactions, the yields are closer to 2.4 percent for this period.[9] Even when we take out the 2.2 percent hit for taxes that nonprofit organizations avoid, these yields are not going to buy much philanthropy.

It certainly does not look better once you take a moment to consider the type of average that is normally quoted when referring to returns on investment. When some financial advisers talk glowingly about the returns provided by the stock market, they may be using what is called an arithmetic mean. So, if Warren Buffet comes to our house for lunch, the three of us could be considered as three of the richest people in America, if we divide his enormous net worth and our tiny holdings by three to obtain an average of personal wealth. If, on the other hand, we were to use a geometric mean to figure out what was going on at the dinner table, the figure would be significantly lower. In other words, using the geometric mean (or, as it is sometimes called, the median rate of return) helps to clarify misunderstandings about markets in which a majority of investors receive worse-than-average returns.

If you're shaking your head over these findings and wanting more historical data, the picture is not all that much better. Three scholars at the London Business School—Elroy Dimson, Paul Marsh, and Mike Staunton—compared stock market returns in the United States with those in fifteen other countries. Since 1990, they concluded the worldwide return on equities has been only 5 percent a year, after inflation. Meanwhile, overseas markets returned less than 3 percent.[10]

At the risk of sounding bearish, some news suggests that the stock market may well be in for a long, multiple-decade period of slow or sluggish growth. Under the Associated Press headline "Some Experts Think Market Will Move Down for Years," Meg Richards notes that some experts see the current pattern of a downturn in the market as part of a much larger bearish trend. If this prediction has any truth, and predictions in and around the stock market are often subject to conjecture, the outlook for invested funds is not great.[11]

Why isn't the stock market the place to be?

Benoit Mandelbrot, the inventor of fractal geometry and a student of stock markets, has been warning since the 1960s that markets are far wilder and much more turbulent than the modern theory of finance would have anyone believe. Survivors of the 2000 market meltdown are living proof of his contentions. Examining the math associated with Mandelbrot's position is fairly daunting even for professional mathematicians, but the bottom line is crystal clear. Money meant to be serving a social purpose should not be gambled away in the wild and crazy environment of the stock markets.[12]

If we have even slightly damped your enthusiasm for capital gains derived from the stock market, we will have accomplished one step in getting you to focus on cash flow rather than always giving priority to the accumulation of assets and liability for your nonprofit institution. But the temptations are many, so here is another cautionary note from the cash flow tool kit.

A wealthy donor has offered you a challenge. He will give you a million bucks to establish an endowment if you match every one of his dollars with three that you raise in the community. Shouldn't you jump at the offer?

You might want to look before you leap. Calculate the cost of raising the three-to-one match, particularly on top of your normal operating expenses, then take a hard look at the spending policy you will need to adopt to sustain the buying power of the funds, and finally figure out how long it will take before you see a penny of appreciation once you have recaptured your original investment.

Then, before accepting the donor's idea of what is good for you, ask yourself whether the donor needs to examine those numbers with you to see the consequences of this request. Show the donor the relatively high cost of raising funds, the relatively low return available from endowments, and the long-term inflexibility of irrevocable trusts as instruments to prevent financial disasters.

In our experience, donors will sometimes, when confronted with the facts, change their minds and offer you a much better deal. For example, the donor may decide to donate the money to be used for operations, with the understanding that you will match it three to one for the same purpose.

Final Thoughts on Endowments

If endowments aren't such a great deal, why does everyone seem to either have or want one? The concept of an endowment is a bit like chocolate cake: wonderful to dream of and delicious to eat, but not always good for you. Just because almost everyone likes chocolate doesn't remove some of the side effects of eating too much chocolate cake.

The things you need to do to create, develop, and sustain endowments have a number of negative consequences. Endowments are costly to raise, require substantial care and feeding, and produce relatively tiny amounts of spendable income, even after your investment has been recaptured. Endowments take 95 percent of the money that could be used for fulfilling your mission and place it in investments that are forever outside your reach. In addition, since the pools of resources they are drawn from are relatively inelastic, they deprive others of needed resources. They do not satisfy your needs for operational funds. They can result in diminution of services. Clients and constituents may suffer.

Still, people always ask us, Wouldn't it be nice to have a large endowment so we won't have to scramble to raise funds each year? Our answer is simply that since the operational needs of the organization continue year after year, and since endowments contribute relatively speaking very little to most institutions' operational budgets, the need to raise funds is not diminished by endowments. Although many donors are asked to contribute on the promise that this is a once-in-a-lifetime gift or a one-time special effort, the reality for most institutions is that they will be back at the door the next year, still needing operational funds to fulfill their mission.

Everyone knows at least one organization that has an endowment that provides lots of operational money. These stories have become legend in the nonprofit world. Development officers at conference cocktail parties whisper about so-and-so with an endowment that is the envy of the crowd. But if you examine the relationship between the mission of the organization and the size of its endowment, it is often clear that the social purpose and the reach of the institution is inhibited by the volume of cash actually available annually.

Is there an alternative to capital accumulation?

Yes indeed. The alternative to all this hoarding is to spend the money on the operational requirements of fulfilling your mission and use your fully secured credit as a tool for managing your anticipated financial risk.

Does it really make sense to send 95 cents out of a hard-earned or hard-raised dollar to Wall Street? Doesn't the commercial world have access to enough capital without the tax-exempt dollars that are donated to nonprofit organizations? For those of you who crave the excitement of gambling or investment in the stock market, there is also an alternative. Nonprofits can use their funds and their credit in a more exciting way. Chapter Fourteen provides a case study on the use of credit to create a new venture, and it is not for the faint of heart.

CHAPTER FOURTEEN

USING CREDIT FOR VENTURE

Of all the uses of credit by nonprofits, borrowing to provide funds for a new venture is perhaps the least familiar to most administrators and their boards. The notion of going into debt to start or develop a nonprofit institution can seem like a very risky financial strategy to pursue. Yet, as with all strategic considerations, it is vital to examine alternatives and options before deciding on one course of action or condemning another that appears unfamiliar at first glance.

U.S. administrators can learn from international experiences with the use of credit to fund ventures. For example, in Japan, where debt financing plays a major role in private enterprise, nonprofit high schools and universities are often debt financed. After World War II, the Japanese needed to rebuild their educational system and no grants were available from the government. Schools borrowed and created the educational system that we see today. During a period of rapid expansion in the mid-sixties, over two-thirds of all private secondary and higher educational capital outlay was loan financed.[1]

In this chapter we discuss the use of fully secured credit to advance an institution or a program—and the commitment that individuals need to make this practice possible. A small private school is our case study in the use of credit to venture.

In the United States businesses routinely borrow, as do larger nonprofit organizations. The small to midsized organizations seem to be the most debt averse, yet it is precisely this group that has the most to gain from the skillful and safe use of credit. Smaller nonprofits need to employ credit as part of their overall financial strategy. That strategy may also include venture, and while the subject is taboo for many, those that have tried it find much to commend in the use of credit.

One cautionary note: Many of the financial terms used in the nonprofit world have been appropriated from the commercial sector and applied with a different meaning in their new context. When added to a predisposition of some board members to call for businesslike practices, the level of confusion can be considerable. For example, no investment is allowed in the nonprofit sector. The IRS code specifically prohibits any sale of equity by nonprofits. Therefore, when someone says that they are investing in a nonprofit, they actually mean that they are providing a gift or grant or that they are loaning funds with the expectation of being repaid. While it is true that some business practices are highly applicable to nonprofit organizations, the two types of organizations are fundamentally different, which makes the use of language especially important when the topic is using credit for venture in the nonprofit sector.

Social entrepreneurs can play a powerful role by acting in concert with, but not within, the nonprofit sector. By *social entrepreneurs* we mean those well-intentioned men and woman who wish to apply their success in business to some of the burning issues in the nonprofit world. While we do not question the personal skill or financial sophistication of these socially oriented entrepreneurs, as noted in Chapter One, we are skeptical about the direct applicability of commercial practices to nonprofits. However, we do believe these creative folks can often provide the means for nonprofit organizations and agencies to use their capital much more effectively. For example, an entrepreneur can do this by buying a building used by a nonprofit institution and leasing it, in some cases at concessionary rates, to the benefit of both the owner and the organization.

By taking away the incentive of nonprofits to accumulate capital and thereby deprive others of its use, social entrepreneurs can have an enormous impact on society. Removing the burden of ownership by nonprofits of concretized capital in the form of buildings and equipment, social entrepreneurs can actually increase the capability of nonprofits to provide services.

In this case study, borrowing was used to provide funds for a new venture. This use of credit allowed a new private school to get off the ground and flourish. Again, the critical role of collateral from creditholders encouraged the bank to become a strong partner and friend of the new school. This case also demonstrates how a local socially motivated developer was willing to construct a new campus for the school and then rent it back to the school on a long-term lease. The school was spared the time and energy of conducting a major capital campaign in its early years of existence, and it still obtained the facilities that it needed and would need for years to come. In this case, the social investment made by the developer clearly aligns with the needs of the institution.

Case Study: West Sound Academy

When Ed Frodel taught in the public schools, he was the most popular humanities teacher in the district, and graduates of his classroom often returned to express their gratitude for his wisdom, kindness, and remarkable energy. But after years of teaching in the public school system, Ed began thinking about establishing his own school, a small institution that would bring together the best of the arts and sciences. Within six months after his decision to pursue his dream, Ed had informally recruited a small cadre of individuals to act as a board for the new institution, had filed for nonprofit status, and had set about planning for the launch of a new private school.

The board, composed of local businessmen and educators, found a temporary facility at a nearby private camp. They hired an experienced educational administrator, Nellie Baker, and an outstanding collection of gifted teachers who ensured that the school would be well staffed.

When they put out the word that West Sound Academy was accepting students, eighteen families immediately signed up for a grade 6–12 program. Each family paid $10,000 for the first year. The school was on its way.

With a sense that things would work out for the best, the board and staff waited for enrollment to grow. Their plans had called for forty students, so their faculty numbered sixteen full- and part-time teachers under contract. Gradually, though, it became clear that fewer students than anticipated would attend.

A brand-new school, still untested, was just a little too challenging for most parents. The tuition was steep, although certainly not out of line with what other private schools in the area were charging. The temporary location at the camp facility, while beautiful and compelling, was too impermanent for others. The location required buses and mini-vans and all the logistics associated with student transportation. In sum, all the elements that needed to mesh were almost, but not quite, in place.

At first, both Ed and Nellie thought about finding new board members, hopefully with very deep pockets, to improve the financial situation of the school. But those people seemed in scarce supply, and things needed to move fast. So they began to explore some of the financial assumptions underlying the program. It seemed clear that enrollment would grow over the next four or five years and that the school could break even by year seven or eight. Until then, though, funds were needed for operations, and even concerted fundraising for the new school wouldn't meet their needs.

We were called in as consultants by Ed and Nellie, to help them look over their situation. Needing to clarify the assumptions that had gone into the budget and to see the relationship between ongoing income and expense over time, we asked right away for a cash-flow budget instead of an annualized budget.

Since time is always a major consideration in the fiscal workings of nonprofit institutions, seeing only an annual budget does not give you a clear picture of the progress of the organization through the year. It's a bit like the state of internal medicine before MRIs and CT scans: a lot of poking and probing and guesswork.

As we used the Cash Flow Forecaster to piece together the school's cash flow, we charted the figures on a monthly basis, calculating total income, total expense, and a monthly cumulative total. These rough figures made it obvious that when a certain month arrived, unless something really radical happened, the school would be unable to continue.

As the realization sank in, both Ed and Nellie began to review their options. It was clear that the salaries for the faculty under contract far exceeded the tuition fees. Expenses that could not have been anticipated, such as having to—at the insistence of neighbors—improve the country lane leading to the camp, had cast the budget completely askew. No one on the board had fundraising expertise, and no grants were in sight for a school without a track record. Even a special event to raise funds would not come close to covering the needed expenses. All the goodwill and idealism that had energized the board and staff suddenly seemed to hit a brick wall.

Yet all reports were that individual students were having a remarkably productive time. Blessed with fine teachers and unimaginably small class sizes, children were dazzling their parents with their enthusiasm, interest, and learning. The school was working academically, if not financially.

After the consultation, Ed and Nellie prepared a long-term cash flow forecast, seven years out, that would give them a sense of when the projected income from enrollment would begin to intersect with the expenses of the program. This information would also tell them how to begin to structure the plan for saving the school in the present.

Clearly, the school's board and staff would need to raise funds wherever and whenever they could. A push for increased enrollment the coming year was also mandated. In addition, two forms of borrowing seemed appropriate for the school. The school needed to establish a line of credit to meet current annual obligations like payroll and vendors' bills and they needed a long-term loan to buy time until the school could break even.

After pulling together some financial projections and talking to the board, Ed and Nellie scheduled a meeting with the branch manager at North Sound Bank (now Frontier Bank), an institution with strong ties to the community. Nellie indicated that West Sound Academy was interested in a business loan that could be drawn on for the first four or five years of the program and then converted to term debt for a payback over a five- to ten-year period—in effect, a mini-mortgage. To make her case, Nellie brought along the budgetary projections created using the Cash Flow Forecaster. After a quick explanation of how the school used the cash flow–based instrument for budgeting, forecasting, and monitoring, the banker asked Nellie to walk him through the figures.

The banker understood that West Sound Academy planned to draw down on the note over a multiple-year period, paying interest only. The payback on the note would start in earnest after the breakeven point was reached.

But when it came time to talk about collateral, things must have started to look very strange to the banker, since the school, unlike most businesses, had no physical assets of interest to the bank. Individuals—parents, friends, members of the board, and others—would collateralize the loan. They would purchase certificates of deposit at the bank and hypothecate, or pledge, these funds to the school for use as collateral. The bank would pay these individuals the interest due on their certificates of deposit, but the entire pool of funds would be available as collateral for the school to draw on.

The banker loved the idea. As he said candidly, "Hey, I have limited risk in this deal. It is up to you to shoulder that responsibility. My major concern is that we keep the cost of processing all those certificates of deposit reasonable." When reminded that his bank ordinarily solicited certificates of deposit, he confessed that it all looked good, and if West Sound Academy was willing to mobilize the collateral in a highly liquid form (and cash is as liquid as money gets), then, with approval from his bank's credit committee, he was ready to lend.

Normally, bankers pay careful attention to two factors: the quality of collateral and the risk involved. With collateral in the form of certificates of deposit and stocks and bonds in his vault, the quality of collateral was clearly not a problem. But what about the risk? The quality of the school's management, the competitive state of the local economy, the sophistication of the business plan, and the capability of the school to generate and follow good fiscal reports and plans were all discussed. It was obvious that without a crystal ball, no one had all the answers. However, the banker felt comfortable with the collateral and with the level of coverage, meaning that he would have a dollar in the vault for every dollar that was loaned.

With an agreement to lend in hand, it was time to call a meeting of parents and staff and explain the creditholder concept. Two weeks later, after receiving a handsome invitation to attend a meeting at the home of the parents of one of the school's students, family members, board members, and staff arrived for an evening of reports, discussion, and beautifully prepared desserts.

As headmaster, Nellie reported on the progress of the school and described the plan to use a multiple-year loan as a bridge to the future success of the program. There was some discussion of the fact that students were doing well and that the school was meeting a critical need in the community. Then Nellie intro-duced the creditholder program as a way for individuals to help the school to ob-tain credit.

In the case of West Sound Academy, the business loan would require com-mitments of at least one year, and participation for even more years to help col-lateralize the term loan. It was explained that the collateral needed to match the financial cycle of the school. Even though not every family had the means to par-ticipate, there were eighteen students, as well as board and staff members and oth-ers who supported the concept of the academy. These people could ensure that the first year's requirement would be met, and the school would solicit creditholders in the second and third year from new parents and others in the community.

Parents supported the idea, and some were willing to make pledges on the spot. One parent pledged to buy a $10,000 certificate of deposit, and another fam-ily agreed to purchase one for $20,000.

Once West Sound Academy formed a creditholder group to place an amount equal to the first year's loan in the bank, North Sound Bank was happy to lend. The next year, when additional creditholder funds were required, more cred-itholders jumped on the bandwagon, having seen the success of the school. As the school grew and met its enrollment forecasts, it was able to sustain its credit with an ongoing creditholder program.

The write-up of the West Sound Academy creditholder program that was shared with parents and grandparents of new students and with interested com-munity members is included in Exhibit 14.1.

Once the operational needs of the school were addressed, securing a suitable facility became an increasing topic at parent meetings and around the staff lunch-room table. This led to action on the part of the board and senior staff.

A New Facility for West Sound Academy

As everyone knows who visits either a public or a private school, facilities are al-most always a major issue. West Sound Academy was no exception. The tempo-rary setting of the first year was remarkably picturesque, but it was also very challenging for the school's staff. All the classrooms and offices had to be packed up on Friday to allow the camp to function during weekends, and then reassem-bled prior to classes on Monday—an exhausting routine.

During this initial year, a lovely parcel of property came to Ed Frodel's atten-tion. Located next to a small art college, the parcel was owned by a family who was interested in selling but who had a long history of protracted negotiations and unresolved deals. With his usual enthusiasm Ed began to court the owners, and even-tually the school was able to strike a deal to purchase the land.

EXHIBIT 14.1. OVERVIEW OF THE WEST SOUND ACADEMY CREDITHOLDER PROGRAM.

Make an Investment in Your Community and Your School
We are asking parents and caring community members to invest in West Sound Academy by becoming Creditholders. The term *Creditholder* refers to friends, associates, and other community members who agree to provide cash or securities as collateral for West Sound Academy's loans with North Sound Bank. The Creditholder program lets your cash or stock work for West Sound Academy while it continues to appreciate for you.

The Strategy
As our financial partner, North Sound Bank is providing a short-term line of credit and long-term business loans to West Sound Academy. These loans help West Sound Academy, which operates on a school year cycle, operate smoothly during the summer months when no tuition revenue is earned, as well as sustain overall operation of the school during its growth years, until tuition income from increasing enrollment is adequate to fund all expenses.

Our strategy is precisely the same as that which a family adopts when it purchases a home and secures a mortgage. By using a portion of our annual income from tuition, fundraising, and grants to pay down our loan, we are able to offer our students the benefits of enhanced educational opportunities now and to use our increased earning power effectively over the coming years.

It is important to understand that, so long as our loan with the Bank is not in default, the individual Creditholders own their own certificates of deposit or pledged stocks and bonds. These can be withdrawn at the discretion of the individual, following the normal rules that banks place on certificates of deposit *and* the ability of West Sound Academy to find replacement collateral. It is West Sound Academy's responsibility to maintain enough collateral for its borrowing. An individual Creditholder's funds will be not required for the entire term of the loan as long as West Sound Academy is able to bring in new Creditholders and meet its financial obligations.

West Sound Academy will actively recruit new Creditholders each year and adjust the level of participation as the loan is gradually amortized so as to limit the risk and exposure to each Creditholder. By increasing participation, we protect each other and West Sound Academy. As enrollment increases and the number of Creditholders increases, the total responsibility for each becomes relatively small while ensuring that our school has the capital required to sustain our educational programs at the high levels expected by students, parents and teachers.

How a Cash Pledge Works
The Bank purchases an FDIC-insured certificate of deposit (CD) in your name at the prevailing interest rate. The CD is invested for a minimum of 12 months and automatically rolls over at the end of the term.

• Interest from the CD belongs to you and may accrue to the CD. As a Creditholder you will therefore have access to the interest if you so designate.

• Through a Creditholder Agreement, Creditholders place the CD as security for West Sound Academy's line of credit and loan. All paperwork can be handled through West Sound Academy.

EXHIBIT 14.1. OVERVIEW OF THE WEST SOUND ACADEMY CREDITHOLDER PROGRAM, *continued.*

- At the maturity date of your CD, you may request that West Sound Academy replace your CD with collateral from another Creditholder. West Sound Academy commits to finding a replacement as quickly as possible; however, your CD will not be released until replacement collateral has been posted.

How a Stock Pledge Works

A Creditholder's stock certificates are pledged to the Bank for a period of 12 months or more. The Bank issues a receipt for the stock, which remains in your name.

- Dividends and any growth in stock value belong to you.

- Through a Creditholder Agreement, a Creditholder pledges the stock as security for West Sound Academy's line of credit and loan. Most paperwork can be handled through West Sound Academy, though stock certificates should be sent via overnight courier or brought to North Sound Bank.

- The Bank reviews the market value of the stock quarterly. Should there be a loss in stock value, West Sound Academy will be responsible for providing additional collateral to compensate for the change in value.

- If you, as a Creditholder, decide to discontinue participating in the program prior to the repayment of the debt, West Sound Academy will make every effort to replace the stock with collateral from another Creditholder. West Sound Academy commits to finding a replacement as quickly as possible; however, your stock will not be released until repayment collateral has been posted.

Risks to Creditholders

CDs and stock belong to Creditholders unless West Sound Academy is no longer financially able to meet its obligations on its loan from the Bank and defaults on its debt, in which case the following will occur:

- West Sound Academy will offer Creditholders the opportunity to replace the pledged CD or stock with funds to cover the amount of the original pledge.

- North Sound Bank will have the right to keep all or part of the pledged CD or stock, as well as any dividends or increase in stock value, to apply in payment of the defaulted loan.

- West Sound Academy will repay to Creditholders the value of any collateral taken by the Bank, subject to West Sound Academy's financial ability to do so.

- A Creditholder's ability to directly control the CD or stock is limited by West Sound Academy's ability to replace pledged funds with new collateral and West Sound Academy's financial ability to keep the loan in good standing with the Bank.

- West Sound Academy strongly advises all potential Creditholders to consult with their financial and legal advisers prior to making this commitment.

Reporting

West Sound Academy will keep you informed of our progress and success on a semiannual basis.

How to Become a Creditholder

Fill out the creditholder agreement and send it to Rebecca Wright at West Sound Academy.

West Sound Academy

To support the school's financial vision, I pledge a certificate of deposit, or stocks or bonds, to North Sound Bank according to the following arrangement:

Amount of CD: $_____

Amount of Stock: $_____

Amount of Bonds: $_____

Term of Pledge:

One year   _____
Two years   _____
Three years _____
Four years   _____
Five years   _____

Approximate date I will open my account with the bank: _____

Name: _____ Date: _____

The school still needed a facility to use before the land could be developed, however. A board member had located a space in a small shopping mall that had formerly housed a large, modern hardware store. The quality of the space was excellent, and with some serious sweat equity and a reasonable amount of funds, the space could be adapted to classrooms suitable for the school's second year. Enrollment had doubled, as projected, and the new space, although time- and energy-consuming to prepare, would serve as a good temporary home.

It was during the remodeling of the temporary space that Ed approached us about dealing with the land and the plans for the new campus on the hill. We suggested that we visit with the banker again and see if anyone in the development community might be interested in taking on the project and leasing it back to the school. The banker quickly grasped the idea that we were talking about a conventional commercial construction lease-back arrangement. He suggested a couple of names, and suddenly Ed's eyes lit up.

One of the names the banker mentioned was Tim Ryan, the grandfather of two of the school's students. A successful builder and developer, he frequently constructed buildings for medical groups, which then leased them back from him. His buildings were always of excellent quality, well finished and attractive. "Why, Tim Ryan is down at the hardware store right now, helping us put up drywall," Ed said. We suggested that Ed have coffee with him and see whether the idea of building and leasing back the campus would interest him.

In an hour, a call came in from Ed. He had approached Tim and found that he was willing to sit down with us the next day, at the bank, to discuss the arrangement. That meeting was quick and to the point. Tim wanted to see the multiple-year cash flow projections. He had a few questions about enrollment, but he was plainly smitten by how well his grandchildren were doing at the academy and was already turning the site plans over in his mind. He proposed that he run some numbers and get back to us in a week.

With an architect doing some preliminary thinking about a site plan and the number of buildings, and with the site near at hand, Tim and his staff used their own experience to scope out the project. The result was a meeting with Tim, Ed and Nellie, and another board member. Tim showed all of us the numbers generated by his accountant, his analysis of the costs, and his estimate of the lease payments. The pieces all worked on paper. The deal constituted a practical and reasonable effort for all the parties involved.

Yet, as so often happens, the project ran into some immediate obstacles. The school had chosen a local architect who was approaching retirement, and with one thing and another the drawings and specifications were late. With fees running up and the work still not done, the developer became increasingly uncomfortable with the pace. His construction firm had other projects to fulfill, and the delays were simply unsupportable. He stepped back from the school project, which threw the school's board into a quandary. Some wanted to proceed, others were reassessing the value of remaining in their current site with a long-term lease arrangement. Parents became concerned by the debate, and soon two sides emerged with contrasting ideas about what was best for the institution.

Into this breach stepped Ed Frodel. Although he had spent his entire life teaching, Ed did some serious financial homework and decided that he would act as the developer. He formed a company, and he reenlisted Tim Ryan to work with him to arrange the financing and to construct the campus. Ed and Tim found a new architect, worked with the County to obtain permits, and made necessary improvements. With support from the Board and parents, Ed and Tim put all the pieces together and built a brand-new campus, under budget and on time—a remarkable accomplishment for Ed as a first-time real estate developer. Clearly a background in humanities and a great deal of perseverance can be a great combination.

The school moved into its new campus, with a lease arrangement that was designed to work for both Ed's company and for the Academy. West Sound Academy was approaching its seventh year, with enrollment as projected in the cash flow forecast, with expenses right in line with projections, and with the promise of positive cash flow in the coming years. The decision by the board to move the school to the new facility was paving the way for increased enrollment in the new and vastly improved facilities.

Within a year of the move to the new facility, the board decided to institutionalize the creditholder program by making it mandatory for all parents and students. A figure of $3,000 per student was established, and the funds could be placed as a certificate of deposit at the local bank or as stocks and bonds pledged for this purpose (see Exhibit 14.2).

The board and administration were aware that some parents of students on financial aid might not be able to mobilize the required sum of $3,000. So when ten families indicated that they did not have the means to participate in the creditholder program, the board—unsurprised—came up with a novel solution. Two board members put together enough money to place $3,000 for each of these families in certificates of deposit at North Sound Bank, and the ten families were asked to come up with a 2 percent interest payment up front to be added to the interest accruing on the certificate of deposit. The cost per family to be enrolled as a creditholder was $82 per year, a sum that was well within each family's budget. The interest paid by the parents was turned over to the board members who had provided the capital, and the school was able to maintain its mandate that all families participate.

As the school was rolling out its new mandatory creditholder program, the bank officers responsible for the account made a proposal to the school. Given the regulatory requirements associated with the outstanding loans in the name of the school, the bank was burdened with considerable paperwork. Unlike a line of credit, the term debt that the bank was carrying needed to be constantly documented and assessed. Why not approach the creditholders and ask them to roll their certificates of deposit into a small number of jumbo accounts? The accounts would be in the name of the school, instead of the individual creditholders, the paperwork would be drastically reduced, and the bank officers felt that the large consolidated accounts would clearly merit a higher rate of interest. The interest could be shared with the school in exchange for the minimal maintenance efforts that would be required of the bookkeeper in keeping track of the individual creditholder accounts. The bank was prepared to assist the bookkeeper in setting up the accounts on her computer, and it seemed that everyone would benefit from the consolidation. A few details still had to be worked out, but none that both parties felt couldn't be solved. The board accepted the proposal.

Review of the Case

The use of credit for venture is hardly a path for risk-averse people to travel. Yet it is instructive in the sense that by demonstrating commitment to the survival of the school, creditholders were able to provide the key element necessary to move ahead. With no support from local foundations or corporations, and with limited support from individual donors, the school was still able to use its ability to foster commitment in the form of creditholder dollars to obtain working capital from the bank.

This case study ended with the small private school moving into a new campus custom-designed for the school, and that sets the stage for the closer look at nonprofit sector real estate strategies we provide in Chapter Fifteen.

EXHIBIT 14.2. CREDITHOLDER INSTRUCTIONS.

WEST SOUND
ACADEMY

P.O. Box 807 • Poulsbo, Washington 98370 • (360) 598-5954   fax (360) 598-5494
www.westsoundacademy.org • *www.paaf.org*

Dear Parent,

As outlined in the admissions packet, the West Sound Academy Board of Trustees has made participation in the West Sound Academy *Creditholder Program* mandatory. The *Creditholder Program* is one of the simplest ways to contribute to the school's financial well-being. As a creditholder, you deposit money which is placed in a Frontier Bank Certificate of Deposit issued in your name. You retain ownership of the CD and you continue to earn interest on your investment.

Through your participation, you join other WSA parents and caring community members that help guarantee the loans needed for the school's start-up. The loans were and *are* part of a well-reasoned business plan and financial partnership with Frontier Bank.

Securing our loans requires a $3,000 creditholder deposit from each family—the Board has made this level of participation mandatory. In lieu of purchasing a Certificate of Deposit, some families place equivalent securities with Frontier Bank. Like the CD, these securities are held in the owner's name by the bank with all dividends and earnings accruing to the owner. And then when your child leaves the school, your CD or stock is returned to you in full—a nice savings account for college!

The *Creditholder Program* has allowed the school to grow and prosper because parents in previous years pledged funds as collateral while their children were at West Sound Academy. We're pleased to welcome you for your turn at this valuable task.

The enclosed flyer, "Step-by-Step Creditholding," details the enrollment process. Jim Kolb is also available to answer any questions.

We look forward to your joining us in this innovative program.

Sincerely,

Board Chair

CHAPTER FIFTEEN

OWNING VERSUS LEASING

Real Estate Strategies

Own or lease? This is a perennial issue in the nonprofit sector. Of all the financial strategies that administrators and their boards are asked to consider, real estate matters may be the most costly and have the longest-lasting consequences.

In this chapter we offer you a range of real estate choices and show you how cash flow thinking and tools, by focusing on operational questions, can cast new light on the relative merits of ownership or leasing. We also discuss capital campaigns, tax-exempt borrowing, and good old-fashioned leases, as well as gifts of buildings and land. We wind up with suggestions about what to do if you already have a building.

In keeping with our goal to make financial matters, even very complex ones, simpler and easier for you, we worked with Alan Bicker, an expert on tax-exempt financing, to develop the Real Estate Calculator. This electronic tool links up with the Cash Flow Forecaster and is also included on the CD that accompanies this book. The software incorporates the cash flow principles we have been discussing. The relative cost of money, the role of inflation, and issues of time and timing all play an important part in this analysis. This means that the questions built into the Real Estate Calculator all operate in a cash flow context as you explore capital campaigns, ownership, sale and lease arrangements, and different types of financing.

We are advocates for nonprofits' leasing real estate and equipment. While not categorically opposed to building ownership, we remain convinced that leasing can often provide the best opportunity for a nonprofit institution to fulfill its mission. Our rationale for this is linked to some of the fundamental issues that make real estate questions confusing and difficult for nonprofit organizations.

For starters, any comparison of the cost and benefits of real estate in the nonprofit sector is dictated by three considerations:

- The hard issues that establish the actual financial costs and benefits of any option
- The special circumstances that apply to a specific institution, which may make one choice more attractive than another
- The soft or subjective issues that represent the values and wishes of the members of the board and staff

With so many different issues in play, it is no wonder that real estate questions in the nonprofit sector are complex. However, that does not mean that we can't identify the issues and compare and contrast them. The Real Estate Calculator enables you to go from cash flow budgeting and forecasting to a series of different scenarios that compare the costs and the benefits of various ways of dealing with real estate.

Using this tool you can see if a capital campaign, with all the trimmings, is right for you. Or you might discover that leasing is just the ticket, saving you time, energy, and money. For those attracted to tax-exempt financing, particularly those that qualify, this is an option that you can explore with the instrument. Sale and leaseback is an increasingly popular real estate strategy for businesses, and it might be perfect for your institution, especially if access to working capital means more to you than sitting on a paper asset that has limited value to furthering your mission.

Key Questions

The advantage of pulling all this information together in a piece of software is that you can accommodate the special aspects of your particular situation with some hard numbers before giving sway to the blind blandishments of property ownership. You've probably figured out what we prefer here, but it's useful to take a closer look at some of the pros and cons associated with leasing versus owning buildings and equipment.

How can board and staff members make sound decisions about real estate?

Owning property has a lot of emotional appeal to folks just trying to get their mission accomplished. It feels safe and secure to own your facilities and equipment. And, after all, isn't it everyone's dream to own their own property?

For some, ownership is like a merit badge, a sign that you have finally arrived. The new building is a landmark, a signal that you are here in the big time. Talking about real estate evokes plenty of powerful feelings. *We will never give up our building, we own it, and would never consider leasing,* one particularly passionate nonprofit leader told us when we asked whether she had considered the financial consequences of leasing versus owning a facility. And this was after we'd listened to an hour-long litany of woes about the boiler, the roof, the cost of fuel, the drafty window frames, the inadequate spaces, and on and on. Chalk up another one to our foolish questions.

The soft issues of value and preference often get confused with the hard, strictly monetary issues. While the building is a tangible asset, it is important to realize that the financial value of a building is realized only when it is sold. Unless, of course, you decide to rent the building to someone else, in which case you get to be both a mission-oriented nonprofit and a landlord. In the nonprofit arena, when a building is sold the proceeds are not distributed as they would be in a business, where they might be used to line the pockets of the owners of the enterprise. Instead, the sale proceeds are typically used for funding program expenses or for acquiring a new facility. Because many nonprofits do not pay taxes, depreciation of the facility is essentially meaningless, since it has no tax benefits for a tax-exempt organization.

All right, all right, we know that your accountant is not going to let us get away with defaming depreciation, but truthfully, how many nonprofit organizations are prepared to establish plant funds to compensate for the real declining value of a building? (*Plant funds* are reserves designed to provide money for replacement and renovations of facilities.) Few nonprofits can afford to sustain large liquid plant funds, and even if they could, the costs of renovation are not deductible.

An article in the *New York Times* headlined "For Nonprofits, Owning Is Becoming the Wave of the Past" noted that a growing number of nonprofit organizations have been selling their buildings in New York, partly because real estate sales in the city are strong and can provide funds for critical missions, but also because many nonprofit organizations realize that leasing space can be much easier and less expensive than keeping a property in good condition.[1]

When the topic of leasing versus owning comes up in discussions with our clients, one issue always emerges quickly. We cannot count the number of times we have been told: "Control is important to us. If we own our building, we have complete control." Yet ownership and control are not necessarily the same thing. For example, owning property that you can't afford to maintain can have disastrous effects on your program budget if the roof starts to leak, or the foundation shifts.

Surely you can remember dealing with a nonprofit that owned a building it could not afford to operate, or could not maintain in excellent condition—the problem is endemic in the nonprofit community. Serving two masters—social purpose and fiscal solvency—makes it difficult to allocate resources to a plant fund when the orphans are hungry.

Control, on the other hand, can be secured through well-crafted long-term leases that bind the parties to a set of understandings that are workable and fair. By spelling out terms and conditions in advance, a nonprofit organization can plan for its future expenditures without worrying about unanticipated disasters. Although some believe that contracts are made to be broken, we still have faith that a properly designed lease, with an option to renew, can go a long way to ensure that both the nonprofit organization and the property owner are protected.

After discussions of control, the second most popular real estate–related topic for many board and staff members is the uniqueness of their organization's needs and requirements. It is undoubtedly true that each nonprofit institution has specific needs and circumstances when it comes to facilities, but some conditions with a big impact on any organization's real estate decisions can be generalized.

For example, if your institution wishes to acquire a building, and you have access to wealthy donors willing to contribute enough funds to purchase or construct the facility, it might make sense to explore the feasibility of conducting a capital campaign. If the campaign has a high probability of success and if the costs both in time and effort can be endured up front, this approach may be the least expensive choice. After all, if someone else will pay for your facility, and if the only expenses are meeting the annual operating costs plus a little extra for a plant fund, this is likely to be cheaper than renting or acquiring a conventional mortgage.

Notice the whole series of conditions that can have a profound effect on the choice—access to wealthy donors being the most obvious. The ability to conduct a campaign that is cost-effective is another, and this condition is influenced by factors that may be beyond the control of the institution, such as the number of capital campaigns simultaneously under way within a community or the state of the economy, particularly as it affects wealthy donors. Moreover, you have to consider the time the campaign will require, along with the time for construction, if that is the option at hand.

What about the costs of a capital campaign?

Everyone wants a capital campaign. After all, having others pay for your facility while you maintain the tax advantages of being a nonprofit can seem pretty compelling. Not only that, the process has been fine-tuned over the years by handsomely tailored consultants in graciously appointed offices across the nation.

Still, capital campaigns have their own risks, and even though you rarely see publicity about campaigns that stall or fail, it happens. For obvious reasons, news about a capital campaign that failed to reach its goal is just the type of information that most nonprofit organizations try to conceal in their public statements.

A study of capital giving to nonprofits in the late 1980s and early 1990s pointed out that the demand for capital giving is apt to outstrip the supply.[2] Although several years have passed since this study was conducted, the findings still are highly relevant. More research on the impact of regional capital giving needs to be done. In the meantime, this study is to be commended as a landmark.

The capital giving study reached five main conclusions:

- Capital giving is growing significantly faster than overall giving.
- The aspirations of nonprofit organizations for capital donations would appear to outstrip future donors' giving capacity in the region under study.
- Many campaigns will likely fail or fall significantly below their targets; alternatively, if they succeed, there will be a significant shift in charitable giving that may negatively affect many organizations.
- Foundations played a major role in the growth of capital giving. This increase was made possible by unusual growth in assets in the period under study.
- Capital campaigns have the effect of redistributing total charitable giving, reducing income to some recipients and increasing income to others.

What this study highlights is the problem many nonprofit institutions face when considering a capital campaign. The goal of getting the money up front from a capital campaign may prove to be elusive in the face of intense competition from other campaigns. You always run the risk that your efforts will be less than successful. In which case, it may not be possible to raise all the funds needed to actually construct, buy, or renovate the facilities.

Capital campaigns are also very costly in terms of time. Capital campaigns can take three to five years in some cases, and while all this is going on, those dollars for operations still need to be raised year after year. Cash flow analysis demonstrates how important it is to keep a sharp eye on operational expenses during any fundraising effort, particularly a capital campaign.

For an institution contemplating a capital campaign, the first consideration is the cost of raising money. The actual costs of raising funds are a matter for considerable speculation within the nonprofit sector. Successful capital campaigns must include some additional funding to account for donor fatigue after the goal is achieved. Some campaigns even include an endowment to provide operating funds in the future. Mobilizing all that money up front can be very expensive and time-consuming.

What else is there to do if we don't run a capital campaign?

Other options are available to nonprofit organizations that choose to own— each with financial advantages and disadvantages. This is where the Real Estate

Calculator comes in so handy. It spells out the pros and cons of each choice in fiscal terms.

One alternative should be familiar to anyone who has ever owned or thought about owning a house. In place of a capital campaign, some nonprofit organizations simply obtain a conventional mortgage from their bank. Any institution planning to enter into a conventional mortgage should be keenly interested in the current cost of money. The amount of interest to be paid over the life of the loan can be a substantial concern, even if interest rates are not too high. Unable to trade off any of the finance costs through a tax deduction, the nonprofit with a conventional mortgage will pay for the building, the financing, and the expenses associated with facility maintenance. These are hard costs that need to be weighed against the tendency to want to own facilities for a variety of softer reasons. Perhaps this is why practically every nonprofit institution in America would like to have a facility named after Melinda Gates, Paul Allen, or Warren Buffet, assuming of course that the honoree would contribute the money to remove the burden of the mortgage.

When discussing conventional mortgages, it is important to underscore again the implications of the cost of money. Selecting a variable interest rate option today, in an effort to take advantage of the great disparity between short- and long-term interest rates, may be striking a bargain with the devil. Your institution is now subject to the interest rate risks of the capital markets. Too many administrators and their boards have been talked into variable rate deals, believing that current rates will never return to their historical levels. Some of us are willing to bet that they are wrong.

Which brings us to a real estate option that seems ideally suited to the nonprofit world. This alternative is to pursue a tax-exempt bond to pay for your facilities.

Just saying *tax-exempt financing* sounds sweet to many administrators. The reason why tax-exempt financing often pencils out better than other choices is that the cost of money is lower. And, as you know, the cost of money is an essential consideration in cash flow thinking. If you compare two mortgages, one with tax-exempt financing and one without, it does not require a genius to figure out which is the better deal. But, here again, the circumstance of the institution plays a part. The nonprofit that has a strong financial track record and good credit is going to be much more attractive to the folks who package the bonds that ultimately underwrite the mortgage. So, as the nonprofit institution proceeds with its exploration of tax-exempt financing, its own fiscal position may be a key factor in determining if the financial arrangement is possible.

Not all nonprofit organizations are eligible for tax-exempt financing. A variety of reasons including certain religious affiliations or a history of leasing to for-profit tenants may be an obstacle to this type of financing. It makes sense to consult a bond attorney to make sure that you qualify before diving headfirst into a tax-exempt transaction.

All the up-front public disclosure of information involved in tax-exempt financing may be uncomfortable for institutions that are guarded about their financial laundry. In some cases it may interfere with fundraising efforts, and in others it may signal previously undisclosed excesses that were masked by clever accounting practices. Bond issues, for example, require full disclosure on an ongoing basis. If the bond issue is rated, a rating can be reduced based on poor performance by the nonprofit institution. Rest assured that sophisticated donors will search bond rating histories of organizations before contributing funds.

Is there any downside to tax-exempt financing?

All other things being equal, it is usually cheaper to borrow at a tax-exempt rate and to avoid paying property taxes than it is to mobilize a capital campaign or to create an investor group to own and lease back the facility. Tax-exempt bond financing as a consideration starts with a simple threshold: your institution must qualify for the bond. This determination can usually be established quickly. If you do qualify, and this is not an inconsequential hurdle for some organizations, the combination of no property taxes and low interest rates seems like an unbeatable one-two punch.

What may not seem so unbeatable are the fees associated with tax-exempt financing. In many cases the bonds that you are seeking will be packaged by a specially designated agency that will trigger the tax-exempt component of the transaction. This agency may also be assembling a number of different financial packages and aggregating them to reach a high enough financial threshold to make the costs associated with the activity worthwhile. All this activity and the special role that attorneys play as bond counsel can quickly result in some hefty fees. The annual payment of a fee for the life of the loan is another consideration that prudent board and staff members need to keep in mind, as visions of tax-exempt sugar plums dance in their heads.

A serious real estate–related problem that may be looming on the horizon is the free ride that many nonprofit institutions get when it comes to property taxes. Oh the joys of not paying taxes. The delicious sense of getting away with something forbidden to others. The delight at beating the system. But as we all learn sooner or later, blessings tend to come with a built-in curse. In most major metropolitan areas of the country, nonprofit institutions are exempt from property taxes but still require the services that local government provides. As the federal budget continues to build mighty deficits, cities across the nation are finding their own revenue bases inadequate to address what are euphemistically called "unfunded mandates." The consequence of this economic push and pull is that some cities are considering imposing some type of alternative tax on nonprofit institutions, a tax that will ultimately have to be paid, indirectly, by the supporters of the institution. And it is worthwhile to remember that leaseholders often wind up paying property taxes that are disguised as rent.

One helpful alternative to these clumsy levies would be to encourage nonprofits to sell and lease back their facilities. Commercially owned real estate would be placed back on the tax rolls, benefiting the cities. Private owners can, in many instances, deduct a portion of the taxes from their federal returns; in essence, robbing federal Peter to pay local Paul.

Alternatives to Ownership

The free lunch aspect of tax exemption may be coming to an end fairly soon. Cities—Boston and Pittsburgh, as two examples—have been successful in supporting large numbers of nonprofit institutions, such as colleges, universities, private schools, religious entities, hospitals, and community development organizations that are trying to transform blighted areas. These cities have paid a heavy price in the provision of services with a lack of counterbalancing income from property taxes. This state of affairs may not be sustainable in the long term. If and when municipalities start to recapture revenues from nonprofit institutions within their boundaries, the costs of facility ownership may rise dramatically.

Sale and Leaseback

From a cash flow perspective, a sale and leaseback arrangement might work well for you. In this case, if the deal is attractive enough to potential investors, and if the time value of money is factored in, this approach puts money in your pocket for the building and establishes a long-term rental relationship.

If you take a portion of the funds paid as part of the sale and prepay your rent for a number of years, you can take advantage of the loss of money's value over time (net present value). In other words, a smart landlord and an equally smart nonprofit tenant would both benefit from the prepayment of rent. In five years, the present value of a dollar might be 85 cents. If the institution prepays the rent, the landlord gets the advantage of the current dollar, and therefore should lower the overall rental to reflect this bonanza. Lowering rent by using current dollars also strengthens the nonprofit institution's bottom line. The arrangements between landlord and tenant should reflect that mutual benefit, and a written agreement is the best way to ensure that both parties remember the terms and conditions.

The circumstances that make sale and leaseback favorable include having a building of sufficient value to attract the investors willing to engage in this type of transaction, or having a credit history strong enough to justify investors' purchasing a building to suit the institution. In all cases the sale and leaseback option results in structuring a long-term lease. An additional ingredient is time. This method of acquiring the monetary value of a suitable building through sale and the long-term protection of leasing can usually be transacted in a fraction of the time necessary for a capital campaign.

It is important for leaders in the nonprofit institution to understand that the market for this type of sale and leaseback transaction is already well defined. CRIC Capital and its affiliate, Nessen & Associates, are examples of firms that routinely broker sale and leaseback deals for larger nonprofits.[3]

Sale and leaseback has become an increasingly popular approach for commercial entities interested in using the monetary value of their properties as a source of working capital. Nonprofit organizations that have traditionally relied on government contracts may want to explore this approach as growing deficits continue to exert downward pressures on government spending.

So, pitting the capital campaign against the sale and leaseback arrangement requires that specific circumstances be in play to allow the choice to be useful. It is easy to declare a capital campaign. It may be much more difficult to conduct it and still sustain the annual fundraising necessary to keep the doors open. On the other hand, the conversion of facilities into immediately available working capital can be explored with little or no cost to the institution.

Traditional Leases

So far, we have looked at choices that involve ownership, through a capital campaign, a conventional mortgage, or a nonconventional (read tax-exempt) mortgage. The only significantly different choice was the sale and leaseback arrangement.

In a traditional lease, the cost of financing the deal is also a factor that may ultimately influence the cost to the nonprofit institution. While it is true that rentals are a function of what the local market will bear and therefore not just a matter of landlords' adding up costs to establish the price, the cost of money is still a major consideration. If the financing costs more because interest rates are higher, then it will have some impact on the cost of the lease. Another circumstance is the availability of space in the local real estate market. If vacancies are plentiful, leases tend to be cheaper. If space is tight, costs go up. Availability and interest rates are factors beyond your institution's control.

We advise our nonprofit clients to try not to own things that are not disposable. Leasing is possible in many different forms, and concessionary leasing is often less expensive than commercial equipment rental. The reason for not owning is simply that there is no incentive in the nonprofit world to own. Ownership has no tax advantages for tax-exempt organizations. Depreciation takes place, but your institution funds it at the cost of fulfilling its social purpose. When things wear out or need to be replaced, it makes more sense to have people who can derive benefit from investing do so, rather than burdening the organization and the people you serve with increased costs. This does not mean that every single nonprofit organization should lease. What we are suggesting is that the comparison of different options to ownership should be given a fair hearing before the court adjourns.

Leasing has its charms. It is incremental, in the sense that you only have to raise and pay the rent once a month, and that can provide more money for your mission. Leasing also shifts the liabilities for ongoing maintenance to the landlord, which can be a blessing. Leasing means living light—not owning the facility with all its attendant headaches. For many nonprofit institutions, the flexibility of leasing means that when it's time to move on because you have outgrown the space, you can fulfill the terms of your lease and move on.

Many people believe that leasing facilities is ultimately more expensive than owning them. This impression is often reinforced by unrealistic sentiments regarding ownership. Often ignored are the expenditures necessary to conduct a successful capital campaign. In addition, if future operating funds are placed in an endowment, this capital is being used inefficiently. Finally, the costs of future maintenance on buildings are often minimized. Many people shy away from leasing, because they believe that when an organization rents a building, it is charged an amount that is intended to cover the landlord's property taxes, interest fees, insurance costs, and profit. Avoiding leasing for this reason ignores the basic economic laws of supply and demand.

The rent or lease payments received by a building owner are determined not by the cost of the building, the interest charges, or the insurance fees. Property owners do not set rents on a cost-plus basis that guarantees them a profit; rather, they charge what the market will bear.

Many nonprofits in expensive, high-occupancy urban centers do face a sky-high market for real estate. This is a serious problem, particularly because it is difficult if not impossible for individual institutions to adopt strategies that will adequately address this problem. We believe that the only realistic answers are systemic ones—that is, measures that encourage the formation of capital markets that reward socially motivated investors for investing in owning the physical plant of the nonprofit sector. There is no reason why a wealthy nation cannot expand its markets, using existing or only slightly modified tax incentives, to encourage investment in commercial ventures that own and lease back facilities to nonprofit organizations.

In many ways, this idea for systemic change is actually just an extension of the type of thinking that originally created tax-exempt financing. With Real Estate Investment Trusts (REITs) using the capital from endowments of large institutions or foundation holdings, this change could be brought about on a city or regional basis.

Real estate markets differ from state to state. Proponents of ownership usually claim that renting is cheaper in some states and ownership is less costly in others. But no one can offer evidence that the laws of supply and demand that govern the real estate market differ significantly across state lines. The value or price of a commercial building is determined by the annual income generated by rent or lease payments. So when rents are low, buildings sell at low prices; conversely, when rents are high, buildings command high prices. Rents and purchase prices move together; thus a building purchased cheaply can also be rented cheaply.

Yet many nonprofit managers would have donors believe that when rents are dear, they can purchase buildings cheaply. If this is the case, according to some economists, such as James Bennett and Thomas DiLorenzo, who have studied this issue, then those nonprofit managers are definitely in the wrong business—instead, they have "vast fortunes to be made in real estate."[4]

Partnership with Socially Motivated Investors

Socially motivated investors can do well by doing good if they participate in creative leasing arrangements with nonprofit organizations. An institution with a strong projected revenue stream can benefit from leasing offered on concessionary terms. In this case, a socially motivated person or a group of socially motivated people offers a nonprofit a lower rate than the market might bear, while still deriving some of the benefits that come from owning real estate. The depreciation, the interest on financing, the cost of operations and maintenance expenses, all have a tax consequence for the owner that can sweeten the deal.

Meanwhile, private ownership of the physical plant of the nonprofit world would free institutions to pursue their mission unencumbered by the demands of real estate ownership.

A foundation, an institutional endowment, or even a donor-directed financial service organization might be persuaded to enhance the credit of a nonprofit institution by providing a "deficiency guarantee." This terrible-sounding term is actually a very good thing. It means insuring a credit in which an unrelated party agrees to cover the cost of the rent in the event that the nonprofit is unable to do so. When this type of insurance is in play, the socially motivated building owner has a reduced risk and can therefore obtain cheaper financing. With less expensive money available, the socially motivated landlord should be able to offer the nonprofit a lower rent.

In an unconventional lease, circumstances may require that you balance two factors. One is the willingness of a socially motivated (in contrast to a purely profit motivated) landlord to offer the nonprofit institution a preferential deal on the real estate. The second being the obtaining of insurance provided by foundations, endowments, or by donor-directed financial service firms. With one or both of these opportunities, the nonconventional lease can be of great benefit to the nonprofit institution and not a bad deal either for the landlord or the financial players providing insurance.

From a strategic standpoint, as an administrator you may be asked to run the numbers on leasing and to develop a business plan aimed at local partners, potential investors, and affiliated agencies and institutions. The plan should include a long-range forecast that demonstrates the institution's ability to generate income to pay its operating expenses—particularly the rent. Investors motivated to participate may bring a sense of social purpose to the initial meeting, but they will need to be convinced that the investment is solid before proceeding. It is sometimes helpful to develop before-and-after tax scenarios for potential investors. Using a combination of the Cash Flow Forecaster and the Real Estate Calculator can make developing your numbers and your plan a relatively painless exercise in business planning.

In some instances, a financing plan developed in cooperation with a local bank makes a compelling case. If you can arrange for the financing to be assumed by investors, some risk to the bank is mitigated and additional credibility is attached to the deal.

A number of funding institutions can make concessionary rates available to organizations with ongoing cash flow. These sources may also enhance the position of the lender or the investor. In some cases, tax-free bonds may be available from a local municipality or agency, which can reduce the costs of interest and make the investment more attractive.

The goal of this strategy is to ensure that the nonprofit organization is able to secure long-term control of space, maximize the use of its own capital, and reduce its immediate and long-term expenses through the payment of rent to an owner who can absorb the primary advantages of ownership. In this way, the social purpose of the nonprofit organization is preserved as the focus for community support.

The techniques for doing this are not new. In 1970, Ginnie Mae Pool No 1, the first Government National Mortgage Association, issued mortgage-backed securities and mortgages, and passed homeowners' monthly loan payments on to investors. To make credit available to folks who were a trifle too low on the lending totem pole, at least by the 1970s standards of banking institutions, Congress was able to create an agency that lowered the bar just enough to unleash a torrent of home ownership. The impact of this no-cost-to-the-taxpayer program has been enormous, and it continues to resonate decades later, as real estate continues to lift the general economy after the stock market meltdown in 2000.

We talk more about Ginnie Mae (and Fannie Mae and Sallie Mae) in Chapter Nineteen, but for now let's leave the door open for some consideration of how socially motivated individuals, or perhaps those intriguingly named "high-engagement philanthropists," might play a constructive role in the ownership and management of the physical plant for the nonprofit world.

Using the Real Estate Calculator to Support Decisions

The Real Estate Calculator will help you compare and contrast different scenarios in which hard issues, such as costs that can be nailed down, are examined. The educational information provided in the software will inform your choices by giving you a sense of the pros and cons associated with owning versus leasing. This information can then be matched up with your specific circumstances to guide you in making a decision in the best interests of your institution.

What the Calculator cannot do is to help you assess the importance of the subjective issues, those values that often tip board and staff members one way or another when confronting real estate questions. If you believe that owning a building is more important than anything else, then there really isn't much of a contest. Regardless of the cost or long-term benefit, this value, which we refer to as "the Great American Dream syndrome," makes attempts at comparison meaningless. However, if you are willing to look beyond the gut issues and to balance the costs and benefits of ownership and leasing, then comparison is the only way to go.

Although it is not an everyday occurrence, wealthy individuals are increasingly deciding to address their own capital gains issues by donating a building to a nonprofit institution. This raises some very provocative questions from a cash flow perspective.

If someone wants to give your institution a building, what should you consider before leaping at the opportunity to acquire the facility? Accepting gifts always seems like a wonderful idea. After all, everybody loves presents. If someone wants or needs to give you a building, you can accept with gratitude, especially if you have made provision for someone else to own and operate it. Why not arrange the donation and then turn the depreciation and expenses in the building over to a businessperson who can use the tax credits. Because you wish to control the space, find someone who will accept the value of the building as partial prepaid rent and utilities for a period of time. You get to control the space on a long-term lease, the donor gets to deduct the value of the building from this year's income taxes, and the businessperson gets the opportunity to enjoy the tax benefits of ownership.

Gifts of land are another category entirely. Often the donor will request that the land be maintained in perpetuity, with or without financial provision for its stewardship. So the tiny nonprofit Land Trust, which struggles to get a five-person quorum at its monthly meetings, is granted a couple of hundred acres of pristine wildlife refuge along with the responsibility to maintain it as a public benefit forever. In this case, the group typically has no option to sell the land or to develop it. As Clara Miller has so wisely pointed out in her article on gifts of property, this is the type of present that requires plenty of forethought on the part of the recipient and some serious plans for how the future financial responsibility associated with this land will be managed.[5]

If your institution already has a building, why wouldn't you want to keep it? You can keep the building, of course, but you might want to consider—just consider, mind you—the possibility that your institution might be better off if you sold the building to an interested party, secured a substantial long-term lease that gave you lots of control, and used a significant portion of the proceeds from the sale to fund your rental for many, many years. Then, when the roof fails in the next snowstorm, someone else's insurance can cover the costs, and someone else (who can derive a tax benefit) can take care of the consequences. While all this is happening, you can continue providing a public good.

Ownership is often justified by assuming that property can be acquired and held as an investment that will yield future profits. That really doesn't apply to a nonprofit, though—nonprofit organizations are meant to provide social benefits through their mission, not to compete as tax-exempt real estate holding companies. For this reason, social purposes should have first claim on all donated funds. Buildings do not lower program costs, and the funds used to acquire buildings are no longer available to pursue the institution's mission.[6]

If your nonprofit were a business and had equity to offer, then the building would serve that purpose. But because your organization is a tax-exempt nonprofit, all the building has is a paper asset value. You can sell the building, but you will not distribute the proceeds; instead they will be used to lease or buy or build another space, or they may be converted into program funds to help fulfill your mission at some future date.

However, all this said, the world still assigns a value to property. The value of your building or property, if properly appraised, can assist you in obtaining certain types of financing. The potential resale value of the property, particularly if it can be adaptively reused by a variety of other consumers, can help to make your case for a bond or for conventional financing.

And last but certainly not least, there is the important issue that some donors will not support operations, but they will fund buildings. Some nonprofits use the "edifice complex" to rationalize acquiring real estate. They claim that contributors are willing to donate for bricks and mortar, but not for less concrete purposes such as research or operating expenses.

Many cultural organizations, colleges and universities, and hospitals tell us that they find it easier to raise money for buildings than for worthy but less permanent and visible purposes such as scholarships or operating funds. However, often the edifice complex is actually encouraged by the conventional wisdom of development officers and fundraising consultants, not the donors. When nonprofits analyze the long-term costs and benefits of owning versus leasing, the financial gains of leasing are often compelling. These numbers, presented in conjunction with the costs and risks associated with conducting a major capital campaign, are often attractive to donors with business acumen.

Real estate is a very intriguing topic and nowhere more so than in the nonprofit sector. As this chapter demonstrates, cash flow thinking opens the door to rethinking some of the conventional approaches to real estate, and it provides the tools necessary to weigh the relative financial risks and rewards of different alternatives.

If all this talk about real estate has whetted your appetite for more cash flow thinking, then Chapter Sixteen, which pulls together all the elements of strategy based on cash flow thinking, will be right down your alley.

CHAPTER SIXTEEN

DEVELOPING EFFECTIVE STRATEGY FROM CASH FLOW TOOLS AND PRINCIPLES

In this concluding chapter of Part Two we provide an example of how our tools and the principles of cash flow thinking work together in addressing the financial crisis of one organization. The building blocks of our approach appear throughout Part One and Part Two, but as a quick reminder we enumerate them here.

- Use the Cash Flow Forecaster to develop a cash flow–based budgeting, forecasting, and reporting system, to supplement the financial systems currently in place.
- Apply the differential cost of money to financial circumstances. If different categories of money have different costs, it makes sense to use the cheapest dollar to stop the bleeding, before incurring greater costs to earn or raise funds.
- Remember that inflation is a factor that cannot be ignored, and plot your financial course to take inflationary variables into account.
- Include time and timing in every financial strategy.
- Form a creditholder group to provide the collateral that you need for fully secured borrowing at the bank.
- Gain, use, and sustain short-term and long-term credit from the bank as an alternative to large cash reserves, endowments, or building and equipment ownership.
- Use the Real Estate Calculator to revisit the value of owning physical facilities.

- Consider the value of a sale and leaseback strategy for generating needed work-ing capital or retiring accumulated debt from property that you currently own.

With these thoughts in mind, here's a look at the circumstances surrounding one institution to show how we would use our cash flow–based thinking to develop a financial strategy to address the situation.

A Symphony in Trouble

Recently a newspaper reported on the financial plight of a symphony orchestra in a major metropolitan area. While it is hardly fair to attempt to diagnose and discuss an organization from information that comes only from the media, we thought it might be instructive to compare our approach to the symphony's situation with the strategy outlined in the newspaper account.

Let's start with the basics. The newspaper reported that the symphony's $130 million endowment had been a victim of a depressed market, which resulted in a $40 million loss. This in turn deprived the institution of $10.1 million in annual income—a sum that normally makes up close to 24 percent of the symphony's budget.

According to the newspaper, the short-term problem for the remainder of the season was a potential cash shortfall or deficit, which is not permitted by the symphony's bylaws. The institution's financial buffer, the Annual Reserve Fund, was exhausted. The cash reserve had topped $5 million dollars three seasons earlier. Consequently, the newspaper noted, the symphony would either have to make deep cuts or raise money without borrowing—which is also prohibited by the bylaws.

It might be said that the symphony pursued a fiscal strategy based on all the classical elements of capital accumulation. The institution built a substantial en-dowment, had significant cash reserves, owned its building, and used its by-laws to prohibit deficits and borrowing.

Perhaps the most telling comment in the newspaper report was, "The struc-tural problem is caused by the depressed stock market, which affects the sym-phony's nearly $90 million endowment." That statement strikes to the heart of the difference between an approach focused on capital accumulation and our ap-proach, which focuses instead on gaining access to working capital. In the capi-tal accumulation mind-set, the problem is almost always seen as outside the organization. It is typically characterized as a lack of money, or in this case the poor performance of the stock market.

The tactical response of the symphony board, as reported in the newspaper, seemed entirely consistent with its long-standing policy of encouraging capital accumulation. The plan involved increasing fundraising efforts, encouraging marketing to boost earned revenue, reducing costs, and collaborating with other institutions to save office expenses.

In addition, it was reported that the symphony planned to increase the rate at which it withdraws funds from its endowment corpus to 8.5 percent. Although even at that rate, the fund would potentially yield only $7.6 million. That still left $6.3 million to be raised to avoid a deficit.

Would the symphony be able to raise sufficient funds to solve its short-term problem? We earnestly hoped so for the cultural life of its community. But what about the long-term consequences of a strategy based on capital accumulation? Will the stock market come back? Will cash reserves be replenished with new donations? How will the symphony's strategy of capital accumulation serve it in the future? These are some of the broader questions that need to be judged in developing a successful strategy.

Orchestrating a Cash Flow–Based Strategy

We believe that the most fundamental obstacle to the fulfillment of mission in the nonprofit world is lack of access to working capital. In other words, lack of access to the operational money people need to spend to implement their mission. The key to our approach is seeing the way the external climate for fundraising and earned income meshes with the institutions' internal policies and practices to result in success or failure. We believe that the destiny of organizations is much more in their own hands, particularly the degree to which the board and staff make provision for having the money they need, when they need it.

Our approach, with its emphasis on cash flow and access to working capital, suggests a very different course of action for the symphony:

- First, we would urge the administration of the symphony to adopt a cash flow budgeting, forecasting, and reporting system to avoid nasty surprises in the future. Using the Cash Flow Forecaster would be a step in the right direction for creating a system to supplement the existing accounting system.
- Second, we would urge the symphony's board to discourage any further contributions to the endowment fund; it is simply too inefficient to be effective in a time of need.
- Third, we would suggest that the symphony change its by-laws to allow for shortfalls or deficits, which happen to even the best of organizations from time to time. And while they are at it, we would suggest changing the by-laws to allow

for fully secured borrowing, which is an inexpensive alternative to building a costly cash reserve.

- Fourth, we would propose that the symphony create a creditholder group composed of supporters and subscribers and establish a fully secured line of credit equal to 20 percent of the annual budget, which on $32 million is close to $6.4 million. That's not simple, but it's not as daunting a task as some might imagine for a well-known and generally well-supported symphony.

- Fifth, we would ask the symphony to consider extending its creditholder program to take what is left of the immediate deficit and convert it into long-term debt, which can be paid off in a disciplined manner over the next five to ten years.

- Sixth, we would recommend that they start to organize a campaign to petition the state legislature to increase the pay-out rate on restricted funds in endowments. Currently, statutes in their state place a ceiling of 7 percent on payouts per year. If the newspaper article is correct, the symphony will be required to cap its payout at 7 percent, not the 8.5 percent reported. That represents an additional $1.35 million that must be raised. (Remember, not all states have legislation that addresses the payout rate for endowments.)

- Finally, we would suggest that the symphony continue to explore ways to earn more income, to raise operational funds, and to cut expenses. One alternative would be to sell the physical plant to a group of culturally motivated investors and music lovers, and then lease it back. A sale and leaseback arrangement for the symphony's building would need to be carefully calculated. But with some help from the Real Estate Calculator, the fiscal feasibility of this approach could be ascertained quickly.

The cash flow–based strategy that we suggest here would result in significant savings to the symphony over time. Currently, the institution is burdened by using very costly funds that produce remarkably low returns. These low returns are not just a result of the interest rates the investment can earn, they also reflect the original cost of raising the capital and the higher annual rates of inflation in the nonprofit sector.

Our cash flow–based strategy shifts the policy environment from one of unrealistic hope that shortfalls will never happen or that borrowing will never be necessary to one that says we will organize ourselves to use whatever resources are available to make this institution succeed.

If society wants the symphony—and other nonprofit institutions—to do more with less, then the approach we are discussing will be of interest, because it is simple, practical, and affordable. It works with both little and big institutions. It enhances donors' sense of predictability. It opens the door to better analysis and more effective research. And it offers new and different approaches to long-standing systemic issues that create the underlying conditions that we experience as symptoms.

Since we believe that the most important strategic issue for the vast majority of nonprofit organizations is that they lack access to the working capital that they need, we recommend a variety of strategies that can increase the amount of working capital available to nonprofit institutions.

In Part Three, we explore strategies currently being used to generate working capital. We also propose some new approaches to place more working capital in the hands of nonprofit institutions.

PART THREE

FINANCIAL FUTURES IN THE CURRENT WORLD OF PHILANTHROPY

Access to working capital is certainly one of the most important issues confronting nonprofit organizations today. Our cash flow–based approach to obtaining working capital is completely incremental. You can use just part of it or you can take it to the limits we discuss in Part Three. Our approach builds progressively, so each step in the process sets the stage for the next.

Some organizations do nothing more than adopt a cash flow budget as a supplement to the conventional budgets that they are asked for all the time. Other organizations integrate the cash flow principles and tools that we offer and create financial strategies that save them time and money. The creditholder concept, which at first seems a little odd, has been embraced by scores of institutions. Decision makers have found that having a liquid asset at hand is a wonderful way to ensure a warm welcome from their banker. This is especially nice when it comes time to set up a line of credit. When disaster strikes, the use of term debt that is fully secured by creditholders has been a lifesaver for many organizations in trouble.

In the same vein, a grasp of cash flow thinking using the Real Estate Calculator and the Cash Flow Forecaster is particularly useful when board and staff members want answers to financial questions. And having a sense of the value of using credit instead of building an endowment or large cash reserves leads some organizations to prosper in creative ways.

Throughout this book we have placed special emphasis on strategies that promote self-sufficiency for nonprofit organizations. Being able to go to your local bank for a line of credit when you need to bridge gaps in operating support is certainly something that is well within the power of even the smallest organization. The same can be said for managing risk with credit rather than with accumulations of costly capital. Our approach is designed to be directly applicable for both large and small institutions that wish to use their own resources to obtain unrestricted working capital. It demands that decision makers think about money in a new way, but that seems a small price to pay for increased fiscal security.

In this final section of the book, we explore the issue of access to working capital on a different level. For some nonprofit decision makers, these ideas may seem a bit removed from their daily reality. Trust us, the comments that we make here are highly applicable to every nonprofit organization regardless of size.

Our assessments of philanthropy are firmly rooted in the basic cash flow principles that we present throughout this book. Using the concepts of the cost of money, the role of inflation, and the impact of time and timing, cash flow thinking allows us a new lens with which to understand contemporary philanthropy. And all nonprofit organizations today operate within a broader context that is heavily influenced by concepts of what constitutes useful philanthropy.

In the chapters of Part Three, we explore how norms in the system of philanthropy and the wider society act as constraints on nonprofit organizations' efforts to obtain working capital. Foundations, government agencies, corporations, donor-directed funds, and individual donors provide only a small portion of the working capital needed by nonprofit institutions.

Philanthropy as an approach to address vital issues in society has adopted a curious position. One of the most commonly cited statements—"We are not interested in providing funds for day-to-day operations"—is a financial obstacle for many institutions seeking to fulfill their mission. This leads us to an issue that we have been advocating throughout the book:

- *Nonprofit institutions need higher levels of working capital to fulfill their mission.*

As one means to obtaining unrestricted dollars for operations, more and more nonprofit institutions are pursuing earned revenue activities. We examine some of the challenges facing social entrepreneurship and propose some alternatives that go beyond the recommendations we have made up to this point.

One strategy that we propose is a simple piece of legislation to make billions of dollars of working capital available to large and small nonprofit institutions. The legislation would compensate society for the deductions accorded to charitable contributions by encouraging the investment of tax-deducted dollars in projects and programs that benefit the public.

For those with an appetite for engaging with the legislative process, our strategy should be fun to contemplate as a worthwhile way to accomplish some important reforms in our society. For those who like to stay at arm's length from the political fray, our strategies may only provide an amusing topic for the next panel at the annual conference. Rest assured, you can still use our cash flow thinking in ways that work best for your institution, without having to plunge into political strife.

Finally, foundations and donor-directed funds contribute only a portion of the gifts and grants obtained each year by nonprofit organizations. Clearly there is a need to go beyond the boundaries of the philanthropic world to expand access to working capital. This leads to our final area of consideration:

- *Nonprofit institutions must reach beyond the world of philanthropy to a much broader basis of societal support.*

We propose the creation of new financial markets that focus on the public interest, in contrast to markets that serve corporate interests. These markets already exist in specialized areas, such as housing and student loans. They use conventional financing procedures through local banking institutions to provide loans. These loans are aggregated, converted to bonds, and sold upstream to investors. As a response to public needs, this mechanism has already demonstrated remarkable success in addressing social problems. The use of markets to provide home loans for people formerly defined as uncreditworthy, or student loans to assist individuals in attending college, are immediate examples. Experiences with micro-credit in the international arena reinforce the value of credit-based concepts. These can serve as an alternative to the current system of philanthropy, with its emphasis on grants to the few and preoccupation with chasing investment returns in the commercial marketplace.

It's a whole new world opening up, and you can glimpse it in the coming chapters. We hope that you see a role for yourself as you explore the role of cash flow thinking in the days ahead.

CHAPTER SEVENTEEN

EARNED REVENUE AND DISCOUNTS

We live in an entrepreneurial society, so it's not surprising that administrators and their board members are likely to be champions of earned revenue strategies. However, the key is to make sure that earned revenue strategies are in fact strategic. By this we mean that they actually generate unrestricted income without demanding more time and energy than they are worth.

To see the strategic aspects of earned revenue approaches, it is necessary to explore the link between earned revenue for access to unrestricted funds and the overall impact that this has on an institution's cash flow. The school holds an auction, the hospital has a white elephant sale, the environmental group sells 100 percent organic T-shirts. All these efforts are attempts to raise more unrestricted money.

In this chapter we explore some of the constraints to earning revenue and offer a few cautionary notes about nonprofit earned income strategies. We demonstrate how focusing on cash flow helps highlight the importance of working capital to nonprofit organizations—which brings us back to the cost of money as an operational issue.

Everybody loves a bargain, but the question is, *At what cost?* We feature a small section on this generous though sometimes misguided tendency for nonprofits to give away the store by offering deep discounts.

In "The Looking-Glass World of Nonprofit Money," Clara Miller notes that at a time when both government and philanthropy are encouraging all sorts of social enterprise and earned income models in the nonprofit sector, the "world of nonprofit management needs to be better understood."[1] Miller writes that non-profit organizations are placed in a difficult position when it comes to relating their prices to the expenses that they incur. In commercial ventures you close an un-profitable business, but in the nonprofit sector this lack of profit is just par for the course. Mission drives nonprofits, and as a result institutions continue to offer shelter, medical care, disaster relief, and other services to people who are unable to pay for them.

Moreover, other factors contribute to the lack of profitability. As noted ear-lier, much of the nonprofit field is labor intensive or requires highly skilled prac-titioners. It also suffers from the loss of economies of scale. You can't simply ramp up the numbers in the quest for profitability. Miller sums up the problem neatly: "If we increase class sizes to 100, all kindergartens will be profitable."

And it is not just profitability that influences the decisions made in the non-profit arena. Although administrators must be attuned to the regulations that apply to grants, some board members are not aware that grants often come with *strings*—assorted restrictions—attached to them. Fewer are aware of the tax implications of unrelated earned revenue in the nonprofit sector.

In many nonprofit situations, third parties—government agencies, founda-tions, individuals, or corporate contribution committees—dictate how their money will be spent on the consumers of the service. The consumers of nonprofit ser-vices are often the elderly, the homeless, parentless children, impoverished adults, and others without the means to pay the full cost of the service. Other consumers are better off, but may still be unwilling to pay for the full cost of the opera, or their children's private school education. Third parties make up the difference in much of the nonprofit world, and as the old saying goes, "The one who pays the piper calls the tune." In the nonprofit world the role of third-party payers re-moves some of the administrative discretion characteristic of commercial ven-tures. This, in turn, means that when nonprofit organization board and staff members decide to develop commercial-style enterprises, their choices and their decision-making powers may not match those in the purely commercial fields.

Perhaps the most obvious example of these constraints is illustrated by the decision to set prices in the nonprofit enterprise. In the nonprofit sector, prices to consumers are often inelastic, regardless of who pays. Just how much more can children or low-income people be expected to pay? The consequence is that as more service is provided, the financial position of nonprofits can be seriously com-promised. It is the moral imperative, rather than any expectation of profit, that keeps nonprofit staff on the job.

Miller makes the key point that price inelasticity presents a double jeopardy situation for management. The problem is that there is a lack of profit-generated working capital to fund growth and a continuing need for larger subsidies as growth takes place.

Subsidizing the Lack of Working Capital

To make up for their lack of access to working capital, nonprofits tend to develop subsidy businesses. Losses in the mission-driven component stimulate the creation of secondary businesses. These are meant to make up the difference in unrestricted funds between income from other sources and expenses. As a consequence, bake sales, special events, parking lots, gift shops, bookstores, and bingo are scattered across the nonprofit landscape. Of course, the auction and even the car wash have costs of their own, and these only add to the complexity of the administration of nonprofits. Yet these secondary activities are so completely integrated into our thinking about earned revenue that many board members focus their attention almost exclusively on mini-enterprises of this type.

As noted earlier, it costs money to raise money and to earn money. The vast majority of large businesses in American society operate with a relatively small margin of profit. Margins of 5 percent, 6 percent, or 7 percent are not uncommon in the ranks of competitive corporations. Do nonprofits, already strapped for cash, have the money to invest in running a store that will bring in a surplus of less than 10 percent? Many do not, and those that do often fail to grasp how time-consuming and demanding successful business undertakings can be. Will the time and effort devoted to obtaining revenue be a drain on the organization and the social purpose for which the organization was chartered? In other words, when does the quest for income overwhelm the mission of the institution?

In boardrooms across the country, earned revenue strategies are hatched and fueled by the idea that nonprofits can be more efficient than businesses. The role of volunteers is often cited in these discussions. Volunteers admittedly reduce some costs, but they also add costs through turnover and the need for flexible scheduling and efficient coordination. In the short run, volunteerism may be great, but in an entrepreneurial environment, in the long run it is not necessarily more cost-effective than a paid workforce.

Administrators who try to find ways to streamline the core activities that generate earned revenue must be alert to the dynamics of service-related enterprises. One of the paradoxes of the service sector is that as the supply of facilities and practitioners increases, demand often increases too. A glance at public education or health care demonstrates how this phenomenon works. Providing more doctors and medical services seems to condition consumer expectations to demand more and often more expensive service. For administrators dealing with this circumstance, the delicate balance between cost cutting or costly reinvestment must be part of the strategic equation.

Here again, the Cash Flow Forecaster can benefit decision makers by allowing them to create different income and expense scenarios rapidly. Sensitivity to trends and patterns of cash flow that are at odds with expectations can be very useful to administrators who are struggling to understand why sometimes expenses appear to be outpacing income, even as income increases due to greater utilization of services.

After the grantmaking wave of the 1970s, a new interest in earned revenue swept across the nonprofit sector. All sorts of schemes were proposed and adopted. Many of them generated income, but often at great cost to the sponsoring organizations.

Why Offering Discounts May Not Be a Good Idea

One of the characteristics of earned revenue strategies in the nonprofit world is that they are often accompanied by a desire to induce attendance or sales by offering discounts. The hospital gift store offers a 20 percent discount to individuals who have joined the hospital foundation membership. The social service agency holds an annual yard sale that features a 25 percent discount to anyone who has contributed funds in the past year. The color catalogue from the environmental group offers a substantial discount for purchasers of fair trade products. The examples of discounting are endless.

Perhaps nowhere in the nonprofit world is the practice of offering discounts on a regular basis more evident than in the subscription campaigns run by nonprofit theaters, operas, symphonies, and ballet companies. Subscription campaigns have a short and checkered history. They were conceived as a way to fill seats and the organization's coffers to cover seasonal deficits and to front the costs for new productions. Instead, they have proven to be costly and, in many ways, questionable as a financial strategy.

Here's why. When an organization offers a discount of, say, 15 percent to subscribers, it is taxing itself at a higher rate of interest than a bank might charge to lend. Added to the discount are the costs of the subscription campaign, which can be as much as 5 percent of the annual budget. Having two campaigns, one for fundraising and the other for subscribers, frequently confuses both donors and subscribers.

One evening, we got a call at dinner from a local theater asking us to subscribe, offering a 15 percent discount to do so. I assumed that this campaign probably cost at least 5 percent to conduct, so the net cost to the theater was 20 percent.

Less than an hour later, we got a call from another telemarketing firm, working for the same theater, telling us how much our donation was needed to cover costs. We did a little math on the phone, and, sure enough, the difference was close to 20 percent. I suggested that the theater not offer financial discounts, but the person on the other end of the phone wanted a pledge, not free advice.

The next day, I called the manager of the theater and made an appointment to discuss this interesting paradox. During our meeting, I asked how the theater's board and staff had arrived at a 15 percent discount. He said the number had sounded like it would be a good inducement to prospective subscribers.

At that point in the discussion, I explained that I had, some years earlier, conducted an informal survey of subscribers in a citywide assessment of subscription campaigns. My results suggested that few subscribers were greatly influenced by the discounting of their ticket price. In fact, the vast majority told me that they supported their cultural institutions and liked to subscribe in order to get preferential seating or greater flexibility in ticket exchange, and would be just as happy to get a nonfinancial perk such as a cup of good coffee and a cookie at intermission, or more flexible ticket exchange, or invitations to special events. I suggested that the theater check with its own subscribers to confirm or deny my statements. I pointed out that my research indicated that the people who are most price-sensitive are the single-ticket purchasers. Yet most theaters charge them the highest prices and offer them the least benefits.

"Drop the financial discounts," I said, "and serve them fresh roasted coffee and cookies instead." The theater manager eyed me coldly and said, "Just how do you propose that I find the money I need to pay off last year's deficit and to pay for this year's productions?" I answered, "Look, form a creditholder group who will support your mission; then go to the bank and engage in a little fully secured borrowing. See if your budget and balance sheet don't look better in a year. Get your money below prime, rather than paying the equivalent of 20 percent in interest through all those discounts and campaign costs."

Together we did the math, and the figures were impressive. The theater manager said he would try it, and as I was leaving I suggested that he drop day-of-performance single-ticket prices for a while to bring in new audience members and see if attendance increased. A year later, the theater was functioning much better, having effected each of these changes, and its telemarketers called us only once to solicit funds—of course, still in the middle of supper.

Leaving the arts aside for a moment, there are some very straightforward reasons why nonprofit organizations should carefully weigh the benefits of discounting when they attempt to earn revenue. Financial discounting that is not accompanied by serious attention to the cost in relation to its benefit frequently results in time and effort being wasted with little gain. Establishing discounts as part of supplemental earned revenue activities without carefully surveying the market for the goods or services may lead to providing benefits to those who do not need them. For a nonprofit institution to subsidize people who can afford to pay full price seems illogical when every dollar of earned revenue is so difficult to come by. Finally, discounting is a self-imposed form of taxation. It raises questions about decision makers' not weighing all the choices available to them when deciding to participate in an activity whose stated purpose is to raise unrestricted funds for a worthwhile cause.

There is a tremendous curiosity about earned revenue in the nonprofit field and a substantial literature has developed that provides encouragement and some helpful tips. Much of this activity seems to us to be evoked by a desire on the part of nonprofit institutions and their supporters to find a self-determined method to mobilize working capital. This makes complete sense when the funding environment is as turbulent as it has been in recent years. In Chapter Eighteen, we offer an approach based on cash flow to address many of these same issues, but on a very different level.

CHAPTER EIGHTEEN

CASH FLOW STRATEGIES AND PHILANTHROPY TODAY

Turning an eye to the world of philanthropy, cash flow sensibility brings new insights. In this chapter we take a hard look at the track record of U.S. philanthropy, exploring the efficiency of an approach that has financialized giving. The accumulation of capital by large nonprofit institutions and their methods for managing their money also comes under criticism from a cash flow perspective. Our intent is to suggest changes in the rules of the game, rules that characterize philanthropy in the United States. And to make this practical, we propose specific steps that can be taken to help these ideas become a reality.

Changing the rules promises a significant increase in the amount of working capital available to nonprofit organizations to pursue their mission. We believe that the consequences of these changes will have a profound effect on nonprofit institutions and will enhance the quality of life for everyone.

The Track Record of Philanthropy

A glance at the record of U.S. philanthropy should be enough to demonstrate why capital accumulation is an inadequate strategy for accomplishing social purposes. As a corporate form, philanthropy, in the modern sense, is three-quarters of a century old. In many respects, it has not proven successful in solving fundamental social concerns, despite being one of the key sectors designated to address these issues.

The problem, as both critics and advocates agree, is that there is simply not enough money to address complex issues. Yet this is only true if one accepts the conventional way in which funding institutions have chosen to handle their money. Foundations and donor-directed funds emphasize investment. From a fraction of the investment interest, grants are made. Given this system of managing capital, it is no surprise that funders are always having to say no to most applicants. Existing money management practices clearly dictate a shortage of money compared to the working capital needs of the nation's nonprofit organizations.

Currently, the assets of nonprofit organizations, including institutional endowments and foundations, are valued at over $2.1 trillion.[1] However, less than 5 percent of the invested portion of these financial assets is available to be spent on mission-related activities in any one year. Too little money, particularly in relation to inflation, is available within the system to meet the needs of most individual institutions and the social, cultural, and environmental purposes they address.

The 1998 study conducted by the Internal Revenue Service Division on Statistics of Income is worth another look, particularly for its observation that the financial assets of the nonprofit sector are heavily skewed toward the largest 5 percent of nonprofit institutions. They held close to 90 percent of the financial assets of the sector and derived close to 80 percent of the revenues. The IRS study further demonstrates that the pool of all gifts and grants available to the nonprofit world is not increasing as fast as the rate of inflation in the nonprofit sector. The pie is not growing fast enough for the current population of nonprofits, and more nonprofit organizations are being added to the rolls each year.

At a time when the need for access to funds for operations has never been greater, the current system of philanthropy simply does not provide adequate resources for most institutions. This situation is growing ever more troubling, and it will not decline in importance unless a sea change such as the one proposed in this book is undertaken.

Defining Issues in Modern Philanthropy

Judging from the heated debate and the flood of new reports on the topic, one of the current hot-button issues in philanthropy is the percentage of assets that foundations are required to give to charities each year.

Some watchdog organizations are trying to pressure grant makers to increase their payout rate by a percentage point or two. Others have testified at congressional hearings to eliminate rising administrative costs from the payout calculation. Foundations steadfastly respond that any increase in the current 5 percent level will seriously threaten their ability to exist in perpetuity.

That the rhetoric and resistance surrounding the issue is so intense is surprising, because in the grander scheme of things, the stakes are low. Rather than quibble over payout, the time has come for nonprofit organizations and their congressional allies to urge foundations, financial service businesses with donor-directed funds, and the largest 5 percent of nonprofit organizations to use their invested funds as a source of working capital for other nonprofits. Currently these funds are invested in Wall Street, in offshore hedge funds, and in many other ventures, mostly commercial. Clearly we need to question the logic of this allocation of resources that steers the majority of the invested funds away from the nonprofit sector.

For years, we have been told that the investment of assets and the distribution of a portion of the interest earned is an efficient and effective means to deal with social and cultural concerns. But the 1998 IRS study reveals that this approach is not working. According to the study, roughly 93 percent of the accumulated assets of foundations and approximately 55 percent of the assets of larger nonprofit groups are in various forms of savings and investments. Relatively little of that capital is directed to accomplishing social purposes. Instead, a pattern of hoarding has developed. The result is that illness, hunger, and homelessness are permitted to stand side by side with unimaginable accumulations of wealth by large nonprofit institutions. As endowments grow, tuitions continue to climb, the costs of health care rise, and the gap between the haves and the have-nots continues to spread.

A fundamental rethinking of how available capital can best be used to fulfill social goals is needed. And that requires a reexamination of philanthropy's underlying premises and practices: the basic rules of philanthropy.

Rules develop for a variety of reasons. One of the established rules of philanthropy is the notion of investing contributed money and paying out a portion of the marginal interest that is earned each year. This is a financial policy that emerged during the early days of the last century, when modern philanthropy was being born. This rule was consistent with the transformation of charity to philanthropy. It reflected a growing tendency to see the world in both corporate and financial terms.

In this metamorphosis, acts of kindness directed at the poor, the suffering, the uneducated, the orphans, and the widows were deemed by the founders of the new philanthropy to be less than sufficient. These worthies decided to change the face of charity by introducing corporate sensibilities. The idea that charity needed to be tempered by a scientific rationalism has created today's landscape of foundations, and more recently the financial market-assisted donor-directed funds. All of these instruments of philanthropy use the investment and payout model, much to the disadvantage of the aforementioned orphans and widows.

The Downside of Investment-Powered Philanthropy

It's all about time. Suppose we focus on little Kim, a child who is starving. Current philanthropy, if it is willing to provide support at all to a nonprofit seeking to assist Kim, offers the institution an opportunity to compete with other institutions to acquire a grant from a pool of funds that constitutes roughly 3.5 cents on the dollar. After all, the nickel-on-a-dollar return characteristic of conservative investments has to be reduced by the money management fees, the administrative expenses of providing grants, and all that other overhead that goes into sustaining the lifestyle of the foundation, or of the financial services industry. Kim is likely to die before anyone finds the funds for a square meal. This example is not meant to hector the funders, rather it demonstrates that many social concerns, like hunger, natural disasters, and manmade violence require an immediate response. The need for services is inherently time based.

Michael Porter and Mark Kramer's calculation that a dollar placed in an endowment, a donor-directed fund, or in a foundation will return a social value equal to a dollar in somewhere between forty and a hundred years has to count for something. Remember, the same dollar contributed and spent this year generates a social value of one dollar. The time measures reflected in this calculation, between the value of the invested dollar and the dollar that is spent this year for mission, are actually quite profound.[2]

Say you donate one dollar to a foundation or to an endowment. That dollar will probably be invested in Wall Street, and perhaps a nickel or less will be used to accomplish a social, cultural, or environmental purpose. You, however, will receive a tax credit for your contribution that can reach as high as 50 cents on your dollar. You feel good about your giving and ignore the full consequences of your act.

But there is another way of thinking about this. Every time Bill and Melinda Gates contribute a dollar to their foundation, we all forgo 50 cents in tax revenues that might have been used for other purposes. In effect, American taxpayers are subsidizing an approach to philanthropy that rewards this behavior with a 50 percent deduction, even though the consequence is that the investment and payout approach locks away 95 cents and contributes less than 5 cents per year to address social and cultural issues. As if that were not unfortunate enough, the foundation is allowed to deduct the cost of money management fees, administrative overhead to make grants, and an inflation-fighting percentage that gets returned to the investment pool. In short, the nickel becomes roughly three and a half cents in a hurry.

Someone who really understands that time and money are linked is Warren Buffet, the investor par excellence. Buffet recently made headlines when he agreed to donate the bulk of his $44 billion fortune to the Bill and Melinda Gates Foundation and four other philanthropies. What is so interesting, from a cash flow perspective, is that Buffet did not give the money to the Gates Foundation to hold until the next Ice Age. Instead, he mandated that his annual contributions must be spent within the year they are received. The value of time and money are inextricably merged in his generosity.

Shortly after the news reports of Warren Buffet's gifts were released, the Gates Foundation came under intense scrutiny in a January 7, 2007, article that took the foundation to task for funding good works with returns from firms that contribute to social ills.[3] At issue were the paradoxical policies of the world's largest foundation. While the efforts of the philanthropic side of the institution were being commended, the investment of its endowment in holdings was criticized as reaping vast financial gains every year from investments that contravened its good works.

This double-edged sword of investment and grant making is the signature of contemporary philanthropy. More on this point later, but for now, it's worth a glance at the people who handle most of the investments in the nonprofit endowment and foundation sectors. The world of commercial markets is dominated by greed and fear, according to all the pundits who routinely write about the investment community. Does it really make sense to send the hard-won dollars that have been rendered tax-exempt for charitable purposes to Wall Street? Placing large and small investments in the hands of the greed-and-fear guys seems odd, when you consider that the nonprofit world and its foundation friends are supposed to be all about selflessness and hope.

Greed and altruism, fear and hope, these are counterbalancing factors in understanding some of the tensions that characterize contemporary philanthropy.[4] This is a genuine problem, in part, because of the motivation of high-end donors. Lucy Bernholz, in her book *Creating Philanthropic Capital Markets: The Deliberate Evolution*, notes the mixed motivation of the Rockefellers in attempting to decide how to handle their vast wealth.

> The factors in these kinds of calculations—the ability to provide for
> future generations, the opportunity to build (or continue) a family tradition
> of philanthropy, avoidance of income, estate, or inheritance taxes, the
> exemption of assets, pursuing a social purpose or making a contribution
> back to the community remain key elements in philanthropic decision
> making.[5]

These are all competing and in some cases paradoxical concerns. Yet philanthropy is a curious form of charity. Most of the money is locked away, and a trifle is granted annually. The current rules of the game, rules reflected in the practice of investment and payout, ensure that the poor, the infirm, the undereducated, the homeless, and those poisoned by environmental degradation will always be with us.

The idea that the principal vehicle for generating philanthropy would be a trust fund seems intuitively sensible. After all, doesn't everyone want a trust fund? It's probably true that those of us who do not have one would love a trust fund. Daddy or Mum's solicitor would act on our behalf, investing all that money in blue chips, while we lived graciously on the interest. Living—perhaps not as grandly as we would like—but still well enough to stifle our spouse's whining and incur the gentle envy of our friends.

It's also true that excesses abound in the society around us. If you haven't looked at yachting magazines lately (with their multimillion-dollar custom-designed, high-performance floating palaces) you really should see what the wealthy are up to these days. These examples of flagrant conspicuous consumption notwithstanding, the metaphor of a trust fund, with investment and payout, has come to dominate the hopes and dreams of many American nonprofiteers, whether board or staff. It is the metaphor of choice for most private foundations and the investment committees of institutional endowments.

Call us puritans, but we believe that this ill-suited model has some terribly painful consequences for institutions and for the communities that they serve. Because, unlike individuals with trust funds, nonprofit institutions have real needs that exceed the sub-nickel returns from the stock market.

If we define the problem confronting nonprofit institutions as lack of money, then the current approach to the investment and payout of accumulated capital has some small merit. After all, any money is better than no money, and a small-ish amount of money year after year certainly seems desirable on first glance. The problem, as we see it, is stacking up the money available each year in relation to the needs that are out there.

Less than a nickel on the dollar is simply not nearly adequate to address the concerns that today's nonprofits confront, and there is no reason to believe that it will be adequate in the future. After all, with almost three-quarters of a century of experience, this system has contributed to an enormous inequity between small and large institutions. The rich institutions keep on getting richer, even as many of them hoard funds and manage their money inefficiently. The smaller organizations struggle with inadequate resources, even as they emulate the larger institutions in their quest for cash reserves, endowments, and the ownership of facilities and equipment.

The chief beneficiaries of philanthropy, under the investment and payout model, are the corporations and the stock markets. As we have seen, the nonprofit sector has a great deal of money—and a great deal of that money is invested in corporations. Without seeming pessimistic, the corporate grasp of the global economy—as Nareena Hertz in *The Silent Take Over* and David Korten in *The Post-Corporate World* note—comes at a heavy price to the world's populations and its resources.[6] The amount of spendable money available to nonprofits is a fraction of the assets being invested in Wall Street, offshore hedge funds, and other venues that produce little or no social, cultural, or environmental benefit—and in some cases are just making the problem much worse.

Again, we believe the problem confronting nonprofit institutions is not a lack of money, but rather a lack of access to working capital. Is this just a matter of semantics? We believe that it is not.

Access to working capital—to the money needed to operate—is a complex matter, with many facets. In a broad sense, however, we believe that these complexities can be reduced to some fundamental issues. Working capital can be obtained in a variety of ways, by raising money through gifts and grants, by earning money, and by borrowing.

Gifts and grants are vital to the existence of most nonprofit institutions and will continue to be important in the foreseeable future. Our problem is not with fundraising and all the perfectly excellent people who make their living as development officers. Rather, it is with the wider system of money management that doles out the dough. Given the prohibition on investment in the nonprofit world created by the nondistribution clause of the IRS regulations, the next logical source of working capital is from gifts and grants. Part of the problem is that the nice institutional folks making those grants (mainly at foundations, but increasingly in donor-directed funds lodged in stock brokerages and other financial service providers) have only a very small percentage of their fund's wealth available to be used for social purposes. This is because the lion's share of the money is dedicated to investment, not to achieving any direct benefit in the social, cultural, or environmental arenas.

Another component of the problem is the willingness of nonprofit institutions to solicit and then hoard contributions that could be used to accomplish the demands of mission, rather than feathering the institution's nest as cash reserves and endowments. It is not the act of raising the funds that we challenge, it is the allocation of raised resources to inefficient and ineffective accounts.

For many nonprofit institutions, earned revenue, coupled with gifts and grants, constitutes the bulk of each year's income. Yet earning this money can be difficult, and sometimes it is just not profitable for nonprofit institutions. The commercial sector provides countless depressing examples of the kinds of margins that can be expected from earnings, after the costs of business are paid. The use of profits as a significant source of working capital is hard to justify as a business strategy for most nonprofits. In the past, large medical insurers, such as Blue Cross of California, have been willing to leave large sums of money on the table, multiple millions in some cases, to shift from tax-exempt status to for-profit status. Why? Because they have determined that access to working capital from the marketplace is worth more to them in the long run than the advantages of their tax-exempt status. In their own words, they need capital from money markets to compete.

Social entrepreneurship is a hot topic in the nonprofit conference circuit right now. Pundits and earnest young entrepreneurial visionaries point to the opportunities available for nonprofit organizations to increase their earned revenue. And some of the arguments for more earned revenue sound pretty good, but time and time again, the lack of access to the private capital market inhibits the dreams of these Horatio Algers of the nonprofit world.

Cash Flow Perspective

Observers note that three types of capital are generally required by nonprofit institutions:

- Capital for facilities, to fund the building or acquisition of buildings or equipment
- Permanent capital for endowments and capital reserves as well as the pools of money that community development organizations use to invest in housing and business development
- Working capital to cover expenses during periods of low cash flow or to fund strategic investments in the organization's capacity[7]

Since we have a cash flow perspective, we would like nonprofits to do the math on the ownership of facilities and equipment, and consider whether some form of leasing is a suitable option for them. If it is, then money that was formerly required for buildings and equipment might just be used for program purposes. After the rent is paid, of course.

You already know what we think about the inefficiency of endowments and cash reserves. In addition, we believe community development organizations will be able to more readily acquire funds to invest in housing and business development directly from the capital markets created to accommodate the investment of the portfolios of foundations, donor-directed financial service providers, and institutional endowments.

Nonprofit organizations and philanthropists might want to consider meeting halfway. But before nonprofit organizations address the philanthropists, a little cleaning of the nonprofit stables, capital-wise, is necessary. So, let's think about cutting way down on the capital campaigns, the endowments, the cash reserves, and the holdings, and see if we can't enlist our colleagues in talking about options that increase the amount of working capital available to us.

Now, you probably won't hear applause from the money managers at the foundations, the investment managers running the donor-directed funds, or the investment committee at Yale as we suggest a new approach to enable nonprofits to gain access to working capital. That's the one form of capital that most everyone, but not us, believes is the hardest to raise. We demur on this point, because we believe that once we as a nation decide to get a fair share for the public interest, working capital will be much more plentiful.

CHAPTER NINETEEN

CASH FLOW STRATEGIES AND PHILANTHROPY TOMORROW

All strategy must have a purpose and a goal. In this chapter, we discuss a simple yet potentially powerful new idea for affording greater access to working capital for nonprofit institutions.

As we note in the Preface, our approach to financial management comes down to one statement: all you need to do is understand and manage your cash flow, learn how to bridge gaps or deal effectively with surpluses, and work to make all the resources in the nonprofit world flow more efficiently.

If you have followed our step-by-step approach to cash flow thinking, you are now prepared to consider financial management in a new way. The tools and principles in this book will assist you in doing just that. Your institution will be self-sufficient if you adopt cash flow strategies in your own approach to financial management.

For many decision makers, our methods and tools will be used to expand their organization's range of fiscal choices. For others, the final aspect of our approach may be especially appealing, in a different sort of way. It now seems clear that making all the resources in the nonprofit world flow more efficiently is in everyone's best interest. To do this, individuals from many sectors of society need to agree that it makes sense to change the rules to allow greater access to working capital for nonprofit institutions.

This is not to say that each person reading this book needs to subscribe to this idea, we hardly expect that. Instead, we would simply like to offer a seat on the bus to anyone who cares to join us. For those not riding, the cash flow thinking, the tools and the principles, will still work well for any institution that adopts them. The immediate benefits of cash flow thinking will show up as increased efficiency and effectiveness. Everyone will have a better understanding of their organization's financial documents. The budgeting, forecasting, and monitoring functions will be significantly streamlined and improved. The opportunity to create a creditholder group to provide collateral will mean the bankers will welcome the groups' requests for a line of credit or a term loan. Organizations will be able to use credit as an alternative to cash reserves or costly endowments, and real estate and earned revenue strategies will be sharpened by cash flow sensibilities.

All these results and more are possible for decision makers who chose to adopt cash flow thinking. For those with a desire to see improvements in the larger system, the simple rule change we propose here may take a little longer.

Changing One Rule of the Game

How can changing one rule afford greater access to working capital across the board? We know that foundations and endowment funds invest the majority of their funds in stocks, bonds, and other assets that provide a portion of the total capital available to corporations and other commercial enterprises. So here's our idea:

> Mandate that funds that have been granted tax-exempt privilege
> be invested in activities associated with the public good.

In other words, ask Congress to change the rules so as to keep the money in the nonprofit world, within the sector that benefits mankind or local communities rather than multinational corporations. We propose that this legislation be called "A Fair Share for the Public Interest Act."

The legislation would state that any contributed funds received by a nonprofit institution and retained for more than two years would need to be fully invested in bonds and other financial instruments issued to create working capital for organizations that qualify for credit in the nonprofit sector.

To allow time for the markets to ramp up the working capital needs of the nonprofit world, in the first five years, 25 percent of the new contributions to foundations, endowments, or donor-directed funds would be invested in these efforts. The percentage of increased participation would rapidly accelerate after the first five years. By the seventh year, 75 percent of the portfolios would be invested in the nonprofit sector, and by the tenth year, 100 percent would be invested in capital markets designed to benefit nonprofit institutions.

Please note we are not suggesting that anyone take a penny away from any foundation, endowment, or donor-directed financial service firm. We are simply proposing legislation that would require that any funds held more than two years be invested in activities that directly benefit the public interest.

One short-term alternative for endowments, funds, and foundations that have been formed with company stock or other commercial investments that they are loath to relinquish would be to allow them to insure the borrowing of nonprofit institutions. Over the ten-year period, all the commercial investments held by these endowments, funds, or foundations would be gradually committed to serving the public good.

By changing this one rule, capital that enjoys a tax deduction to fulfill social purposes would be compounded in its social value. After all, this is just asking for a fair share for the public interest in exchange for the tax benefits obtained by donors. In this way, the public interest will be served, and funds set aside—by foundations, institutions, and financial service corporations—will be made available to the tax-exempt sector.

Apart from the struggle to obtain the legislation, the key to making this approach work is the willingness of nonprofit institutions to form creditholder groups to collateralize their borrowing. Imagine, the alumni of good old Tech U. banding together to create a collateral pool that would mean their beloved institution could borrow whenever it needed funds. Talk about the gift that lasts and lasts.

This idea is not as far-fetched or fanciful as it might first appear. It is in some ways like the charters to Fannie Mae or Sallie Mae, credit-based programs that have successfully made housing and student loans available to millions of U.S. citizens. Through insured or enhanced short-term and long-term credit, issued directly or indirectly by foundations, donor-directed funds, and large nonprofit endowments, working capital can be made available to financially strapped charities and other nonprofit institutions.

Access to Credit and Social Benefits

The case of the federal program that made security-backed mortgages available to middle-class people, known as the Ginnie Mae Pool No 1, is instructive. After issuing more than 380,000 mortgages over thirty years, the pool was closed in the year 2000, with only ten mortgages in default. The aggregate value of these defaulted mortgages was less than a motorcycle costs today. The notion that a bond-backed loan program could create the basis for a profound change in American home ownership—with bankers, investors, homeowners, and the government all winning—is a prime example of how well credit-based strategies are suited to dealing with social concerns.[1]

This new approach, of course, would require more American nonprofit groups to learn how to gain access to credit. Organizations would substitute borrowing and the use of credit for endowments, cash reserves, building and equipment ownership, and the attendant costly capital campaigns that each requires. Fundraising would still continue, although without emphasis on capital accumulation.

Under this new approach, businesses and entrepreneurs would be encouraged to invest in buildings and equipment that would be leased to nonprofit organizations. Given access to working capital, those nonprofits would be much more attractive as tenants. Indeed, a new class of social entrepreneurs would arise to become the owners of buildings and equipment used by nonprofit organizations. Such an arrangement would free nonprofit groups from the liability of ownership while giving them the benefit of controlling their space. What's more, it would provide a suitable and appropriate focus for community-minded, venture-oriented philanthropists.

Access to working capital is a perennial problem for nonprofit organizations. The costs and time associated with raising operating support are formidable, donor resistance to providing working capital is problematic, and increased competition for funds is driving up the cost of raising them. Over the past twenty years, available funds from all gifts and grants have barely kept pace with inflation. For small and midsized institutions, that has been especially burdensome. Being able to obtain working capital at the local bank will allow institutions to focus more directly on accomplishing their missions.

By using their assets both directly and indirectly to provide credit and working capital to smaller nonprofits, foundations and large institutions would be fulfilling their social purpose. They would also be operating with far lower levels of risk, since investing in securities will prove to be safer than playing around in a very volatile stock market. Among the investors in the bonds will be the foundations, donor-directed funds, and large nonprofit groups. From their earnings on these investments in a publicly focused market, foundations and funds would continue to give out grants to worthy organizations.

In short, a break from the old system of commercial investment and payout of marginal interest could ensure a much brighter future. With the use of credit and prudent borrowing by nonprofit organizations, more people could be served, and worthwhile goals that might have been thwarted by lack of funds would have a better chance of being achieved. In the end, such an innovation just might make everyone's lives simpler and easier.

Role of the Proposed Legislation in an Overall Plan

We believe that access to working capital—obtained by nonprofits using cash flow budgeting and forecasting—opens the door to the use of credit enhanced by insurance provided by the portfolios of foundations, endowments, and donor-directed financial service funds. This approach in turn opens the door to the creation of markets that can act as a powerful financial resource for nonprofit entities.

We envision the creation of special capital markets, markets set up to be used by commercial investors interested in owning the physical plant of the nonprofit world and by all nonprofits seeking working capital. The core investment in this market would be mandated to come from the billions of dollars currently held by private foundations, donor-directed investment funds, and nonprofit endowments.

Some bonds already are tax-exempt or are issued by nonprofit institutions. They may not be as sexy as high-tech offerings, but they tend to be less risky, and they are productive over time. Yet for most nonprofit organizations, entering these markets at scale is simply too expensive and complex to be worthwhile. So it's back to the bake sales and the dreams of a mysterious bequest that might solve all the institution's financial problems.

Clearly organizations face impediments to entering existing markets. By and large, nonprofits engage in activities that are not commercially viable. They are not going to earn the kinds of revenue that the markets—as they are currently configured—desire. But nonprofits, year in and year out, provide valuable services for which they obtain revenues, and the cash flow they deal with is not inconsequential. Colleges and universities, hospitals, private schools, and a host of other nonprofits have the means to use working capital to their advantage and also the means to repay their borrowing on a regular basis. What these nonprofits share is the inability to muster the kinds of assets that easily convert to a liquid form usable either as collateral or as inventory. Moreover, the scale of borrowing is small, relative to the size of commercial offerings.

Nonprofits that have their borrowing insured first by creditholders and then by foundations, endowments, financial service donor-directed funds, and other large capital pools will be much more attractive to markets. If tax-deductible funds are required to be invested in these markets, the volume of transactions should make it worthwhile for enterprising folks to create and manage these markets.

The fiduciary rules that money managers adhere to when it comes to maximizing returns for nonprofits may need to be modified for funds that have been given special license through their tax-exempt status. When claims are made that investments in offshore hedge funds are consistent with fiduciary rules, some serious questions need to be asked about the purpose those rules serve in addressing the public good. Or—to turn the argument around—if trustees follow conventional fiduciary rules to maximize profits, then normal rates of taxation should be applied to recapture the social benefits lost in the transaction.

The implications are fairly straightforward. The rules that appear to encourage the growth of only a small portion of the field's institutions would be challenged. A conceptual shift and an off-the-shelf mechanism—perhaps like the original Ginnie Mae or her much more sophisticated sisters—might help to alter the outcomes in the nonprofit world.

All private foundations and endowments held by the largest of the nonprofit institutions are the beneficiaries of a tax code that rewards contributions with substantial tax deductions. Capital accumulation in this country has been largely abetted by a tax code that creates incentives for people to donate money, particularly large sums of money, to philanthropic purposes. This proposal in no way should be seen as inhibiting the generosity of donors. Nor is it a call for an elimination of the federal tax credits that spur some larger gifts. Instead, by changing the rules, we can encourage capital that enjoys tax-exempt status to be invested in fulfilling social purposes. It makes working capital available to institutions that need to borrow. And because of the guarantees built into the system from the creditholders, the foundations, and the endowments, the money that is available as working capital should be reasonably inexpensive. As in other capital markets, when you remove risk, rewards tend to diminish and capital is less expensive.

Of course, nonprofit organizations will still have to raise funds and earn income. After all, cheap or not, borrowed funds still need to be paid back. However, the increased efficiency of using a borrowed dollar until an earned or raised dollar comes in will improve the financial functioning of most nonprofit institutions.

Productivity is being heralded as an aspect of the commercial economy that is driving the growth of our society. This is despite the growing prevalence of two-income families and the numbers of people working two and three jobs to make ends meet. Almost all of us are working longer hours than our parents did. Yet increases in productivity are hard to cite in the nonprofit sector. As William Baumol pointed out back in the 1960s, the nonprofit sector is very labor intensive. This is especially true in the arts and cultural arenas. You still need five players to perform Mozart's String Quintet in G Minor, just as you did in 1787.[2]

Or, for that matter, does anyone want to place more kids in overcrowded classrooms, or more patients in maxed-out emergency rooms? How many more clients can we add to existing caseloads for exhausted social workers? Labor is a fact of life in the nonprofit sector, at least until those marvelous new service robots enter the mainstream.

However, productivity in the nonprofit sector could be significantly increased if less time had to be spent on cobbling together emergency fund requests to raise the money to meet next week's payroll, or crafting unreadable financial reports that confound rather than illuminate the financial picture.

The current system of philanthropy is often unresponsive to applicants for its funds. Only a fraction of the proposals submitted are funded, and the usual reason stated is lack of money.

That leaves a couple of alternatives. You can believe that there really is too little money available and just accept your fate. Or you can keep doing the same thing, which means applying and applying and trying to be nice to foundation program officers on the few occasions when you have the opportunity to consort with them. Another alternative is to work hard for legislation to change the system— to work toward a change that actually encourages foundations and donor-directed funds as well as individual donors to direct their tax-exempt funds to benefit the nonprofit world.

A Better Tomorrow

Imagine a different tomorrow for U.S. nonprofit institutions. A future in which more mission is accomplished for less money. An economic environment in which social, cultural, and environmental concerns are featured along with the nightly news from Wall Street.

Consider what this future might look like in practical terms. It all starts with the individual nonprofit institution. The board and staff have a comfortable grasp of the institution's financial past, present, and future cash flow. They receive and comprehend financial reports that make sense to everyone because they are cash flow oriented. The reports translate into strategies for growth and development and also for managing risk.

By using a forecaster that projects money and time into the future, the institution uses its monthly actuals for income and expense to create rolling forecasts that address unexpected bumps in the road. Accrual accounting is still the norm for many institutions, and their accountants still report periodically to the board and staff and conduct institutional audits. Quarterly, or at the midpoint of the year, or annually, everyone sees the financial statements prepared by the accountants that reflect the assets and liabilities of the institution.

However, the board and staff rely on cash flow and cash flow reporting at their monthly meetings. The bookkeeper drops each month's income and expense actuals into the forecaster to help board and staff make strategic and corrective choices. The institution is lean; it does not accumulate capital that is not needed for its core mission. Instead, it relies on creditholders who support the mission of the organization by providing access to inexpensive and rapidly available credit through their placement of collateral in the institution's bank. An annual campaign, which is fully integrated into the annual giving program of the institution, ensures that creditholders as well as donors have an opportunity to participate in supporting the mission of the institution.

Access to working capital comes from the partnership formed by the institution with its bank, as a result of the high quality of collateral that is made available by the creditholders. The money to deal with immediate concerns is borrowed when needed and paid back when not. The banker is an ardent ally of the institution and is always on the lookout for opportunities in the community that will encourage and support the mission of the institution.

The institution owns little that is not disposable. It leases its space under a long-term agreement that is flexible and works well for both the organization and the landlord. In this case, the landlord is a small team of socially motivated investors who use their commercial skills and background to maximize their participation in a joint venture that brings benefits to them as well as to the institution that they support. The socially motivated investors talk among themselves all the time about metrics and quantifiable outcomes, but are sensible enough to drop the coded language when dealing with the nonprofit's board and staff, who frankly have better things to do with their time than adopt a new jargon.

When the institution applies to the local foundation, it is eligible for grants-in-aid just like any other applicant. It may or may not obtain funding. Some things never change, since the amount of spendable funds that the foundation has available each year is a function of an endowment that was established when Henry Ford was still offering the world any color Model T it wanted, so long as that color was black. This foundation participates in the nonprofit sector in two additional ways.

First, the foundation has made provision for a portion of its portfolio to be used to insure the bank-based borrowing of nonprofit institutions. In some cases it receives a modest fee for this insurance. Rather than setting up a program-related investment division, with all the costs and training associated with this process, the foundation relies on the experience and prudence of professional bankers, all trained and paid at someone else's expense. The bankers understand nonprofit organizations, since they are doing so much more business with them each year. They make bankable loans that can be packaged and sold upstream to investors, much like the mortgages that are handled by Fannie Mae.

Second, the foundation invests a majority of its funds in bonds that are offered as a result of borrowing by nonprofit institutions. It does this to accommodate a piece of legislation passed by Congress that says, in effect, if we, the American people, grant generous tax deductions for contributing to a foundation, donor-directed fund, or an institutional endowment, we expect that all these donated funds will be used to promote social, cultural, and environmental purposes in the public interest.

The money that becomes available as a result of this legislation stimulates a new market, one in which tax-exempt organizations find access to the working capital that they need. Whether the bonds are tax-exempt or not, the market is active, and annual reports on Harvard or the Sisters of Mercy Hospital are read with interest by investors and by analysts. The result of all this activity is that the lion's share of money that is in the hands of private foundations, financial service firms with donor-directed schemes, community foundations, or institutional endowments is used directly as working capital by the nonprofit sector.

Having a serious stake in the financial future of nonprofit institutions causes a different set of behaviors within the community of funders and donors. There is intense interest in making sure that nonprofits succeed, that they function effectively and fulfill their mission while remaining solvent. Technical assistance programs, underwritten by the funding sector, bring consultants a bonanza of new contracts. In this case, however, results are directly related to the ability of the nonprofit institutions to perform as economic entities able to meet their bond obligations. Consultants need to get beyond the ever-popular mission exercises or the eternal strategic planning retreats. Instead, a premium is placed on work that can be measured in financial terms.

The old ratio is reversed. Instead of the majority of the financial assets of the nonprofit world being invested in corporations and less than 5 percent made available for donations and grants, now virtually all the invested funds are available to provide working capital that drives the nonprofit sector forward. The remaining fraction, after all the administrative costs, money management fees, and other institutional overheads are deducted, is still available for grants.

The market that sells bonds to cover the borrowing of nonprofit institutions operates just like other markets. (There may be some scandals and abuses, just as in any other human endeavor. After all, hardly anyone makes the evening news for their good deeds, but gossip and bad behavior always capture a wider market of viewers.) This market, like the ones stimulated by the "Merry Maes," Fannie, Ginnie, and Sallie Mae, serves an important commercial purpose as well as a social purpose that brings benefits to the service sector and to the overall economy.

Investors buy these bonds, and for their participation, they get returns that are reasonable, if not heart-throbbingly high or low, and also the right to display a bumper sticker that proclaims their financial support for their favorite school, or hospital, or environmental cause, or whatever tickles their fiscal fancy.

Nonprofit organizations have access to the working capital that they need, and because so little of their money is used for accumulating capital in the form of cash reserves, endowments, buildings, or equipment, they are able to provide higher and higher levels of service, with high-quality jobs unlike the work that is being moved offshore by corporations more interested in profit than jobs back home. Pay scales start to climb, but that is a correction, not an indication of the greed that has settled as a permanent cloud on corporate compensation practices.

The services provided by nonprofit organizations, whether fee-based or grant-driven, allow for a greatly expanded sense of mission. Goals are set higher. Plans are crafted that have a realistic chance of succeeding, and people in communities throughout the nation and even across the planet are afforded the benefits of a sector that begins and ends with their needs and wishes.

Pretty picture? You bet it is, but it is also one that we can all work together to craft and realize. Just combine some cash flow, some collateral, some credit from the banks, a pinch of insurance, and some encouraging legislation to foster a market for working capital bonds, and this can become a reality, someday. In the meantime, seize the day and let's work together to make all the resources in the nonprofit world flow more efficiently.

Our purpose in writing this book is to provide new insights into money matters and practical information on managing money effectively and efficiently. Our goal is to help you obtain more mission for less money, by changing the way you think about money and its management.

We have talked at length about the importance of shifting to cash flow budgeting and forecasting. We have tried to make a case that borrowing—when it is fully secured by creditholders—is a reasonable alternative to cash reserves and endowments. We have attacked the notion of capital accumulation within the nonprofit sector and suggested that in some cases you might be better served to lease buildings and equipment rather than own them. Finally, we have posed some questions about the expectations that many have for earned revenue in the nonprofit world.

A simple piece of legislation designed to increase access to working capital for nonprofit institutions has been proposed. New markets can develop if this legislation is enacted. And those markets will serve the society and its institutional participants well. Cash flow strategies are the key to success in the nonprofit world.

NOTES

Chapter One

1. Yogi Berra in a television commercial, complete with quacking duck.
2. A. Levitt, *Take on the Street* (New York: Pantheon, 2002).
3. D. Gardner and T. Gardner, "The Motley Fool: Be Careful When It Comes to Accruals," *Seattle Post Intelligencer,* November 5, 2006.

Chapter Four

1. S. Strom, "After Years of Cash Flow, Universities Hit an Ebb," *New York Times,* March 13, 2003.
2. J. Hope and R. Fraser, *Beyond Budgeting: How Managers Can Break Free from the Annual Performance Trap* (Boston: Harvard Business School Press, 2003).
3. R. Lowenstein, *When Genius Failed: The Rise and Fall of Long-Term Capital Management* (New York: Random House, 2000).
4. J. Zweig, "Peter's Uncertainty Principle," *Money Magazine,* Nov. 2004, p. 144. For those who have not read Peter L. Bernstein's *Against the Gods: The Remarkable Story of Risk* (New York: Wiley, 1996), make a point of adding it to your list to understand the critical relationship between gambling and investing, all made possible by the development of probability theory.

Chapter Five

1. P. L. Bernstein, *Against the Gods: The Remarkable Story of Risk* (New York: Wiley, 1996), p. 6.
2. B. Mandelbrot, *The (Mis)Behavior of Markets: A Fractal View of Risk, Ruin, and Reward* (New York: Basic Books, 2004); R. Lowenstein, *When Genius Failed: The Rise and Fall of Long-Term Capital Management* (New York: Random House, 2000).

Chapter Six

1. Association for Health Care Philanthropy, *Annual Report on Giving*, 2005, p. 11.
2. H. Gardner, *Changing Minds: The Art and Science of Changing Our Own and Other People's Minds* (Boston: Harvard Business School Press, 2004).
3. Association for Health Care Philanthropy, *Annual Report on Giving*, 2005, p. 10.
4. J. A. Paulos, *A Mathematician Plays the Stock Market* (New York: Basic Books, 2003), p. 31.
5. G. Vickers, *The Art of Judgment: A Study of Policy Making* (London: Chapman & Hall, 1965).
6. T. A. McLaughlin, *Streetsmart Financial Basics for Nonprofit Managers* (New York: Wiley, 1995), p. 58.
7. H. Lipman, "Measuring Endowments: How the Survey Was Conducted," *Chronicle of Philanthropy: The Chronicle of Education*, Special Edition on Endowments, May 27–28, 2004, p. B2.
8. M. L. Herman, G. L. Head, P. M. Jackson, and T. E. Fogarty, *Managing Risk in Nonprofit Organizations* (New York: Wiley, 2004).
9. K. Phillips, *Wealth and Democracy: A Political History of the American Rich* (New York: Broadway Books, 2002).

Chapter Eight

1. R. Reich, "A Failure of Philanthropy: American Charity Shortchanges the Poor, and Public Policy Is Partly to Blame," *Stanford Social Innovation Review*, Winter 2005.
2. K. Phillips, *Wealth and Democracy: A Political History of the American Rich* (New York: Broadway Books, 2002).
3. A. Meckstroth and P. Arnsberger, "A 20-Year Review of the Nonprofit Sector, 1975–1995," *Statistics of Income (SOI) Bulletin*, Fall 1998.
4. P. Arnsberger, M. Ludlum, and M. Riley, "Current Research in the Nonprofit Sector," *Statistics of Income (SOI) Bulletin*, Tax Stats—2005 Special Study in Federal Tax Statistics. (The *SOI Bulletin* is available from the Tax Stats section of the IRS Web site, www.irs.gov/taxstats.)
5. L. Bernholz, *Creating Philanthropic Capital Markets: The Deliberate Evolution* (New York: Wiley, 2004).
6. D. Marni LaRose and B. Wolverton, "Donor Advised Funds Experience Drop in Contributions, Survey Finds," *Chronicle of Philanthropy*, May 15, 2003.
7. Association for Health Care Philanthropy, *Annual Report on Giving*, 2003.

8. Association for Health Care Philanthropy, Annual Report on Giving, 2005.

9. V. Pareto, *Manual of Political Economy* (New York: Augustus M. Kelley, 1971. Originally published 1906.)

10. Reich, "A Failure of Philanthropy."

Chapter Nine

1. M. Dropkin, *The Cash Flow Management Book for Nonprofits* (San Francisco: Jossey-Bass, 2001). This book briefly discusses Peter Drucker's comments on cutting expenses without considering the potential consequences. .

2. H. P. Tuckman and F. C. Chang, "How Well Is Debt Managed by Nonprofits?" *Nonprofit Management & Leadership 3*, no. 4 (Summer 1993).

3. L. Calder, *Financing the American Dream: A Cultural History of Consumer Credit* (Princeton, NJ: Princeton University Press, 1999).

Chapter Ten

1. T. D. Wilson, *Strangers to Ourselves: Discovering the Adaptive Unconscious* (Cambridge, MA: The Belknap Press of Harvard University Press, 2002).

Chapter Thirteen

1. H. Hansmann, quoted in P. Brimelow, "Professor Scrooge: Colleges Cry Poor Mouth to Their Alumni Even While Their Endowments Soar," *Forbes Magazine,* Oct. 19, 1998.

2. H. Hansmann, quoted in M. Cottle, "Too Well Endowed?" *Washington Monthly,* September 1998, p. 5.

3. L. Harvy, "Big Gifts and Rising Stocks Fuel Growth," *Chronicle of Philanthropy,* Special Supplement on Endowments, May 27–28, 2004.

4. M. Kramer and M. Porter, Letter to the Editor, *Chronicle of Philanthropy,* July 27, 2000.

5. Harvy, "Big Gifts and Rising Stocks Fuel Growth," p. B2.

6. Association for Health Care Philanthropy, *Annual Report on Giving,* 2005.

7. W. J. Baumol and W. Bowen, *Performing Arts: The Economic Dilemma* (Boston: MIT Press, 1966).

8. J. G. Dees, *Enterprising Nonprofits: A Toolkit for Social Entrepreneurs* (New York: Wiley, 2001).

9. D. Futrelle, "Build Wealth in Any Market," *Money Magazine,* September, 2004.

10. Futrelle, "Build Wealth in Any Market."

11. M. Richards, "Some Experts Think Market Will Move Down for Years," *Seattle Times,* August 30, 2004.

12. B. Mandelbrot, *The (Mis)Behavior of Markets: A Fractal View of Risk, Ruin, and Reward* (New York: Basic Books, 2004).

Chapter Fourteen

1. E. James and G. Benjamin, *Public Versus Private Education: The Japanese Experiment* (London: Macmillan, 1987).

Chapter Fifteen

1. S. Siwolop, "For Nonprofits, Owing Is Becoming the Wave of the Past," *New York Times*, March 30, 2005.
2. M. Blake, *A Study of Capital Giving to San Francisco Nonprofits, 1988–1992* (San Francisco: Walter & Elise Haas Fund, 1994).
3. R. Nessen, *Real Estate Finance and Taxation: Structuring Complex Transactions* (Boston: Robert L. Nessen, 1998).
4. J. T. Bennett and T. J. DiLorenzo, *Unhealthy Charities: Hazardous to Your Health and Wealth* (New York: Basic Books, 1994).
5. C. Miller, "The Gift Horse or Trojan Horse: A Thorough Physical Is Critical," *Nonprofit Quarterly*, Summer 2004.
6. Bennett and DiLorenzo, *Unhealthy Charities.*

Chapter Seventeen

1. C. Miller, "The Looking-Glass World of Nonprofit Money," *Nonprofit Quarterly 12*, no. 3, Spring 2005.

Chapter Eighteen

1. P. Arnsberger, M. Ludlum, and M. Riley, Internal Revenue Service, *Current Research in the Nonprofit Sector*, Statistics of Income (SOI) Tax Stats—2005 Special Study in Federal Tax Statistics, October 2006. Available online: http://www.irs.gov/pub/irs-soi/05eonta.pdf. Access date: April 8, 2007.
2. M. Kramer and M. Porter, Letter to the Editor, *Chronicle of Philanthropy*, July 27, 2000.
3. C. Piller, E. Sanders, and R. Dixon, "Gates Foundation Money Works at Cross Purposes," *Seattle Times*, January 7, 2007.
4. D. C. Johnson, *Perfectly Legal: The Covert Campaign to Rig Our Tax System to Benefit the Super Rich— and Cheat Everyone Else* (New York: Portfolio, 2003).
5. L. Bernholz, *Creating Philanthropic Capital Markets: The Deliberate Evolution* (New York: Wiley, 2004), p. 124.
6. N. Hertz, *The Silent Takeover: Global Capitalism and the Death of Democracy* (New York: Free Press, 2001); D. Korten, *The Post-Corporate World* (West Hartford, CT: Kumarian Press, 1999).
7. W. Ryan, "Nonprofit Capital: A Review of Problems and Strategies," white paper prepared for The Rockefeller Foundation & Fannie Mae Foundation, 2001.

Chapter Nineteen

1. J. Tower, "Ginnie Mae Pool No. 1: A Revolution Is Paid Off," *Bloomsberg News,* as reprinted in the *Seattle Times,* September 19, 1999.

2. J. Surowiecki, "The Financial Page: What Ails Us," *New Yorker Magazine,* July 7, 2003, p. 27.

ADDITIONAL READING

A number of sources contributed to the ideas reflected in this book. This list is provided for those who have some extra time for reading and a compelling need to learn more about where we got some of our ideas about money matters.

Anthes, E., Cronin, J., and Jackson, M. *The Nonprofit Board Book*. West Memphis and Hampton, Ark.: Independent Community Consultants, 1985.

Bolman, L. G., and Deal, T. E. *Reframing Organizations: Artistry, Choice, and Leadership*. San Francisco: Jossey-Bass, 1994.

Bryson, J. M. *Strategic Planning for Public and Nonprofit Organizations*. San Francisco: Jossey-Bass, 1990.

DiMaggio, P. J. *Nonprofit Enterprises in the Arts*. New York: Oxford University Press, 1986.

Dowie, M. *American Foundations: An Investigative History*. Cambridge, Mass: MIT Press, 2001.

Gardner, H. *Changing Minds: The Art and Science of Changing Our Own and Other People's Minds*. Boston: Harvard Business School Press, 2004.

Gladwell, M. *The Tipping Point: How Little Things Can Make a Big Difference*. New York: Little, Brown, 2002.

Hammack, D. C., and Young, D. R. *Nonprofit Organizations in the Market Economy*. San Francisco: Jossey-Bass, 1993.

Hopkins, B. R. *The Legal Answer Book for Nonprofit Organizations*. New York: Wiley, 1992.

Internal Revenue Service. *Statistics of Income, Compendium of Studies of Tax-Exempt Organizations, 1974–87*, Volume 1. Washington, D.C.: U.S. Government Printing Office, 1991.

Internal Revenue Service. *Statistics of Income, Compendium of Studies of Tax-Exempt Organizations, 1986–1992*, Volume 2. Washington, D.C.: U.S. Government Printing Office, 1991.

Kauffman, S. A. *Origins of Order: Self-Organization and Selection in Evolution.* New York: Oxford University Press, 1992.

Kotler, P., and Andreasen, A. *Strategic Marketing for Nonprofit Organizations.* Upper Saddle River, N.J.: Prentice Hall, 1982.

Krugman, P. *The Self-Organizing Economy.* Malden, Mass.: Blackwell, 1996.

Linzer, R. "Borrowing: A Resource for Nonprofits." *Chronicle of Non-Profit Enterprise,* Jan. 1989.

Linzer, R. "Why You Want to Borrow from Banks." *Taft Nonprofit Executive,* Apr. 1989, *8*(8).

Linzer, R. "Endowments: The Other Side of the Coin." *Chronicle of Non-Profit Enterprise,* July 1992.

Linzer, R. "Using Credit to Stabilize Cash Flow." *Journal of the Land Trust Alliance,* Winter 1993.

Linzer, R. "Charities Should Borrow Money, Not Hoard It." *Chronicle of Philanthropy,* Opinion Section, July 24, 1997.

Linzer, R., and Linzer, A. *It's Easy! Money Matters for Nonprofit Managers.* Indianola, Wash.: Port Madison Press, 2001.

Rudney, G. "The Scope and Dimensions of Nonprofit Activity." In W. W. Powell (ed.), *The Nonprofit Sector: A Research Handbook.* New Haven, Conn.: Yale University Press, 1987.

Salamon, L., and Abramson, A. *Managing Foundation Assets: An Analysis of Foundation Investment and Payout Procedures and Performance.* New York: Council on Foundations, 1991.

Schor, J. B. *The Overworked American: The Unexpected Decline of Leisure.* New York: Basic Books, 1992.

Skloot, E. *Smart Borrowing: A Nonprofit's Guide to Working with Banks.* New York: New York Community Trust, 1989.

Stacey, R. D. *Managing the Unknowable: Strategic Boundaries Between Order and Chaos in Organizations.* San Francisco: Jossey-Bass, 1992.

Stevens, S., and Anderson, L. *All the Way to the Bank: Smart Money Management for Tomorrow's Nonprofit.* St. Paul, Minn.: Stevens Group, 1997.

Strathern, P. *A Brief History of Economic Genius.* New York and London: TEXERE LLC, 2001.

Waldrop, M. M. *Complexity: The Emerging Science at the Edge of Order and Chaos.* New York: Touchstone, 1992.

Weisbrod, B. *The Nonprofit Economy.* Cambridge, Mass.: Harvard University Press, 1998.

Williamson, P. J. *Spending Policy for College and University Endowments.* Wilton, Conn.: Common Fund, 1979.

INDEX

HOW TO USE THE CD

SYSTEM REQUIREMENTS

PC with Microsoft Windows 98SE or later
Mac with Apple OS version 10.1 or later

USING THE CD WITH WINDOWS

To view the items located on the CD, follow these steps:

1. Insert the CD into your computer's CD-ROM drive.
2. A window appears with the following options:

   Contents: Allows you to view the files included on the CD.
   Software: Allows you to install useful software from the CD.
   Links: Displays a hyperlinked page of websites.
   Author: Displays a page with information about the author(s).
   Contact Us: Displays a page with information on contacting the publisher or author.
   Help: Displays a page with information on using the CD.
   Exit: Closes the interface window.

If you do not have autorun enabled, or if the autorun window does not appear, follow these steps to access the CD:

1. Click Start -› Run.
2. In the dialog box that appears, type d:\start.exe, where d is the letter of your CD-ROM drive. This brings up the autorun window described in the preceding set of steps.
3. Choose the desired option from the menu. (See Step 2 in the preceding list for a description of these options.)

IN CASE OF TROUBLE

If you experience difficulty using the CD, please follow these steps:

1. Make sure your hardware and systems configurations conform to the systems requirements noted under "System Requirements" above.
2. Review the installation procedure for your type of hardware and operating system. It is possible to reinstall the software if necessary.

To speak with someone in Product Technical Support, call 800-762-2974 or 317-572-3994 Monday through Friday from 8:30 a.m. to 5:00 p.m. EST. You can also contact Product Technical Support and get support information through our website at www.wiley.com/techsupport.

Before calling or writing, please have the following information available:

- Type of computer and operating system.
- Any error messages displayed.
- Complete description of the problem.

It is best if you are sitting at your computer when making the call.